LET US MEET IN HEAVEN

The Civil War Letters of James Michael Barr,
5th South Carolina Cavalry

Edited by
Thomas D. Mays

MCWHINEY FOUNDATION PRESS
McMurry University
Abilene, Texas

Cataloging-in-Publication Data

Barr, James Michael, 1829–1864.
    Let us meet in heaven: the Civil War letters of James Michael Barr,
    5th South Carolina Cavalry / edited by Thomas D. Mays.
        p. cm.
    Includes bibliographical references and index.
    ISBN 1-893114-24-4 (cloth)
        1.Barr, James Michael, 1829–1864—Correspondence.
    2. Confederate States of America. Army. South Carolina Cavalry
    Regiment, 5th. 3. South Carolina—History—Civil War, 1861–
    1865—Regimental histories. 4. United States—History—Civil War,
    1861–1865—Regimental histories. 5. South Carolina—History—
    Civil War, 1861–1865—Personal narratives. 6. United
    States—History—Civil War, 1861–1865—Personal narratives,
    Confederate. 7. Soldiers—South Carolina—Leesville—
    Correspondence. 8. Leesville (S.C.)—Biography. I. Mays, Thomas D.,
    1960– II. Title

    E577.6 5th .B37 2000
    973.7'457—dc21

00-052516
CIP

Printed in Abilene, Texas
United States of America

ISBN 1-893114-24-4
10 9 8 7 6 5 4 3 2 1

Book Designed by Rosenbohm Graphic Design

All inquiries regarding volume purchases of this book should be addressed
to the McWhiney Foundation Press, Box 637, McMurry Station,
Abilene, TX 79697-0637
Telephone inquiries may be made by calling (915) 793-4682

www.mcwhiney.org

In Memory of
Ruth Barr McDaniel

TABLE OF CONTENTS

James Michael Barr Home

Sketches by Elizabeth M. Leyendecker, Great, Great, Grand Daughter

INTRODUCTION

Interest in the American Civil War has waned little over the years. Since the war's centennial in the 1960s, fascination with the subject has grown immensely. Although scholars and the interested public still study the campaigns and commanders, the story of the common soldier continues to captivate students of the war. Soldier's letters and diaries provide readers with an intimate and personalized portrait of the conflict that is difficult to extract from post war histories and official reports. The Civil War letters of James and Rebecca Barr are a valuable addition to this area of study. The Barr family letters shed light on James Barr's military experience as a member of the 5th South Carolina Cavalry while also providing valuable and rare insight on the life of a small-scale slave owner and farmer.

Prior to the Civil War James Michael Barr was a rising yeoman farmer. He was born on December 10, 1829 and raised in the Lexington District of South Carolina near the small town of Leesville. Located near the center of the state, the Lexington District was primarily a rural farming region. Barr's parents, Mary Ann and Michael Barr were prosperous farmers, and by 1860 James too had established himself. In addition to farming, Barr ran a store and a mill on the side. Most land owning farmers in the district owned real estate and personal property valued between $1,000 and $5,000. By 1860 James Barr had accumulated a farm and slaves valued at $26,920. While Barr and his family enjoyed an above average standard of living, he was not a member of the

A CONFEDERATE FAMILY

*This chart maps the relationship between the families of James Michael Barr and Rebecca Ann (Dowling) Barr. The sixteen members who are known to have served in the Confederate Army are marked in **bold face**.*

Michael Barr (1791-1874)
married Mary Ann Minnick (1798-1871)
and had fourteen children:

Caroline Christina Barr (1815-1883)
married Henry H. Spann
sons:
Philip Churchill Spann
John Fletcher Spann
daughter:
Virginia Caroline Spann
William Joseph Barr (1816-1890)
married Leah Bouknight
sons:
Walter N. Barr
John J. Barr
Hesper Ellen Barr (1817-1880)
Elizabeth Barr (1820-1896)
John Wesley Barr (1822-1892)

Mary Ann Barr (1825-1892)
married **Walter Quattlebaum**
daughter:
Mittie Quattlebaum
John Jacob Barr (1828-1846)
James Michael Barr (1829-1864)
married Rebecca Ann Dowling

Daniel Thomas Barr (1832-1909)
Sallie Eloise Barr (1834-1914)
married **Samuel Guess**
Sue Catherine Barr (1836-1868)
married **Joseph Guess**
Henry P. Barr (1838-1870?)

Amanda Barr (1840-1872)

Frank Barr (1843-1843)

Decania Dowling (1803-1857)
married Elizabeth Zorn (1803-1865)
and had nine children

Ellen Elizabeth Dowling (1824-1890)
Sarah Dowling (1825-1899)
Mary S. Dowling (1826-1853)

Elijah Henry Dowling (1830-1906)
married Virginia Caroline Spann

William Preston Dowling
Aaron Decania Dowling (1836-1877)

Charleigh T. Dowling (1838-1904)
married Mittie Quattlebaum
Rebecca Ann Dowling (1840-1921)
married **James Michael Barr**
widowed; married
Tom Warren
John Caldwell Dowling (1843-1931)

planter class (almost all of the planters in the Lexington District owned real estate and slaves valued at more than $50,000 and some claimed estates worth more than $100,000). Barr was on the rise socially as well. On April 12, 1853 Barr was commissioned as a major in the state militia in the Upper Battalion, 15th Regiment of Infantry. Barr would use the title of "Major" in life and, oddly enough, his friends and relatives would continue to address him as "the Major" even as he served as a private in the Confederate army.[1]

On June 21, 1859 Barr married Rebecca Ann Dowling from the Barnwell District, and they settled about one mile north of Leesville near his father's home. Although she was only nineteen when the war began, Rebecca had already given birth to one son, James Dowling Barr, and she would have three more children during the conflict; John Wesley Barr, Charlie Decania Barr, and a daughter who died the day after her birth. In 1863, after James joined the army, Rebecca found herself in charge of managing the farm and slaves. Like many women during the war she lived completely outside her traditional role of wife and mother by also assuming the daunting challenge of running a farm. Many of the letters between the Barrs deal primarily with issues relating to the farm. Early on, James gave Rebecca detailed instructions on every aspect of farming, but by the time his regiment was ordered to Virginia, Barr left the farm's management in his wife's hands. "You will have to sell some bacon and then you can have money to spend," he wrote, adding, "Rebecca, I want you to sell and buy whatever you want."[2]

Indeed, one of the most valuable aspects of the Barr letters is found in their numerous references to the management of slaves. The largest part of the academic research into the peculiar institution of slavery has been confined to studies of the planter class (those owning twenty or more slaves), leaving a somewhat distorted view of the institution. In fact, almost half of all slaves in the South did not live on large plantations. In addition, the majority of Southern slave owners were middle class farmers. For example, in Barr's home county, the Lexington District, there were 609 slaveholders in 1860,

[1] *Eighth Census of the United States: 1860*, Population Schedules, Lexington District, South Carolina, hereafter cited as *1860 Census* (unless otherwise indicated this citation refers to population schedules); Ruth Barr McDaniel, comp., *Confederate War Correspondence of James Michael Barr and Rebecca Ann Dowling Barr* (Taylors, SC: Ruth Barr McDaniel, 1963), 7.

[2] McDaniel, *Correspondence*, 12; J. M Barr to R.A.D. Barr, March 23, 1864. The Barr letters are in the possession of the McDaniel Family.

but only 72 of them owned more than twenty slaves and qualified as planters. The rest, like the Barrs, were middle class or yeomen farmers who worked and lived side by side with their slave families. Barr's letters offer a valuable glimpse into this little understood aspect of slavery.[3]

Barr devoted a good deal of space in his letters to the management of his servants. In 1860 he owned twelve, slaves including four adults, four teenage females, and four children under age twelve. The slaves mentioned in the letters include Anderson (known as Ance), who was in his twenties, his teenage wife Mary, Old Bill, who was in his fifties during the war, Bill's wife Dina, and his sons Jerry and Jess. Among the other slaves mentioned are Cate, Mariah and Jane.[4]

Barr would send his slaves greetings in his letters: "Tell the Negroes 'Howdy' for me and tell them to do their duty."[5] In the same paternalistic tone used by many Southern slave owners, Barr also wrote his wife to "tell the Negroes that I say they all ought to try and see how well they can do. They ought to work well and do it good. This means a good stand and good work and a heap of it."[6] Barr also addressed discipline: "Bill stops too long at Noon." He complained in one letter, "I think one hour and a half plenty time, longer than they stopped when I was at home."[7] After Cate lost a baby, Barr grumbled to his wife; "it is no more than I expected . . . If she did it purposely, it would be enough to hang her for, but laziness I should guess to be the cause . . . It is a great wonder she did not die too. I hope the rest have learned better sense and will take warning."[8] When it came to feeding them, Barr noted, "I can kill two or three beefs next Summer and if the Negroes do not work better, they won't need any meat for if they don't work, I don't care whether I feed them or not."[9] After Bill's son Jerry complained about his weekly meat ration, Barr asked his wife to "Tell me how much meat to give Jerry. I think that I gave him 3 lbs. a

---

[3] *1860 Census*, Lexington District, South Carolina.

[4] *1860 Census*, Slave Schedules, Lexington District, South Carolina.

[5] J. M Barr to R. A. D. Barr, May 27, 1864.

[6] Ibid., March 8, 1863.

[7] Ibid., May 24, 1863.

[8] Ibid., June 2, 1863.

[9] Ibid., January 10, 1864.

week and if that is not enough and he prefers it, I will sell him. Some one wanted to buy him before I left."[10] When the slaves began to pilfer Barr's chicken house, he wrote his wife a stern note: "Tell the Negroes that if you have to write to me again about their stealing your chickens that I will write to Mr. Spann to make them make away with all of theirs. If those that have them don't steal them, they ought to know which ones do it."[11] When it came to comparing his fare in the army to that of his slaves, Barr lashed out: "If soldiers only could fare as well as some Negroes at home. If we could only get two lbs. of bacon we could do pretty well. My Negroes need not complain. What if they had to fare like some soldiers, bad beef and musty meal—course at that."[12]

But Barr was not always a harsh disciplinarian. He brought Ance with him when he served in South Carolina and Virginia and at times gave the slave considerable leeway, even going so far as to permit Ance to live independently and to hire himself out as a day laborer. With this level of autonomy, one must wonder why Ance never crossed Union lines into freedom. But it must be kept in mind that Ance's wife Mary remained with the Barrs in South Carolina, and he thought of her often, even sending along messages in the mail. In October 1863 Barr's brother-in-law included a note in his letter home: "Anderson asked me to write you for him. He says you will please let me know how Mary is. 'I am well and hope you (Mary) are the same.' He encloses $7.50 Seven Dollars and fifty Cents for the use of his wife. Whenever she needs anything she can come to you and get the money."[13] Whatever his motive might have been, Anderson remained deeply devoted to the Barr family for years.

In January 1863 Barr joined what would become Company I, 5th South Carolina Cavalry. From its organization in December 1861 and January 1862, the unit was assigned to the coastal defense of South Carolina. After mustering at Camp Hampton, near Columbia, South Carolina, the company was stationed near the coast at McPhersonville and Pocotaligo. The company originally served as Company A, 2nd Battalion South Carolina Cavalry and later as

---

[10] Ibid., February 18, 1863.

[11] Ibid., June 3, 1864.

[12] Ibid., December 30, 1863.

[13] Charleigh T.Dowling to R. A. D. Barr, October 30, 1863.

Company D, 14th Battalion South Carolina Cavalry. Prior to the organization of the 5th, most of the companies had been posted independently or as part of small cavalry battalions. Other than some light skirmishing around Pocotaligo, the unit had seen no large-scale action prior to Barr's enlistment. Many of the men may have seen service in the unit as a good way to avoid fighting with the large Confederate armies in Virginia and the West.[14] Their good fortune did not last long, however, for in the spring of 1864 the 5th South Carolina Cavalry was ordered to the front in Virginia and became part of Brigadier General Matthew C. Butler's Brigade in Major General Wade Hampton's Cavalry Division. Barr would then participate in some of the most severe fighting of the war as Union Lieutenant General Ulysses S. Grant drove relentlessly on General Robert E. Lee's army and Richmond. In the spring of 1864 Barr saw action in Virginia at Chester Station, Drewry's Bluff, Atkinson's Farm, and South Side. He also took part in some of the largest cavalry engagements of the war, including the Battles of Haw's Shop, Atlee's Station, Cold Harbor, and Trevilian Station, where he was wounded.

Initially Barr found camp life rather pleasant, even going so far as to complain about an abundance of food. At one point he carped, "we are needing something from home, but we get plenty of good beef, but I am tired of it. I have to throw away some of it at times to keep it from spoiling."[15] Prior to the arrival of his slave Ance, Barr stated "I seat myself again this Wednesday morning to write you how I am getting on. I am quite well and getting on tolerably well, considering that I have no Negro to wait on me."[16] In the spring of 1864, when the regiment reached Virginia, many of the men were shocked at what they found. Barr recorded "I think Cavalry service is the hardest service out here as we fight any way and always on the go."[17] He later added, "We get plenty to eat, but we see a hard time here. We are now in the War sure enough. We have seen service since we have been in Virginia. The Cavalry says

---

[14] Lewis F. Knudsen, Jr., "5th South Carolina Cavalry Regiment (Provisional Army of the Confederate States), 1861-1865: Muster Roll, Officer Registers, and Muster Roll Records and Events" (Columbia, SC: Lewis F. Knudsen, Jr., 1999), 63.

[15] J. M. Barr to R. A. D. Barr, May 24, 1863.

[16] Ibid., July 8, 1863.

[17] Ibid., May 29, 1864.

[18] Ibid., June 5, 1864.

the service is much harder here this Spring than it has ever been."[18] Barr was not the only member of the 5th South Carolina Cavalry to be staggered by brutality of the war in Virginia. Captain A.B. Mulligan of Company B, wrote home in June 1864: "I did not think it possible for men to undergo so much exposure with out breaking down. . . . We are getting so that we can lye down in a mud hole & sleep about as well as we used to in or beds." He then added, "We who are just from North & South Carolina have just begun to realize the war."[19]

Religion played a major role in Barr's life, a faith he shared with his wife: "I think you ought to go to the Church whenever, you can," he wrote Rebecca, "it is a place that all ought to go whenever they can."[20] While Barr was a Methodist, Rebecca was a Baptist (no small difference in the 1860s). In one letter Barr insisted, "My Dear Rebecca, I am now a stronger Methodist than ever." Barr then recanted and apologized to his wife, "My Dear One, let me not influence you to join my Church by saying that I was a stronger Methodist than I ever was. I only spoke as I felt. Prejudice has a good deal to do with it." But Barr was not narrow-minded when it came to his faith: "Yet, I believe some here think that their Church is the only way to Heaven. God pity them and help them to do better than some of them are doing."[21] In time, as the reality of war set in, Barr wrote his wife, "We must put our trust in the Lord. He is able to shield us from the enemy's balls, if he sees fit, and if we never meet on earth, let us meet in Heaven where parting will be no more."[22]

The history of the letters themselves is worth noting. During the war Rebecca Barr carefully preserved all of her correspondence with her husband, including several letters she had written to him. In early 1865, as Union General William T. Sherman's troops burned and pillaged their way across South Carolina, Rebecca found her home in the marauders' path. With the help of one of her slaves, she buried a trunk containing the letters and other family valuables in the middle of the road in front of her farm and then ran a

---

[19] Olin Fulmer Hutchinson, Jr., *"My Dear Mother & Sisters": Civil War Letters of Capt. A.B. Mulligan, Co. B 5th South Carolina Cavalry—Butler's Division—Hampton's Corps, 1861-1865* (Spartanburg, SC: The Reprint Company, 1992), 122.

[20] J. M. Barr to R. A. D. Barr, July 6, 1863.

[21] Ibid., September 3, 1863.

[22] Ibid., July 18, 1863.

wagon back and forth over the spot to hide any trace of its whereabouts. The trunk, letters, and several items of clothing belonging to James Michael Barr survived the war and have been carefully preserved by the family for generations. In the early 1960s Barr's granddaughter, Ruth Barr McDaniel, began to transcribe the letters. With the eye of a professional historian, Mrs. McDaniel painstakingly transcribed each letter in detail, being careful to include the original spelling and punctuation, and published the collection in a book limited to fifty copies entitled *Confederate War Correspondence of James Michael Barr and Rebecca Ann Dowling Barr* (Taylors, SC: Ruth Barr McDaniel, 1963).

The main goal in editing the collection has been to clarify for the general reader and scholar many of the people, places, and events that are mentioned in the letters. Wherever people referred to in the letters have been identified, they are documented in footnotes. As with any collection of letters, a few people are mentioned that, due to incomplete information or the misspelling of their names simply cannot be identified. In describing political and military events of the war I have relied on several general texts, including E.B. Long with Barbara Long, *The Civil War Day by Day: An Almanac, 1861–1865* (New York: Double Day, 1971); Mark Boatner III, *The Civil War Dictionary, Revised Edition* (New York: David McKay Company, Inc., 1988), and Stewart Sifakis, *Who Was Who in the Civil War* (New York: Facts on File, 1988). The original letters between Barr and his family have been included in their entirety, however the genealogical references to the Barr family and other items that would not interest the general reader have been removed. Barr tended to write in a stream of consciousness and therefore many his paragraphs do not flow smoothly. In order to separate clear lines of thinking many large paragraphs have been divided into sentences that contain completely separate ideas. Also the perspective offered is necessarily one-sided, as most of the letters are from James to Rebecca. The reader will, however, be able to infer the content of many of Rebecca's letters to James by his responses.

This study would not have been possible with out the assistance of many people, to whom I owe a great deal of debt. This edition is based upon the painstaking work of Mrs. Ruth Barr McDaniel in transcribing the letters and her sons Raymond and Robert McDaniel, who had the idea of bringing this unique and informative story to a wider audience. I am also indebted to Mr. Lewis F. Knudsen, Jr. of Columbia, South Carolina, who is the unofficial historian of the 5th South Carolina Cavalry. While researching an ancestor who fought who fought with the 5th he has compiled a meticulously detailed muster roll of the regiment entitled "5th SC Cavalry Regiment (Provisional Army of the Confederate States) 1861–1865. Regimental Roll, Officer Registers, and Muster Roll Record of Events." Knudsen's work is based upon the *Compiled Service Records* from the National Archives as well as other sources from the South Carolina Archives and the South Carolina Confederate Historian. Knudsen's thorough research was an invaluable addition to this study. I also owe a debt of gratitude to Mr. Paul Cochran and Ms. Tracy Shilcutt of McMurry University in Abilene, Texas, for their efforts as research assistants. And also to Dr. Tracy Power, of the South Carolina Department of Archives and History in Columbia, South Carolina. And of course I need to thank Dr. Grady McWhiney and Dr. Don Frazier of the McWhiney Foundation Press. Thanks also to my friend and colleague Dr. David Coffey, who edited my work and kept it on track. I also owe a note of thanks to my colleagues in the Division of History and Political Science at Quincy University, who cheerfully granted me the freedom I needed to pursue this study. I would also like to thank my 93 year-old-grandmother Alice Bragg for her assistance in solving the great pender mystery. And most importantly, I owe a debt to my wife Carrie Mays, who has put up with more than I would ever want to admit.

CHAPTER ONE
WE ARE WELL FIXED

In January 1863 in order to avoid conscription Barr traveled to Pocotaligo, South Carolina to join what would become Company I, of the 5th South Carolina Cavalry. Upon enlisting, Barr was recorded as being 35 years old, with dark hair and eyes and six feet in height. Barr apparently joined the company because many of his wife's relatives from her home in the Barnwell District served in the unit. James W. Reed organized the company from men from the Barnwell and Orangeburg Districts. Reed served as captain until the men reorganized and elected new leaders in May 1862. By the time Barr joined the unit was under the command of one of Barr's neighbors and personal friends, Captain Thomas W. Tyler.[23]

Editor's note: Even before enlisting, Barr felt pressure to join the army early in the war. On July 2, 1862 J. Wesley Barr wrote his brother James the following letter from the front in Virginia. Prior to the war John Wesley Barr (1822–1892) cultivated a large farm in the Edgefield District with his wife Sarah and his four children. Wesley (as he was known) enlisted June 4, 1861 into Hampton's Legion in what became Company I, 2nd South Carolina Cavalry. Barr served as a private and chaplain in the company until being dis-

---

[23] McDaniel, *Correspondence*, 8; Knudsen, "5th SC," 82.

charged in 1862, likely due to ill health. After the war he followed his calling as a Methodist minister. [24]

Camp In The Woods
2 Miles from Drurys Bluffs
And 7 Miles from Richmond, Va.

July 2nd, 1862

Dear Brother James:

I suppose you have looked time and time again for a letter from me. Well, I have no apologies to make. I acknowledge that I have been careless and indifferent about writing.

I know you have received the news that we have been fighting for five days already and the fight is not done yet. Though we are not fighting today on the account of the heavy continual rain which it has been doing all day. We have got the Yanks pressed to the wall at last and if it had not rained today I think by this time we would have had the whole of the Northern Army surrendering. They have retreated as far now as they can, they have either to give up or take the James River, for we have them entirely surrounded.[25]

We have lost a great many men in killed and wounded. It is a sight to behold. The Yankee loss is beyond description. We have taken 7000 prisoners and they are still coming in. Major Steadman is unhurt so far. Fletcher is slightly wounded in the leg. I can't begin to tell you of the casualties in some of the companies yet as they are not known yet. Our Squadron has not had to charge yet, so we haven't lost any men yet. But we don't know how soon we may be cut to pieces.

---

[24] *1860 Census*, Edgefield District, South Carolina; McDaniel, *Correspondence*, 271; John A. Chapman, *History of Edgefield County* (1897; repr., Clearwater, SC: Eastern Digital Resources, 1998), 423, 496. According to Chapman, J. W. Barr was the originator of "Barr's Legion."

[25] J. W. Barr's letter dates to the day after the Seven Days Battles around Richmond, Virginia, had ended. By July 2, 1862 General Robert E. Lee's Army of Northern Virginia had successfully driven Major General George McClellan's Army of the Potomac from within sight of Richmond to a defensive position along the James River. The move temporarily eliminated McClellan's army as a threat and opened the way for a Confederate invasion of the North.

SOUTH CAROLINA

James, I don't think you will have to leave as you have no overseer and are attending to Father's business. But if you are, you could get in no better company than ours. The Cavalry has the best chance all the time. If you come, be here in twelve days so I can give you the ropes. You can get a horse here, just bring your saddlebags, 4 or 5 shirts, 3 pair of pants, one coat and over coat. Also one pair of heavy boots or shoes (large at that).

I expect to leave for home in two weeks. I am going to ride through as I want to carry my man home with me.

Ab I think is mending slowly. I will go up to see him in the morning if nothing happens. His father left yesterday.

I am not so well today.

I thought I would have heard from Thomas before now. Tell him I sent his money and furlough by George Studman.

I will close. Write soon and give me all the particulars. I will close hop-

ing these lines will find your family and all our kindred well. I would like to hear from Henry as he was in the fight.[26] Tell Pa and Ma howdy for me and remember me to all.

Good by, your Brother

J.W. Barr.

---

[26] Prior to the war James Barr's brother Henry P. Barr made his home near his parents in the Lexington District, where he and his wife Anna Acklyn Reed managed a small farm and helped the senior Barr run his place. According to family tradition, Henry avoided service by hiring a substitute but was forced to enlist after the substitute was killed in battle. On May 4, 1864 Henry enlisted as a private in Company D, 2nd South Carolina Cavalry. *1860 Census*, Lexington District, South Carolina; McDaniel, *Correspondence*, 272-3.

[27] Anderson, or "Ance" as he was most often called, was the property of James M. Barr. Barr's father had given him the slave on February 25, 1853, when Ance was about sixteen-years-old. Ance remained with Barr throughout the war and lived until the close of the century. McDaniel, *Correspondence*, 11.

Editor's note: James Michael Barr enlisted in Company I, 5th South Carolina Cavalry in January 1863 at Pocotaligo, South Carolina.

Pocatoligo, S.C.
January 19, 1863

Dear Rebecca:

As I may be sent off on picket duty soon, and as I think you will be looking for a letter from me, I have concluded to write this morning to let you hear from me.

We got in Saturday evening and put up our tent. We are pretty well fixed for the present, but I need Anderson. He would take a great deal of labor off from me such as getting wood, tending to my horse, and cooking.[27] Though I am getting on finely so far, we were mustered in yesterday. It is well that we came as early as we did for there is an order out to bring in all the Conscrips that the Act of Congress does not exempt.[28] So you see that all Militia Officers will be sent after. Officers will start today for that purpose. Aaron will have to come. I think, they say here, that his substitute cannot be taken.[29]

---

[26] Prior to the war James Barr's brother Henry P. Barr made his home near his parents in the Lexington District, where he and his wife Anna Acklyn Reed managed a small farm and helped the senior Barr run his place. According to family tradition, Henry avoided service by hiring a substitute but was forced to enlist after the substitute was killed in battle. On May 4, 1864 Henry enlisted as a private in Company D, 2nd South Carolina Cavalry. *1860 Census*, Lexington District, South Carolina; McDaniel, *Correspondence*, 272-3.

[28] In January 1863 Confederate President Jefferson Davis asked Congress to tighten the Conscription Act and to target specifically those who had been previously exempt. Prior to this there had been many ways by which Southerners had avoided service. One could be exempted for working in a number of occupations, including railroad operators, hospital workers, and industrial laborers. In several states, officers in the state militia were exempt as well. Aaron Dowling and James Barr may have taken advantage of this exemption. The wealthy could also find a release by hiring someone from one of the exempted classes to take their place in the ranks. Evidentially Dowling's substitute failed to pass the medical exam.

[29] Aaron Decania Dowling, Barr's brother-in-law, farmed with his wife in the Orangeburg District prior to the war. He enlisted as a private at age 26 into Company I, 5th South Carolina Cavalry, and after the war he settled near Willow Swamp Church in the Orangeburg District, where he farmed until his death in 1877. *1860 Census*, Orangeburg District; Knudsen, "5th SC," 18; McDaniel, *Correspondence*, 274.

Rebecca, I am well and hope you and the children arrived home safely and that you are all well. You must kiss both of our little boys for me. I expect Jimmy will talk often about me.

Tell Henry to have my cotton gined. Mr. D. Shealy I think will gin it.[30] Tell him to pay Pa the cotton I owe him. There is baging in the store house that will do to put it up in. Make them take good care of the sheep and lambs, if there are any. Take good care of the cattle, hogs. I put this in so you may tell Bill, thinking by my writing it back home, he may take better care of every thing.[31] You must have the meat hung up when it will do.

When you write, let me know how all the family is, especially how Pa and Ma is getting on.

Your husband,
J.M. Barr

J,M. Barr
Camp D. Maj. Morgans Squadron[32]
Pocatoligo, S.C.
Care of Capt. Tyler[33]

---

[30] Most likely David C. Shealy, who was a prosperous farmer in the area. *1860 Census*, Lexington District, South Carolina.

[31] Prior to the war James Barr's older brother, William J. Barr (1816-1890) was an affluent farmer in the Lexington District, where he lived with his wife Leah Bouknight and four of their children. Barr worked as a planter, miller, and trial justice. According to family tradition he also served with several of his sons in the Confederate Army. *1860 Census*, Lexington District, South Carolina; McDaniel, *Correspondence*, 270.

[32] Major Joseph H. Morgan, 5th South Carolina Cavalry. Knudsen, "5th SC," 63.

[33] Captain Thomas W. Tyler commanded Company I, 5th South Carolina Cavalry from August 26, 1862 until the end of the war. He was a very successful young farmer in his early thirties when the war began, living with his wife and four children in the Orangeburg District. On June 12, 1864 he was wounded in action at Trevilian Station, Virginia. *1860 Census*, Orangeburg District, South Carolina; Knudsen, "5th SC," 56, 82.

———◦◦◦———

Home
January 25, 1863

My Dear Husband:

When we arrived home Thursday night, I found your letter awaiting my arrival and how delighted to hear from you and to hear you were well, for I was afraid being exposed in such weather as we had last week would have made you sick.

I found all things doing very well, when I got home. Old Dina was sick. She can hardly walk, and Mariah was sick three days during my absence, though she is well now. One of the young sheep had a lamb while we were gone, but she lost it. Old Bill says he thinks it was born too soon, none of the rest have had any yet. They are very backwards. I had the stray cow milked this morning for the first time. She gave a quart, and we did not get all the milk; I think she will make a splendid milk cow, if she could be fed well. Jerry and Jess have been plowing in the Stuble field. They will finish Monday, they say. Jess ploughs well and can keep up with his daddy. He is pleased at the idea of plowing, and says he'd rather do that than any work he ever did do. Bill says he wants to run three ploughs Monday. The hogs don't seem to fatten, and I haven't had the garden prepared for sowing seed yet, though I want to have it done next week if it possibly can be done. Henry Barr says he will carry off a load of our potatoes next week. They are rotting very badly.

I can tell you something I expect will please you. Daniel Mitchell brought Anderson home, and he is now on his way down to you.[34] Brother Elijah came home with me and took Anderson back with him.[35] He left here

---

[34] Daniel D. D. Mitchell was a farmer in his mid thirties who lived near the Barrs in the vicinity of Leesville. *1860 Census*, Lexington District, South Carolina.

[35] Rebecca Barr's brother Elijah Henry Dowling, M.D. was married twice. His first wife was Virginia Carolina Spann and his second was Laura Cannon. He had four children by his first wife. He lived near his sister Rebecca in Lexington and later moved to Charleston, South Carolina. Dowling was an assistant surgeon in Colonel Johnson Hagood's 1st South Carolina Infantry. He resigned May 15, 1862. McDaniel, *Correspondence*, 274; A. S. Salley, *South Carolina Troops in Confederate Service*, vol. 1 (Columbia, SC: The State Co., 1913), np.

yesterday morning, though he said he would not leave Mother to go to Pocataligo until Wednesday. So you need not look for him before Wednesday. Daniel Mitchell did not want any pay for his trouble. So when he offered me the money you gave him for Ance, I would not take it. So he has that much if no more. Anderson sounded very willing to go down to you, but he said he never wanted to go back where he was before. The negroes were all glad enough to get back.[36]

Mr. Spann was here yesterday evening and he says he thinks the better plan would be for you to have Henry to tend to your business as Phill's health is not good.[37] He says Phill is scarcely able to tend to his business, and he says he thinks one would do better than two. He says he will do all he can for me. Anything I want him to do just let him know and he will do it with pleasure.

Your mother got a letter from Tom last week. He was doing very well. He said if you had not gone in the service to tell you to go at once, not to wait til you would be made to go.[38]

John Tom Parrison is dead. He died from a wound in the leg. He was buried at his mother's last week. He did not die at home. He died in the West they say. It almost killed his mother.

Henry Barr attacked Emanual Quattlebaum about talking about you and him, and they had a brief quarrel.[39] He told Henry you were a Col., and if you

[36] Apparently the Confederate Government had impressed some of Barr's slaves to work on fortifications along the coast. As the war progressed most slave owners became very reluctant to lend their property to the government due to the extremely poor conditions the slaves were forced to work under.

[37] Reverend Henry Hammond Spann and his son Philip Churchill Spann lived close to the Barrs in the vicinity of Leesville. Henry was a Methodist minister in his mid fifties and had married J. M. Barr's sister Caroline Christana Spann. *1860 Census*, Lexington District, South Carolina; McDaniel, *Correspondence*, 270.

[38] James Barr's brother Daniel Thomas Barr (1832-1909) farmed in the Rock Well area of the Lexington District. While one family source identifies him as "Daniel Thomas," family letters and military records list him as Thomas "Tom" D. Barr. He enlisted July 8, 1861 at age 29 into Company K, 9th South Carolina Infantry at Ridgeville, South Carolina. Later, his unit reorganized to create Company F, of the South Carolina Palmetto Sharpshooters. He had been severely wounded on May 31, 1862 during the Battle of Fair Oaks (Seven Pines). Barr served until paroled with the unit at Appomattox Court House on April 9, 1865. He had risen to the rank of fifth sergeant. After the war he settled with his wife Nancy Rodella Elizabeth Rawl in the Rock Well community, where they raised eight children. Barr was a planter and trial justice and served as a lieutenant colonel on Governor Hugh Smith Thompson's staff. *1860 Census*, Lexington District, South Carolina; McDaniel, *Correspondence*, 272; R. A. Brock, *The Appomattox Roster* (The Southern Historical Society, 1887).

[39] Emanual Quattlebaum was a farmer in his mid fifties, who lived with his large family in the vicinity of Lightwood Creek in the Lexington District. *1860 Census*, Lexington District, South Carolina.

had ordered them to meet at Williamson's, he would not have gone. He also told Henry if there was any chance in the world to carry him in service again, he would do it certain. Their conversation was so long until I can't tell it all. Quattlebaum is running for Lieut. Col. and John Lee for Major.[40] Henry says he intends to do all he can against him, and I know if I had any thing to say I would never say anything good.

I don't suppose you have heard the news. It is reported Squire Steadman and the Widow Boyd are to be married soon; don't you think that will be a match, this report is said to be true and I don't doubt it.

Walter Quattlebaum stays a time. It looks like he is pleased down there. I am glad I did not wait for him.[41]

This morning looks very much like we might have snow.

We had a very good time coming home. We left Mother's Wednesday morning and took dinner with Sallie Guess and spent the night at the Aarons.[42] We got home the very next night a little after night. The children were both very good traveling. John Wesley was better than I ever saw. He did not seem to tire riding.

Jane had woven out the cloth we left in the looms, and it was done very well. I want to put in forty yards more just as soon as I can get it ready. I got seventeen yards of yellow homespun at Bamberg, paid fifty cents a yard. It is very good cloth.

Jim and Maggie Smith were here last week. Jim bought Jake from his Pa and is to give him fifteen hundred dollars for him.

Henry Barr sold six dollars worth of tobacco while we were gone, though he has not given me the money. I haven't sold any since we have been home.

---

[40] Possibly John W. Lee, a prosperous farmer in his early fifties, who lived near Leesville in the Lexington district. Ibid.

[41] Walter Quattlebaum was J. M. Barr's brother-in-law. He had married Mary Ann Barr and was a successful farmer in the Edgefield District prior to the war. According to family tradition, Walter Quattlebaum was a captain in the Confederate States Army. *1860 Census*, Barnwell District, South Carolina; McDaniel, *Correspondence*, 271.

[42] Sallie Guess was J. M. Barr's sister. She had married Samuel Daniel Dedicus Guess, who worked as a dentist, farmer, and banker. Prior to the war the Guesses and their young son lived in the Barnwell District. Guess enlisted at age 24 with Barr in Company I, 5th South Carolina Cavalry and was carried on the rolls as a "substitute for S. Guess." *1860 Census*, Barnwell District, South Carolina; McDaniel, *Correspondence*, 272; Knudsen, "5th SC," 25.

Sister Ellen paid me the money she was owing you.[43] It was three dollars.

I am feeling very lonely today. No company and it is the Holy Sabbath Day so I can't work to pass off the time; the only thing I can pass off the time with is writing to you. If I could just write all the time I would do very well. I don't know that you can read this letter. It is the worse paper I ever wrote on, and John Wesley is standing by me begging me to take him. Jim often says he wants to go on the coast with Pa. When he awoke this morning, he called Pa. He had forgotten you were not home. You must write to me every week if not more often. If you don't write every week I will be very uneasy about you.

How is Charlie getting on with his neck?[44] I hope he is well.

Sallie Guess gave me half bushel of penders to plant.[45]

I have not sent for Sue nor Mary. I thought Mr. Quattlebaum would bring one when he brought the Negroes home.[46]

The neighbors are generally well.

You must write often to your ever dear and affectionate wife.

Rebecca

---

[43] Ellen Elizabeth Dowling, (1824-1890) was Rebecca Barr's sister. She married Andrew Jackson Cox and lived near Denmark, South Carolina, where they raised six children. McDaniel, *Correspondence, 274*.

[44] Charleigh Thaddeus Dowling, (1838-1904) was Rebecca Barr's older brother. He worked as an overseer in the Barnwell District prior to the war. At age 24 he enlisted into Company I, 5th South Carolina Cavalry, along with his brother-in-law
J. M. Barr. "Charlie" was a companion and messmate to Barr throughout the war. Afterwards, Dowling settled with his wife Margaret "Mittie" Quattlebaum (Walter Quattlebaum's daughter) near Norway, South Carolina, where he farmed and practiced dentistry. *1860 Census*, Barnwell District, South Carolina; Kundsen, "5th SC," 18; McDaniel, *Correspondence, 274-5*.

[45] "Penders," or Pinders as they are more commonly spelled, are peanuts.

[46] J. M. Barr's sisters Susan "Sue" Cathrine Guess and Mary Ann Quattlebaum both lived in the Lexington District. McDaniel, *Correspondence, 271-2*.

Pocatoligo, S.C.
January 29, 1863

My Dear Wife:

When I arrived back to camp from one weeks picket duty, your letter was awaiting my arrival, and I assure you it afforded me great pleasure to hear from you and our dear little boys and to hear that you arrived home safely and to hear that you were well. I am well and getting on finely so far.

Last Wednesday a week, our Company was sent off as pickets and we arrived back to our quarters yesterday evening. So you see we had seven days and seven nights to stand guard and watch for the Yankees. The first part of our time one would stand two hours at a time, but the last three nights two men would watch half the night and two more the other half. So you may think it was very hard, but you must not think that it was so hard on me for I assure you I got along fine with the exception of two hours on Wednesday morning. It commenced sleeting but not whilst standing it was sleeting I got on I think fine through it. It was very cold as we had to stand on the banks of the river and at that time the tide was high enough for the Yankees to land. We were fifteen miles off from Camp.

Charlie was with me. He is getting on finely. His neck is swollen yet. Though on last Thursday night he was amusing himself standing on his head, but at that time his neck was nearly well.

We have had plenty to eat so far. We get beef every evening, I think nearly enough. We also draw sugar, rice and a little soap, enough for our hands and dishes. We also get salt. We will get one candle a week.

I think if I can only keep my health I can get on fine after Anderson gets here. I will look for him this evening.

Mr. Sawyer came yesterday evening and brought a letter for Charlie. Mittie said Elijah stayed with her on his way down and would leave for here this morning.[47] Mr. Sawyer brought Charlie a box. I do not know what is in it as we have not looked over it, but it is large enough to hold three or four hams.

I do not think we will move from here soon. My reasons for it is the account of the picket Post being so far. If the Cavalry should be carried away, then it would be necessary to move the Infantry nearer down.

There are two or three cases of small pox down here. None in our Squadron. I was vaccinated, but it would not take. They have sent them off and scattered the tents of those that were together. I hope it will not get among our men.[48]

Tell Henry if there is no advertisement of the cow at Shealy's to advertise her color and marks. Tell him to put one up at Shealy's, one at Crouts

---

[47] Possibly J. H. Sawyer of the Lexington District. *1860 Census*, Lexington District, South Carolina.

[48] By the time of the Civil War, Small Pox vaccination had become common. A person was "vaccinated" by having a needle first inserted into an infected person's pock and then having the infected needle inserted into a healthy person. If successful, the person would catch a mild infection leaving them immune from the disease.

Mill, and one at J. Spanns Shoe Shop.

Bill must be more careful with the sheep. I know that it was nothing else but carelessness that they lost the lamb. I expect he had the pen so the year-lings could get in and they perhaps killed it. The lambs always die when I am off. So you can see that the negroes are too careless. Don't let the cattle and sheep go together as they may get all the young ones killed. Tell Henry to let my cattle be put in the Hallman field, the field below the mill.

Tell Spann if Philips health is bad that I am perfectly willing for Henry to attend to my affairs.

When you can send word to William tell him to give credit to your sis-ters account.

Bill will soon commence to haul manure for the cotton patches out of lot. Stable manure for the corn.

Walter Quattlebaum will trim my young peach trees. You had better tie more strings to them. The one marked with white string is June Purple Golden Necteren, Purple and White Chinese peaches. The purple has very nearly faded out. [49]

Have all the mold rubbed off the meat, and you would better have the hogs that are up killed for I don't think they will get any better. Keep the meat smoked till it is dry. Don't forget to smoke with Chinaberries.

Don't let any one ride my colt.

Tell Bill that I look to him. Tell him not to have any sticks in the lot. Tell him to be careful with the corn and not let any one get it out unless he is there.

Tell Henry to look after my corn and see how the hogs feed. I don't want the out hogs to get poor that they die.[50]

Have Bill to feed the geese once a day till grass comes up. Keep them in the pasture. Tell him not to let any hogs get in and not let the geese go in the wheat fields. Feed the sheep on peas out of the store. If you feed up all the hull peas, feed some of the shelled ones.

---

[49] Barr is probably referring to the practice of tying young trees to a stake to hold them upright when heavy with fruit. The peach varieties he mentions are only a small sampling of more than fifteen types found in South Carolina at the time. See Lewis Cecil Gray, *History of Agriculture in the Southern United States to 1860*, 2 vols. (Washington, D. C., 1933; reprint ed. Clifton N.J., Augustus M. Kelly, publishers, 1973) II: 191.

[50] "Out hogs" apparently were Barr's free-range pigs. Most southern farmers did not pen their hogs but preferred to let them roam free.

January 30

I had to leave this till this morning as I had to go on parade yesterday and stand guard last night. I am all right this morning and am still well. I can eat very hearty. We are having plenty to eat.

Ance has not got here yet. I look for him today.

I hope this will find you all well. Kiss Jimmy and John Wesley for me. The last word Jimmy said to me at your mother's as I told him goodby, was, "Pa, let me go a piece with you." Elijah said he should go.

Being one week on picket has caused me not to write sooner. Write soon.

Your true husband,

James M. Barr

Pocatoligo, S.C.
Sunday, Feb. 1, 1863

My Dear Wife;

As I am still at camp and have not much to interest me I will write you a few lines. I intended when I came to camp to write every Sunday, but on account of picketing duty I cannot write every Sunday, for when we go we have to stay seven days. We go every two weeks and next Wednesday will be our time, though we may not be sent till Wednesday a week, that is if Captain Caughman's Company reports for duty.[51] They had the itch among them and was moved off some four miles yesterday.

Saturday we had a general Review and Inspection. We had quite a lively time at it. Some of the old Reserves marched in double quick time and even the old ones double quicked out. It appeared that they were short winded.

---

[51] Captain Augustus Henry Caughman from the Lexington District commanded Company F, 5th South Carolina Cavalry. Kundsen, "5th SC," 12.

Brigadier General William Stephen Walker commanded the 3rd Military District of South Carolina, Department of South Carolina, Georgia, and Florida. A native of Pittsburgh, he grew up near Washington, D. C. He served as a lieutenant in the Regiment of Voltigeurs and Light Infantry in the Mexican War until that unit disbanded after the end of hostilities. He rejoined the army in 1855 as a captain in the 1st U. S. Cavalry but resigned his commission to serve the Confederacy. After a year as a recruiter and organizer in Memphis, he transferred to South Carolina, where he received promotion to colonel and took command of the 3rd Military District with headquarters at Pocotaligo. Walker earned the rank of brigadier general due in part to his successful defense of the region from frequent Union raids from the coast.

Albert B. Shaw Collection, Virginia Historical Society, Richmond

After Review, General Walker had his Aids to announce to us the victory that we achieved at Charleston and I know the capturing of one Rebel and destroying some two or three (three I think) of the blockaiding rebels.[52] We were allowed to give three cheers for the victory gained. The signal was the raising of his cap on the point of his sword (by the General). There was a roar

---

[52] Brigadier General William Stephen Walker commanded the 3rd Military District of South Carolina, Department of South Carolina, Georgia and Florida. Walker was a Mexican War veteran and regular army officer prior to resigning his commission to join the Confederacy. In 1864, after taking his command into Virginia, Walker was wounded and captured at Petersburg. After losing his right foot, he was exchanged and returned to duty. Like other Confederates, Barr occasionally referred to Union forces as "rebels." This was logical to some Southerners for they felt that they were the ones who were defending the Constitution and had inherited the fight for liberty from the Founding Fathers.

sent up from the hold-line full half a mile long.[53] I think there is fighting about Savannah too this morning, as we can hear the guns very distinctly.[54] Hope some of the Rams and Ladies gun boats will come around to Point Royal and run the Yankee rebels off. Then we could go over to Beaufort and run the Yankees off our soil, clear off the island.

My dear Rebecca, you must not think that I am not getting on well, for I do assure you that I am getting on finely. You must not think that I am try- ing to flatter you, for in eating line at this time we have more than we want.

Mittie sent Charlie a box of back bones, ribs, and sausages, and sweet cake. Mother had fixed up a good deal, but Elijah told him he could not bring it though he brought a cheese box full. Elijah and Henry Rice have just left.[55] They will spend the night with Mr. Copland. They carried Ellic back with them. Charlie hated to let him go but Mit wanted him. He now wants his old man Jim.[56]

I want you to write often and let me know the news and how you are get- ting on.

Tell Jimmie that Pa saw some Yankees. Kiss him and Johnny for me. Don't let them go off too far with the little negroes. Be careful that they do not go about the wells. If you keep Jane about the house, perhaps it would be well for Dina to take care of them.

Rebecca, if you cannot write, get some one else to write.

Tell Henry he can get the salt for ten dollars a bushel and to get me two bushels.

I have not been sick nor have not had a cold since I have been down. I can eat very hearty, much more so than when at home. I am very pleased so far.

---

[53] On January 31, 1863 two Confederate ironclads, the CSS *Chicora* and CSS *Palmetto State*, attempted to break the Union blockade around Charleston, South Carolina. They were successful in severally damaging two Federal ships, the USS *Mercedita* and the USS *Keystone State*, before withdrawing. The Confederacy then claimed that the blockade had been lifted, but it proved only a temporary setback for the United States Navy.

[54] On February 1, 1863 Union and Confederate forces were engaged about seventeen miles northeast of Savannah at Bull Island, South Carolina. Barr's camp at Pocotaligo was about 34 miles north of Bull Island.

[55] Henry William Rice was Rebecca Barr's brother-in-law. He had married Sara Dowling (1825-1899), and they were the parents of seven children. McDaniel, *Correspondence*, 274.

[56] Ellic and Jim appear to have been slaves belonging to Charlie and Mittie Dowling.

I think I prefer a private.[57]

Hope this will reach you and children well.

Your ever dear Husband,

J.M. Barr

———⊰◦◦◦⊱———

Pocatoligo, S.C.

February 6, 1863

My Dear Wife:

Your letter of the third instant came safely to hand this evening, which afforded me great pleasure in hearing from home, and to hear that the negroes are lying up. I hope they will not lie up when there is nothing to matter.

I am glad to hear that some of my friends think enough of me to inquire of you so often, for in many cases persons pretend to be friends when they are not.

I am sorry to hear of the bad luck with the lambs. I think the way I put them (the ewes) and the way they are fed that they ought not to lose their lambs. Bill ought to know how to feed them shell peas. They won't need many. I don't want them wasted. I told Bill to feed the stock good. Feeding well and feeding to waste are two things. I know Bill is too careless.

Rebecca, I don't know when I can get off to come home. Furloughs are now stopped. We do not know how soon we may have to fight either here or at Charleston but if you get down and I get a letter that you are sick, with the Dr. 's certificate, I might then get off. It would be necessary to have the Dr. 's certificate.

I am glad to hear that you have Lane [Jane] with you, for I know you will not be lonesome.

We are doing very well. We have plenty to eat. We have now some three

---

[57] Although Barr had served as a major and later a colonel in the militia and had the proper social standing for a commission, he stated several times during his early service that he preferred being a private.

hams, some backbones, ribs, and sausages yet, with some three days ration of beef on hand. We get splendid rice. We have not touched the flour yet as we have plenty of flour bread.

Yesterday and last night were very bad. Yet not with standing all the bad weather, which is not half as bad as you think, I am getting on very well so far. When I am in my tent I fare just as well as if I was sleeping in a room. Our tent is closed all but one end and we have a plank floor, so you see we are doing fine. In the day we can go in some of the boys cabins. We will have us a kitchen put up ten by fourteen feet. Then we can shelter ourselves when we are at our tents from the rain and wind, but we will keep our tents to sleep in.

My saddle was condemned by the Inspection Officers, but they have not yet given me an army saddle. I expect I will get one soon.

Ance is a first rate cook. He is the best cook. I know he can beat any of our negroes at home. Capt. Tyler said the other day that he was a fast cook and a good cook.

I want you to have some two pair of good stockings knit to come up near-ly to my knees made out of cotton. I want my leggings. Capt. Tyler said if his wife would make him such a pair he would love her better.

We will go on pickets next Wednesday and will be gone one week. Hope we may have a good week. Thought you may have had a good week, though you may have had bad weather, yet it may not be so here for last Wednesday a week I believe, it snowed a little, very little.

Some one stole three of my chickens the first week. My hens are laying. One lays in George Sandifer's tent. It joins ours[58]. George is not messing with us.

Joseph Guess and Mr. Copeland took dinner with us today.[59] Jo will go home tomorrow. Sam is now at home. He goes home every six weeks. I think if any one will do as he ought he may stand a chance to get home once in three months. Yet there are some men who say they have not been home in five months.

Did I write for Henry to get me salt? Get two or three bushels and don't

---

[58] George W. Sandifer from the Barnwell District served as private in Company I, 5th South Carolina Cavalry. Knudsen, "5th SC," 49.

[59] Joseph Guess was a close neighbor and likely a relative of Barr's brother-in-law and tent mate Samuel D. M. Guess. *1860 Census*, Barnwell District, South Carolina.

pay over ten or twelve dollars per bushel. We have plenty eggs, yet we can get as many as we want down here. They are 35 cents or 37 1/2t cents per dozen. Lard they say is 35 cents per lb., hams 50 cents. Potatoes we would like to have. I am very fond of them and so is Charlie.[60]

Your Dear Husband

James M. Barr

Pocataligo, S.C.
February 7, 1863

My Dear Wife:

Last night was the coldest night we have had since I have been in camp. I am still getting on very well. I am pleased with the service that I am in. I would hate to be in an Infantry Company. Cavalry service suits me better than any service I think I could get in. My health has been very good since I have been in service. Charlie appears to stand it very well, though his neck is a little swollen again. He says it does not pain him.

---

[60] By February 1863 inflation had dropped the buying power of the Confederate dollar to about 20 cents.

If you get down, you had better ask the Dr. to write to me for you. He can state your situation and send a certificate, then perhaps I might get off home for ten days. Tell him why you want him to write. You need not be backward in asking him. I would like to see you, Jimmy and John Wesley. Though I have not been home sick yet, if it was not for your condition, I would be much better satisfied.[61]

I stand camps very well and am very well pleased so far.

Write soon and write long letters. This letter is being written in the night. Don't let any one see it, as it is so bad.

Your Dear Husband

James M. Barr

———⊰∘∘∘⊱———

Pocataligo, S.C.
February 9, 1863

My Dear Wife:

As I will go again on picket Wednesday and will be gone one week, I have concluded to write you a few lines before we leave. Yet our pickets may be run from their post today as the Yankees are bombing tremendously some where this morning, I think on our coast. I hope if they land they will do it before we go on Picket. Then I will not have my cooking utensils and blankets to bring off or to lose.[62] Reinforcements have been going on to Savannah on every train. Four Regiments have passed here.

We are looking for more men here and suppose they will get here today. The officers came on Saturday and one Company will come from Columbia

---

[61] Rebecca Barr's "condition" was pregnancy.

[62] Barr might have been referring to the constant cannonading along the coast that signaled the dash of a Confederate blockade-runner.

to this Regiment. We are now in the 5th South Carolina Cavalry Regiment Company and you must direct the letters the same as you did last. I will tell you when a change is made.[63]

Ance has the mumps. He must have contracted them when in Charleston as there are no other cases here. He is a number one cook.

Last Saturday our Captain made a request for clothing. We are clothed pretty well at this time. I got one large brown blanket, one pair of splendid English shoes, one pair pants, two pair of drawers, two shirts, and two pair of splendid socks. So you see I will have no use for the stockings I wrote to you for. I would like to send the pair of white blankets home or the comfort. I have too many clothes here, more than I can keep well packed.

As for getting home soon, I think it will be a dull chance as it is necessary to keep every one here that they can. Bob Hays tried to get a furlough to go to his Mother's sale, but failed to get one.[64]

The smallpox is still here. There are seven or eight cases at McPhersonville, some four miles from here, in the hospital. One case broke out in a Company near ours and he was sent off. I have been vaccinated some three times but can't get it to take, I intend to try it again.

You did right in sending the letters to Quattlebaum. I hope he was elected and if not, I think he ought to go in the service anyway as he is an able bodied man, much more so than some that's here in service, and is as old as some. The age should be nothing if a man is able to do service, which I know he is.

Tell Pa and Ma for me that I am getting on very well. Tell Henry to write to me. Even if he writes bad that is no excuse. I wrote to Tom a week ago and wrote William a note and let him know the men that wanted to pay their

---

[63] On January 18, 1863 various cavalry companies were organized into the 5th South Carolina Cavalry. The companies then served separately in detachments, guarding the Atlantic coast until 1864. Knudsen, "5th SC," 2-3.

[64] Robert H. Hays served as a private in Company I, 5th South Carolina Cavalry. Hays enlisted at age 35 from the Barnwell District. He was killed in action on May 11, 1864 at Drewry's Bluff, Virginia. Knudsen, "5th SC," 27.

accounts. Send a note to the office and he can get it from there.

Tell Jimmie to be a good boy. Kiss them both for me.

Your Husband

J.M. Barr

———◦◦◦◦◦———

Fraziers, S.C.

February 12, 1863

My dear Wife:

I received your letter this morning on picket post. Lt. Brooker handed it to me (as I was relieved).[65] We stand every other twenty four hours. So you see I will be at Headquarters, which is Fraziers, till tomorrow morning. I will be on pickets four nights and four days. not having a post for the week. We are watching very closely the movements of the Enemy.

I see from General Walkers dispatch to Gov. Bonham that the Enemy had sixty repels [vessels] at Port Royal entrance and says if attacked he will need the three Regiments of Reserves, but the old fellows are very anxious to get off home.[66] I won't say all, for some have volunteered to stay for thirty days longer.

---

[65] E. Booker served as a second lieutenant in Company I, 5th South Carolina Cavalry. Knudsen, "5th SC," 82.

[66] During January and February 1863 Confederate authorities suspected that the Federals were planning a major attack on Charleston or Savannah and called out the old men and boys of the state reserves. General Walker expected an attack in his district at any time. In addition to writing South Carolina Governor Milledge Luke Bonham for assistance, on February 10 Walker wrote to General P. G.T. Beauregard, the commander of the Department of South Carolina, Georgia and Florida, asking for an extension of service for the reserves and reinforcements: "When the reserves leave I will have an aggregate force of less than 3,000 men, so widely scattered over a long line of defense that they could be beaten in detail before being concentrated. Everything points to a most formidable attack, and I offer these suggestions that my position may be thoroughly understood, and that the necessary reenforcements may be ready to assist me in case of attack." United States War Department, *The War of the Rebellion: A Compilation of the Official Records of the Union and Confederate Armies*, 128 vols. (Washington, DC: Government Printing Office, 1880-1901), series 1, vol. 14, p.772, hereinafter cited as *OR*. All references are to Series 1 unless otherwise noted.

My first post was some half mile from the Ferry. This time I will be on four different posts. We are looking for the Yankees to land soon, but we will try and not let them catch us as they did Lt. Banks.[67] At that post they say they can come out and cut our pickets off at any time, as the post is in a corner like.

I would like very much to see Thomas. Tell him, if you get to see him, that I would like very much to have him with me here on a good horse. Then his feet might get right. I mean that the sole might get better for I know he has had some hard times, Tell him I wrote to him some weeks or so ago.

I do not know how much I will weigh, though I saw myself Sunday for the first time since I left home. I have fattened up a good deal. I expect if I live to keep my health that I will weigh two hundred lbs. in twelve months or a shorter time.

Some of our boys and the Yankees had a quarrel from their post this morning. They would curse each other and then talk friends. I could hear our boys. The Yankees asked what regiment they belonged to. The reply by our boys was the Forty-Seventh South Carolina Regiment. Of course we would not tell them.

Aaron has not put a substitute in. His teaching school has, I believe, cleared him as he has been teaching for several years. His occupation has been school teaching I believe a good while though.[68]

You know how long John C. was at your Mothers when Elijah came back or when he left, I don't know which.[69]

Tell Henry to pay Pa his cotton back that I borrowed when at home. Tell him not to use any more of my iron than he can help. Use up some of the old ploughs.

Has an owner come for the cow yet? If not, did any one stick up the advertisement? If an owner comes, they ought to pay for her feed till you milked her.

Tell the people that inquire after me that I am getting on finely, though

---

[67] On October 22, 1862 First Lieutenant Amos O. Banks, Company I, 5th South Carolina Cavalry was captured near Pocotaligo at Cuthbert House. On October 24, 1864 he joined the Confederate Invalid Corps. Knudsen, "5th SC," 6.

[68] Aaron D. Dowling listed his occupation in the 1860 Census as "Farmer." *1860 Census*, Orangeburg District, South Carolina.

[69] Rebecca Barr's brother John Caldwell Calhoun Dowling had been a student living at home with his mother prior to the war. *1860 Census*, Barnwell District, South Carolina.

I have not been in a fight yet and am not anxious to get in one, but if one takes place, I expect to fill my place and do the best I can and trust to the good One to protect me.

Tell Jimmie that Pa has not seen any apples but did get a fine orange off of an orange tree. I believe I told you about it. I would have given one dollar to have it sent to you but could not do it. Charlie and I ate it. It was a sweet orange. I got it in a front yard. Tell Jimmie Pa will bring him a big bullet if he gets to come home soon.

If you get down soon you can tell Dr. Addy that you want him to let me know your situation and to send a certificate saying that he is my family Doctor etc. He knows better how to do than I can tell. Don't tell him I wanted him to write. Tell him you wanted him to try and get me off a few days to see you. I was told that if the Dr. would in such cases they would let one off.

As for summer clothing, I will need pants and cotton shirts. I have two colored ones. I sold the velvet one for seven dollars and bought blankets for six dollars. Lt. Guess wagon was to come down this week.[70] If it comes I told Ance to send the pair of blankets home.

I will close to get this off this evening as it will have to be sent back 16 miles to Pocataligo. Tell Jimmie and Johnny that Pa wants to see them and you too.

Adieu for the present

Your Beloved Husband

James M. Barr

---

[70] Sam Guess, Barr's messmate and brother-in-law, may have also been a militia officer with the title of "lieutenant." He served as a private in the Confederate service.

Pocataligo, S.C.
February 18.1863

My dear Wife:

It is again that I attempt to write you and answer to yours of the 15th, which came safely to hand this evening, but you must not look for a long letter for I have just got back to camp from our picket point and my candle is too high for me to see the lines, and I feel a good deal like going to bed. I don't know what to write you though.

I can tell you something I expect you have not heard. John C. has got in our company. He has been transferred. He got a furlough for seven days. Ance says he will come tomorrow, but he told me he would not come till Saturday.[71] As we have election for 3rd. Lt. tomorrow I expect he has concluded not to miss voting. There are three candidates, Whetstone, Crum and Felder. Whetstone will be elected I believe.[72] I prefer being a private. Tell Phillip if he does go in service to come here.[73] Several men have joined our company in the last few days. Several that belong to companies in Virginia, or they have been attached to it, till General Walker can hear from Va.

I did not take Ance with me on picket as he was pretty bad off with the mumps. He is still pretty sick though the swelling has gone a good deal. The Dr. says he thinks he will be well in a few days. So you see he is not doing me any good, but I hope he will be able to in a few days to attend to his business.

---

[71] Rebecca's brother John C. Dowling enlisted April 11, 1862 at age 18 as a private in Company A, 1st South Carolina Infantry under Colonel Franklin W. Kilpatrick in Brigadier General Micah Jenkins' Brigade. He may not have been entirely truthful with his family for he was listed as absent without leave from his company from November 11, 1862 through the end of June 1863. *1860 Census*, Barnwell District, South Carolina; Salley, *South Carolina Troops*, np.

[72] A. P. Whetstone from the Barnwell District served as a second lieutenant in Company I, 5th South Carolina Cavalry. He was wounded during the Battle of Trevilian Station, Virginia, June 11-12, 1864. J. W. Crum was from the Orangeburg district and served in Company I, 5th South Carolina Cavalry. Several Felders served in the 5th, but there is no record of any of them in Company I. Knudsen, "5th SC," 16, 59.

[73] Philip Churchill Spann, son of Reverend Henry Hammond Spann, was Barr's nephew. He was in his mid twenties when the war began and had been farming near his father's place with his wife Jane and their young son. Philip C. Spann enlisted into Company I, 5th South Carolina Cavalry. *1860 Census*, Lexington District, South Carolina; Knudsen, "5th SC," 52; McDaniel, *Correspondence*, 270.

I am truly glad to hear that Mary will stay with you and others. It has satisfied my mind a good deal for I was uneasy about you, knowing you would not ask any one to stay with you. I hope you may get on well and when I come home to see our dear little boys and a pretty little black eyed girl babe.[74]

Do not feel uneasy for me. A many one has gone in battle and come off safe. Trust I may be permitted to come through if I get in one. I expect we will be moved to Charleston. I don't know how soon.

Tell me how much meat to give Jerry. I think that I gave him 3 lbs. a week and if that is not enough and he prefers it, I will sell him.[75] Some one wanted to buy him before I left. At Mrs. Hayes' Sale a girl and one child brought 2005 dollars. Twelve to fourteen year old girls, 1400 to 1500 dollars, so I heard.

I am still well. I have not been sick a day since or an hour since I left home.

You ought to write twice a week. My being on picket doesn't keep me from getting letters. Some one has to come to headquarters daily.

Your True Husband

J.M. Barr

---

[74] Rebecca Dowling was about eight months pregnant at this time. McDaniel, *Correspondence*, 12.

[75] Prior to the war most adult slaves were fed an average of a half a pound of pork per day. Considering the war and Jerry's age, Barr may have been feeding him a healthier diet than many other slaves had at the time. Eugene D. Genovese, *Roll, Jordan, Roll: The World the Slaves Made* (New York: Vintage Books, 1976), 63.

———◦◦◦◦———

Pocataligo, S.C.
February 19. 1863

My Dear Wife:

This morning about three o'clock about one hundred soldiers, Col. Stevens Regiment, came up.[76] They made their fires all around our camp that is our camping. So you see we are nearly surrounded. These soldiers are Barnwell, Orangeburg, and Colleton men I hear.

Tell Henry I will write him in a few days.

I don't think Bill takes care of the sheep. It is easy to tell smooth tale for they looked too well when I left to die if he had taken the right care of them. Though they can wear cotton instead of wool, which they would rather do than take care of the stock.

You need not have my shoes fixed just now, but keep enough of sole leather to put a sole to them when they are to be fixed. I want them made over putting the same work back on them with an additional sole.

I hear that some fifteen cases of smallpox are in Blackville.

I will close as I can't write to suit myself.

Your Affectionate Husband
James M. Barr

---

[76] Colonel Clement Hoffman Stevens commanded the 24th South Carolina Infantry. Promoted to brigadier general in February 1864, he commanded a Georgia brigade when he was mortally wounded near Atlanta in July 1864. *OR*, vol. 14, p. 814.

Pocataligo, S. C.
February 22, 1863

My dear Rebecca:

I again make an attempt to write you a few lines to let you know that I am well. I have not enjoyed better health for a long time than I now do. I appear always hungry at every meal, not hungry because we have not much to eat. I've had plenty and still have a good supply on hand. We have two hams, two shoulders and all the flour and fruit that I brought with me. We have two large cakes of butter yet, which your Mother sent me by Elijah. We still have a few dozen eggs yet and a good many sweet things from home. Besides, we draw beef every day except Sunday. We get about half a lb. of bacon apiece a week. We get sugar nearly enough to sweeten our coffee. It would be enough but we have it nearly every meal when we are in camp. We draw no flour but get rice and meal. The meal is not good, not as good as ours at home, for it is ground too long.

I see that a good many new recruits are joining the Companies. Several have come to ours and about twenty have joined the Lexington Company.

Another Regiment came to this place yesterday evening. They are North Carolinians. They say their Brigade is all coming here. They are under Cooks. I would much rather have South Carolinians here.[77]

Everything is quiet here for the present. We are well fixed.

My horse is looking well. He has fattened up and by currying and brushing him his hair looks well. Our horses were all appraised yesterday. My horse was appraised at three hundred and fifty dollars, Charlie's at three hundred. Only two horses in our company were appraised higher than mine. Two or three as high. The men in our company have generally good horses appraised from 200 to 400.[78]

---

[77] On February 20, 1863 General Beauregard reinforced General Walker with Brigadier General John R. Cooke's North Carolina Brigade. Ibid., p. 788..

[78] Horses in the Confederate Cavalry belonged to individual soldiers. While the army did not furnish horses, it would reimburse men who lost theirs. In addition, a horseless soldier could find himself involuntarily transferred to the infantry.

Ance is still doing me no good, but I think he is mending. I think he will soon be well unless the weather should get too bad and he relapses. We hire our cooking done. Capt. Tyler's boy is now cooking for us. I hope Ance will soon be able to cook as I would much rather have him to cook.

Tell Jimmie he must tell Bill to take good care of his poney and must not let any one ride it nor throw sticks at it.

I wrote to Henry on the twentieth and said to him to plant twelve acres in cotton and to drill the corn on the other side of the mill. Bill ought to know how I had it done year before last, but I do not know whether he will know or not.

Tell Henry to sell some peas if any one wants to buy, and to get as much as he can but not to take less than two dollars a bushel strick measure.

I would like very much to have my horse down here. If I had him here I would send Sam back. He would have been appraised at about Four Hundred dollars. That is if he is looking well. I wish I could get him here. I may send for him. Let me know how he is looking. Don't know whether I can get any one to bring him to me or not.

It has been raining slowly all the morning and is still raining.

Why don't you write twice a week? Can't you find something to write about? I think you can write what all the Negroes are doing who are plowing, what the rest are doing, how they behave and whether they mind you. Have you any trouble to keep them about the house, especially at night and on Sundays? If so write me and I will write to Henry. But if they are not obedient, you ought to get Henry to correct them.

How are your geese getting on? Do they stay in the pasture? Ask Bill every day whether they do or not. I should have them some where else. I don't want them in the wheat nor in the fields that I want corn in. Are any of them setting? Charlie asked me this day if you had any goose eggs. Let all set and raise all you can. When they hatch, Bill must make Jess Pen them.

Keep a good supply of postage stamps on hand so if I need them you can send them to me. I let Charlie have half I brought from home and gave some for newspapers. Whenever I want a newspaper, ten cts. will buy one, and if I send to the Depot for one, I can make the change with stamps.

For Summer I will need light shirts, homespun will do. Two heavy calico would suit me better than anything else. Hope this will find you as well as can be expected and find our children well. I must write Walter Quattlebaum in a few days.

James M. Barr
Care of Capt. T.W. Tyler
Pocataligo, S.C.
Your dear Husband
J.M. Barr

Leesville, S.C.
Sunday Morning
February 22, 1863

My Dear Major:

I received your letter yesterday evening and was delighted to hear from you and to hear you are well and have not been in battle. I was sorry to hear Ance was still sick. I hope he will soon be able to wait on you. I expect it goes rather hard with you to have to do your own cooking and tend to your horse. I was glad to hear John C. was now with you. I heard he was married, but I suppose it was all a joke.

I saw Tom yesterday. He was here but did not stay more than a few minutes, hardly gave us time to see him. He was on his way to Gants muster ground for the purpose of getting men to go with him. I don't know how many he will get. I heard little Jim Spann was going for one. Tom is looking well. He says old Mr. Rawl is still sick and is as helpless as a babe.[79] I don't think he will ever get well, though the Dr. says he may get up again.

Henry sold your mule yesterday to Daniel Quattlebaum for 75 dollars and he gave a note. I told Henry to give it to William. D. Quattlebaum bought the negro Wesley. Bought him at Haltiwangers sale and swaped him to Jake Shealy for his negro boy and Jake Shealy gave two hundred dollars to boot. The negro man's name was Dan. He is a brother to Quattlebaum's Luissia.[80]

Henry bought you two bushels of salt in Columbia and gave twenty dollars for the two bushels, but I know it will not measure two bushels, put in small sacks.

The men all have to leave for Charleston next Thursday, that is the Militia. I mean the men and boys and some of them regret it very much.

[79] Mr. Rawl was likely Thomas Barr's father-in-law..

[80] Daniel Quattlebaum was a very prosperous farmer in the Lexington District. William D. Quattlebaum from Edgefield had served as a second lieutenant Company C, 19th South Carolina Infantry prior to the 1862 reorganization, when he resigned his commission. Jake Shealy may be J. M. Shealy, who was a middling farmer prior to the war. *1860 Census*, Lexington District, South Carolina; Chapman, *History*, 449.

Some of the poor men say their families will have to suffer as they will be gone during planting season. Walter Quattlebaum is going too. I hope he will go where you are. I hope you will not have to move from where you are although your Pa says he thinks there will be a fight at Pocataligo, though I hope and trust it will not be so. There was no late news in the papers from Charleston.

Soloman Lowman is to be buried at the White Church today. It is said that he died of small pox, though I don't know that it is true.[81]

How delighted I was yesterday when I heard some of the negroes say, "Younder comes Master." I looked and how surprised I was to see Jim Smith and Edd Hays. They did not stop but passed on. I can't imagine what their business was. They went to Mr. Smiths about twelve o'clock and passed by going back in the afternoon. Their stay was short.

I am truly glad you went in service when you did for it would have been awful if you would have gone with the conscripts. I hope they have a fight down there that will whip the Yankees, and surely our men will whip them as they are all ordered to go. Some people think the Yankees will not attack Charleston or Savannah or any other place down there. I hope they won't.

Henry told me to tell you the calves and mules look better than they did when you left, but the sheep do not look as well. He says they don't suffer from the want of anything to eat. Bill says he has been giving them too many peas. He says the reason he thinks so is that they are shedding their wool very badly. We have had one more lamb. It is a very fine one. We have three white ones, one red one that looks very much like a calf. It has a white face and two white feet. Jimmy calls them all his lambs. He asks Bill every day if his lambs are well.

It is now Sunday night. The reason I did not finish it this morning Henry and Anna came.

Mr. Quattlebaum sent after Lue today as he is going off, though she will come back next Thursday. Florence is staying with me till Lue comes back. What do you think?

I let Jimmy go home with Lue. He was determined to go and I could not beg him to stay. I told him I would be very lonely and would cry and he kissed

---

[81] Perhaps S. F. Lowman, who served in Company F, 19th South Carolina Infantry. Chapman, *History*, 456.

me and said, "Ma, don't cry and I will bring you a real fish." I miss the little fellow so much. He is so bad I can't help from missing him. I asked John Wesley tonight where Jimmy was and he said, "gone" just as good as anyone could. He has gotten to be so very independent. He goes in and out of the house just when he pleases. This morning before breakfast, he went out the dining room door and went around to the front yard and was playing in the water that rained there last night. I had him to undress and put on dry clothes. I am so afraid John Wesley will forget you that I talk a great deal to him about you. I would be so delighted if you could see him at some of his monkey motions.

Bill has not yet found the sow I wrote to you about. I don't mean the sow, but I mean her little pigs. Bill sees the sow every day and says he thinks she has about seven pigs.

We have been having bad weather for the stock and the chickens, but when I think of you soldiers being exposed to the weather, how much worse I feel.

I sold four dollars worth of tobacco yesterday, which is more than I have sold in some time. I expect I will sell a good deal this week to the soldiers that are going off. I hope so any way. I hope I may sell it all.

I was coming from the store yesterday and Dr. Addy stopped. I felt quite cheap knowing that Henry had spoken to him to stay at home on my account. Dearest one, I am so anxious for it all to be over with soon, so I can get to see you as I have no chance of seeing you until then it seems. Anna was saying if she was me, she would not want you to come as soon as you heard of it - not before four weeks afterwards, but I told her I would want you to come right away. I would not want you to wait a week. I told her I was not like her. This world is not much pleasure to me without you.[82]

I don't know that you can understand this letter for really my mind is so confused I scarcely know half the time what I am doing.

I am about to close and did not tell you whether we were sick or well. We are all quite well. I feel like I might stay up a month longer, but I hope not. However, it is not as I desire, but it is as the Lord pleases.

Your Pa's family are all well except George. He is not well yet. I hope this

---

[82] Rebecca Barr was a few weeks away from giving birth to her third child when she wrote this letter.

will find you well and still in fine spirits.

Your Wife
Rebecca

Write soon and often. I would be glad to hear from you by every mail, though I don't miss it far.

I forgot to tell you the cause of the negroes complaining about the meat. I was to blame. I weighed off one weeks allowance for two and only gave them three lbs. for two weeks, so you see they had a cause to complain. I don't know what made me make the mistake. I looked on the books where you had it written and found out my mistake and gave them more meat immediately. Nothing more this time.

———$\sim\!\circ\!\circ\!\sim$———

Pocataligo, S. C. February , 1863
[no date on letter]

My Dear Rebecca:

I received your letter yesterday evening and was truly glad to hear from you and to hear that you were well and that all were well. I have been on the grunting orders for two days with my back.[83] The Dr. says it is kidney disease, though I have been up every day, yet I have not been able for duty. I am still weak in my back but feel a good deal better. I write to tell you how I am. Hope you will not feel uneasy for me for I am now mending and feel that I will soon be able to do duty.

Ance is well and has been cooking for us for two days. I can eat as hearty as ever. I don't wish you to feel uneasy for me for I could say I am well, but not being stronger in my back. I thought it best to tell precisely how I am

---

[83] "Grunting orders" appear to refer to light duty.

though. If the fight should come on this evening I think I should be in it, so you may know that I am not very sick. I know you will think he is worse off than he would let me know but not the case.

We do not know how soon we may have to fight at this place. The Yankees may come out in large forces and take the place, but I don't think they can before they get Pocataligo or the railroads. A many a life will be lost. I think we are well fixed and can make a hard fight, but the enemy can land at two points and march on the railroad. If they do they will give us a hard fight. Hope if they do land that the victory may be ours and that without the loss of many lives.

Surely you are mistaken about the price of the mule. I expect it was one hundred and seventy five dollars instead of 75 dollars. If I could have had the mule here I could of sold him for three hundred dollars.

I don't know whether Henry will have horses enough to tend my crop. My colt must be taken care of. I want her to be kept fat. I want her to be as good at three years old as many would be at eight.

I see that the Militia will stay at home a while longer.

I get a paper whenever we want one by paying ten cts.

I am very sorry you were so much disappointed in seeing Jim Smith.

The reason the sheep are sheding their wool (tell Bill) I can tell him. He let them get poor and then started them to mend and then they started to shed. Tell Henry I want the best ones kept, that is of the lambs.

I don't want you to let Jimmy go too far off from home. Tell Jimmy he said he was going to stay at home and take care of Ma for Pa. I hope John Wesley will not forget me.

We are faring well compared to some soldiers. A Regiment came through the other night. It rained nearly all night on them. They had on tents.

Charlie is well. John C. has not come down yet. Don't know what is the matter.

Hope this will find you and the children well, Father and Mother and kindred.

Rev. Mr. Welden preached us a splendid sermon last night, the first preaching I have heard.

Your husband,
J.M. Barr

I am glad William bought the cow for me. If you can, take good care of the calf and good care of the Warren yearling.

We are trying to send some things home to Charlie's. I will send the pair of blankets, one pair of socks, pants, 2 shirts, one pair shoes. If I get them that far, Henry can get them for you.

———◦○◦◦◦———

Editor's note: The following is a letter to Rebecca from her mother Elizabeth S. Dowling.

Spring Town, S.C.
March 1, 1863

Dear Daughter:

I was expecting a letter from you and thought the time long before I received it, but yesterday it came to hand and happy were we all to bear from you and to hear that you were well. We are all quite well, except some of the negroes are complaining from being vaccinated, which I think will soon be well. Sarah and Ellen's families are well, except Sarah's Rebecca.[84] She has fever caused from her being vaccinated.

Dear Daughter, I am sorry to inform you that John C. is still unfriendly. He did not get a substitute, but got a transfer to Capt. Tom Tyler's Company where the Major and Charlie are. Aaron hasn't put in a substitute nor gone himself. He is teaching school.

I suppose you are weaving. I am glad to hear it and hope you may succeed well. Mollie weaves a piece nearly every week. I have just put in a piece of sixty four yds., which weaves finely.

I sowed my garden and the seeds have come up beautifully. I have plants almost large enough to set out.

---

[84] Rebecca Barr's sisters Sarah Dowling Rice and Ellen Elizabeth Dowling Cox. McDaniel, *Correspondence*, 274-275.

Preston has at last named his babe.[85] He named it George Emma Dowling and you can't imagine how fast the babe grows and how pretty it is.

Dear Daughter, let me tell you something of the neighborhood news. Mrs. Hagood is dead. She died last week from a disease of the heart.[86] Elijah was there when she died. She was only sick a few days and without a change. Soon I think Cousin Hannah Michel will die. She has pneumonia. Elijah is tending her. I hope she will recover.

I suppose the small pox is near the Major and Charlie. I hope they won't take it though. I feel very uneasy about them. John C. is not certain his exchange is permanent as Bamberg says he never gave his consent for him to leave his Company.[87]

John C. had a very rainy day to go down. He went Saturday. We have had some very pretty weather so much that they are planting corn, but we may have to plant again.

Now I must tell you that Jake is going to take a wife at Rebecca Zorn's next Saturday night.[88]

I know you are lonely and I will try, if I don't get sick, to visit you some time before long. The children all send their love to you.

Your Affectionate Mother,
E.S. Dowling
P.S. I have never been to see Sarah yet since she came here. I must tell you Aaron Guess is expected home every day. Kiss your children for me.

Your mother E.S.D.

---

[85] Rebecca Barr's brother William Preston Dowling was a practicing dentist in his early thirties during the war. *1860 Census*, Barnwell District; McDaniel, *Correspondence*, 274-275.

[86] This was most likely Mrs. M. Hagood who was in her mid seventies and managed her prosperous Barnwell farm with the help of an overseer. *1860 Census*, Barnwell District, South Carolina.

[87] Captain Isaac S. Bamberg commanded Company A, 1st South Carolina Infantry. He resigned on June 16, 1863. Salley, *South Carolina Troops*, np.

[88] Rebecca Zorn of was Rebecca Barr's aunt. Prior to the war she lived independently in the Barnwell District. *1860 Census*, Barnwell District, South Carolina.

———⊰◦∘◦⊱———

Pocataligo, S.C.
March 2, 1863
My Dear Rebecca:

As I think you may be some what uneasy about me, as I wrote you that I
was not very well and that I was under the Dr.'s treatment, I think it best to
write you a few lines to let you know how I am getting on, as I know it natu-
ral for you to think that I am really worse off than I am. I have fallen off some,
but I am up and about a good deal better than when I wrote you last, though
not doing any duty yet and don't expect to do any for a week. The Company
will do picket duty this week. They will picket from Camp so I will not be so
lonesome. I feel much better and have (had and have) a good appetite.

John C. came down Monday evening. Decanie Cox came with him.
Caney started back this morning. He was well pleased whilest here. John C.
is messing with Charlie and I and will stay in our tent. I sent with Caney the
pair of white blankets, a pair of pants, two white shirts, one you made for me
and one slazy one I drew. I also sent the pair of shoes that Wingard made and
my saddle, as I have no use for two.[89]

If three horses will not do my plowing, I perhaps would better buy
another, though it seems Henry would not have sold if he had not thought
the mules and horse would be sufficient to do it. If I could have told him, I
would have said not to sell.

Bill must take good care of the pigs as well as the other things. I would
not take three hundred dollars for my colt if she is looking as well as when I
left and tell Bill she must not look any worse.

I am surprised at your weaving. You know that you ought not to have
done it and your long walks after the geese. I think you ought not to fatigue
yourself so much. Why doesn't Bill shut the geese up in the pasture and keep
them out of the grass patch? Is the grass any account? If not, I want it planted in something else.

I expect the reason your hens don't hatch is that the eggs are handled too

---

[89] Decanie Cox may have been a relative of Rebecca's sister Ellen Cox. McDaniel, *Correspondence*, 274.

much or the hens have bad nests to sit in. My hens have layed me some forty eggs. One has just gone setting. The Captain has told me several times to let her set. This evening he said he would buy eggs and set her. I told him I would rather have the eggs.

I think it a bad chance for a furlough. I don't know when I will get to come home. I would like to see you and the babies. I dreamed last night that I was home, so you see that I saw you in my sleep.

It has been quite warm down here. We have had several warm days. Have they planted any corn yet? When will they' commence? When you plant sweet potatoes, plant watermellons in the patch.

You need not make me any shirts yet. If I get to go home in a month or two I can buy calico for a couple.

Kiss Jimmie and Johnny for Pa.

Your Dear Husband
J.M. Barr

Poctaligo, S.C.
March the 8th, 1863

My Dear Wife:

I received your letter Friday evening and I assure you it afforded me much pleasure to hear from you and my dear little children. Especially to hear that you all were well. I hope this may find you still enjoying the same blessing; I am now doing very well. I feel nearly as well as I ever did.

We are doing picketing duty this week but our week will be out Wednesday and then other Companies will relieve for two weeks, but we still have other dutys to do which are nearly as hard to do as picketing but not near so dangerous. First, we have our yards to sweep and stables to clean out by nine o'clock every morning. Second, drill and saber exercise on foot at eleven o'clock, taught by a drill Master, a very crabed one at that. I felt like knocking him down once since I have been down here, though I get on with him very well now. The new recruits are very awkward in the saber exercise. Third, drill on horse back which I like very much. Fourth, later in the evening dress parade, either on foot or horse back. Every Tuesday we have Regimental Parade and on Fridays, inspection of Saber and rifles. Our rifles will shoot about one thousand yards. Once a month General Review and Inspection. So you can see that we are kept pretty busy, besides keeping our saber and rifles in fine order to stand the inspection.

We are now very comfortably fixed up. We have two beds up in our tent and have plenty of room in it. We have a regular wall tent now. Ance and a young fellow cut us logs and notched them up some five logs high and then stretched our tent over it which gives us the room.

Ance is making some money washing at five cents a garment, cleaning stalls when he has a chance and buying penders at three dollars a bushel and selling them at six dollars and forty cts. per bushel. He washes very well. I thought I would hire my washing done, but he can do it as well as I could get it done. He then irons them. Speaking of penders, you would better have a good many planted.

You asked me what kind of drawers did I draw and whether they would do for me or not. They are first rate twilled drawers suitable for Summer. I drew a round Jacket yesterday, you ought now to see me stepping about in full uniform of Confederate Grey and my grey pants I brought from home and grey round Jacket with my boots blacked. Yes, blacked for the first time since I left home, though I often have my shoes greased. If you make me any summer pants, I would like something grey. I don't think I would like dimity.[90] If you hire it woven, get a good weaver to weave it.

You say Wesley said the mule was sold too cheap. I know it was and would have written to Henry but I did not think he would sell it. If my letter would have gotten to him in time stating that I wanted my horse, I don't suppose he would have sold. I suppose he can loan me a mule when needed with the crop. If not, I will have to buy again if a crop can't be made without one. They must feed better, drive harder, plough better and if the season is good, I think a crop can be made if the will is good. Perhaps the Negroes may not be in the humor.

---

[90] Dimity was a plain-woven corded cotton cloth usually made in stripes or checks.

We have been having splendid weather down here, rather too warm, not much rain.

Mr. Fink took dinner with us the other day.[91] He was ditching close by and came to see us. He is looking very well. I have ditched one day since I have been down. (Men have to be detailed from each Company for that purpose and for Camp Guard).

I am glad to know that your garden seed has come up. I hope you may have good luck with your garden. And if I get home to see a fine garden, I don't want any thing planted in the cotton patches, but I want a good stand of cotton. Tell the Negroes that I say they all ought to try and see how well they can do. They ought to work well and do it good. This means a good stand and good work and a heap of it.

What did Tom say about his over coat? Did he say he wanted it?

You did not tell me how the colt looked.

You asked me to try and get a furlough and come home. It is a bad chance for a furlough. One man in our company got one the other day for six days. Mr. Abram Hartzog got a letter the other day with the Dr.'s certificate stating that his wife was very sick and he was needed or she wished to see him, He applied for a furlough. It was all fixed, but the General would not sign it so the chance for a furlough is bad.[92]

All is quiet here. I hope the excitement of a fight will soon wear off and that they may soon begin to give furloughs for I would like very much to see you, Jimmie and Johnny Wesley. I would like to see the little fellow to see if he would know me. Suppose though he has forgotten me.

I will be sure to write once a week. You must write often.

Send me a few stamps if you can get them handily. Don't send many at a time, some 5 or 10.

Take good care of salt. Salt the stock occasionally. I bought for next Winter fearing it would get higher. Use the last. How much did I have before? Henry bought two bushels. If I have not much, perhaps I would better get more.

---

[91] Probably George A. Fink from the Lexington District, who was a private in Company F, 5th South Carolina Cavalry. Knudsen, "5th SC," 21.

[92] A. N. W. Hartzog served in Company I, 5th South Carolina Cavalry. He enlisted from the Barnwell District and was wounded on October 22, 1862 at Pocotaligo, South Carolina. Hartzog died in 1881. Knudsen, "5th SC," 16, 27.

I believe I told you not to make any more shirts.

Give my respects to friends. Hope I may soon see them.

All my love to you and the darling boys and kindred.

Your Husband
J.M. Barr

—◦◦◦—

Pocataligo, S.C.
March 15, 1863

My Dear Rebecca:

As another Sunday has made its appearance and as it is such a beautiful day, I shall devote some part of it to my dearest one who is so far from me. Yet we still have the privilege of conversing with each other by the mail.

I am truly glad that you have company so that you may not be so lonely, but it appears that they hit too much together. Don't know though, you are the better judge.

I am now enjoying very good health. I don't think I even had kidney disease. The pain was perhaps caused from riding horseback as I was not accustomed to riding horse back a great deal, I came here to try to be of service to my Country and shall never try to get off unless I prove to be unfit for duty. You may expect to hear of complaining among soldiers where there are so many and among them perhaps a husband or brother or friend to be sick. As they are exposed to all kinds of weather more than at home, but when you hear that they are complaining, you must not think they can't stand camp life. You must think they will become hardened to camps and they will soon become to stand it much better. You say you know I feel lonely and low spirited. I have been sick, but I assure you I was up all the time pretty much as usual. Capt. Tyler was complaining part of the time as he was grunting with his back too.

I did write Henry a letter encouraging him to do better. I hope he may. I want to see if he will say anything to me about it when he writes. Ask him if he read the letter to Pa and Ma, if he said anything more about it, and what did they say to him, and whether he had taken up the crop or not. I think it was just as well for the Negores to work on Thanksgiving Day as it was for us to work here.

Mr. Leaphart can have six head of sheep for one Hundred dollars ($100).[93] Six head. I expect a fine wool one from last years lambs and will give him the pick among the flock. If he wants them at that price, (6) six for $100 dollars, Henry can select them out for him. Tell Henry I don't want to sell my finest wool sheep or the ewes, those that have lambs. Is the grass fit to turn the sheep on, the lambs I mean?

I would like to know what Phillip would take for the Rube Shealy mare as soon as possible, whether he will sell or not.

I am glad Henry thinks he can tend my land so easy. I think three ought to tend it very easily.

I suppose by this time that all my corn is planted as the Negroes had nothing else to do when I left but to prepare the land for planting.

I think there is no use of Bill and Jess looking after the geese eggs. Ask Henry to see if any are setting.

I am pleased to hear that the colt is looking as well as when I left. I was fearful they wouldn't take the care of her that they ought.

How is the corn holding out? I hope it is not wasted.

Did you have your meat well smoked with china berries?

Did they stop the cotton rows at the peach trees? I told Bill and Jerry both. I suppose they did it.

Ance will make a collar for Jim's horse.

Bill must not feed the big hogs so much corn. I told him I wanted him to tend to them good, not to let them die, but not to keep them too fat.

I hope the fruit will not be killed and trust I may get home when there is plenty, but I don't know when I can get home. I would like very much to see you and our little fellows, but it has not been so long yet, only about two months. Time slips off fast.

---

[93] Joseph Leaphart of Lexington was J. W. Barr's brother-in-law. Leaphart married Elizabeth Barr (1820-1896) and they raised seven children. Being in his fifties when the war began, Leaphart was able to avoid military service. *1860 Census*, Lexington District, South Carolina; McDaniel, *Correspondence*, 271.

Tell Henry that I wish he would come down. It would pay him well to come and look around, but be sure to let me know before he comes.

I want my watch. The one William let me have doesn't run half of the time. I want to send my woolen clothes home too as soon as I can get Summer ones. I need a summer round jacket. Mr. Spann has a coat make like I want one. He wore it fishing last Summer.

We get pork and beef every day, bad beef though.

I must now write a few lines for Ance as he is here asking me to write for him. He says ask Henry and George if they have spent the money he left with them, if Henry bought the stockings for his wife, and what he paid. And he wants John to make him a good pocket knife with a good finish and send it by Henry if he comes. And to tell you he has made ten dollars and twenty-five cents since he has been here. I expect he wants the Negroes to know it. He wants to know how his wife is.

I received a letter the other day from Thomas. He wrote about the sixth of March. He says that he left Mr. Rawl very low and his family with scarlet fever. I don't like that. I got his over coat. I have put it in my valice. I hope Henry will come down that I may be able to send it home. He said he was well and started on a sixty mile march.

I saw yesterday nine Yankees. They were prisoners that were captured a few days ago, a Lieutenant, one sargent and seven privates. They were captured over on Hilton Head. I believe they were the signal core. They were halted at the railroad and our boys gathered around to see them. They looked very much cut down. There was one that looked like he was a great rascal. When they were ordered to march one said, "I suppose they are done with the show." I understand that some one said to them they were glad to see them. They answered that, "you will have the pleasure of seeing a great many more in a few days."

What has become of the raw hide I left in the store house? If Pa is not tanning it, I want it sent to Fulmer 's Tan Yard.

I hope this may find you enjoying as good health as I could expect knowing your situation. Trust that Jimmie is well and that he was not sick after you wrote. As for John Wesley, I hope he is well and how I would like to see the little fellow. Would like to see you all, but it may be three months more before I can realize that pleasure for furloughs are scarce and few between.

Give my love to Pa and Ma and remember me to all inquiring friends. My love to you and the children.

Remaining as ever
Your dear Husband,
J.M. Barr

———∞∞∞———

Pocataligo, S.C.
March 20, 1863

My Dear Wife:

I, this evening, have just received a letter from Dr. Addy stating that you were confined on the 17th and that we have another fine son and that you and the babe were doing well.[94] You can't imagine what pleasure it gives me to know that the long dreaded time has come and gone and to hear that you are doing so well. I hope you will still continue to mend.

I would like very much to see you and our dear little children and I hope and trust it will not be long before I get to see you at our home. I don't think there is any chance to get a furlough now, but as soon as the excitement of a fight at this place wears off, I think I can get a furlough. I think it will take some five or six weeks for it to wear off. I only have one chance to get off soon and that is a slim one. That is to hire some one for two or three weeks and if I could find such a some one, the question is whether the Captain would take him for a few days or not.

I am well and getting on finely, not needing any provisions. We are getting plenty of pork, bacon and beef. We have been having plenty potatoes, paying from $1.00 to $1.50 for them per bushel. I don't want the tobacco kept if you can sell it.

---

[94] On March 17, 1863 Rebecca Barr gave birth to a son, Charlie Decania Barr. McDaniel, *Correspondence*, 12.

Don't want any hand sent on the Coast. I would rather pay a fine.[95]

You had better hire some one to weave out your cloth and turn Jane out.

I suppose I have plenty of clothing for Summer if I could get home to get them. I would like to have a round Jacket, but you must not bother yourself about that now as I will not need them yet. I suppose I can get home by the time that I need them.

I want you to write me as soon as you can or get someone else to do it and let me know how you are getting on. I will wait anxiously to hear.

Your Devoted Husband
James M. Barr

---

[95] The Confederate Government had been impressing slaves in order to build coastal fortifications.

———◦◦◦◦—

Pocataligo, S.C.
April 12, 1863

My Dear Wife:

I am now in camp but very much fatigued. We got back here this morning about one hour before sun. No doubt you have seen by now of the destruction of an armed Yankee steamer in Coosaw River. The steamer was destroyed near where Joseph Guess lived on Thursday morning.[96]

Wednesday evening about six o'clock we were ordered to Chisolm Island. We were halted near the Island after a hard ride in a canter, but in fine spirit. I never saw men in better humor, keen for a fight. We spent the latter part of the night bad as we were halted in an old field and there was a heavy dew and it was cold. We had no blankets and with little fire burning from straw and log finding we could get. About day the artillery opened on the boat. We have taken two prisoners and got one that was killed. He was burned badly. All his clothes were burned off of him, balance escaped, but some drowned.

Thursday morning we were ordered back to camp. Friday about two we were ordered back to the Island and got there about dark with two days rations. We halted and hitched. We marched across the Island about two miles and halted at the house place where Joseph Guess' overseer lived. With rifle and spades and shovels there we worked till day break throwing up breast works.

At day we marched back to our horses and Saturday night we were marched back to the Island to split the artillery. We succeeded in getting off with one of the guns, a brass twenty-five pounder, worth a good deal to us.

---

[96] On April 9, 1863 a small force of Confederates under artillery Captain Stephen Elliott engaged the Union armed transport steamer *George Washington* on the Coosaw River. Elliott's command consisted of two artillery batteries supported by six companies of the 48th North Carolina Infantry and five companies of cavalry, including Company I, 5th South Carolina Cavalry. Early on the morning of April 9 Elliott's force found the *George Washington* after she had been left behind by her gunboat escort. At dawn, Elliott found an easy target and after a few rounds, the *Washington's* powder magazine ignited leaving the boat aflame. The Federals raised a white flag and used the cease-fire as an opportunity to flee to the safety of the opposite bank as the ship burned to the waterline. Elliott's men captured two severally burned prisoners and the body of a third. *OR*, vol. 14, pp. 282-283.

There were two more on the boat, the Yankees having taken them off. The day we wanted the other two, the Yankees found us out and commenced shelling us or shelling about the wrecked steamer. At our picket post the shells could be seen too well as they came in a direct course for us. The shells looked beautiful. Solid shot fell in about two hundred yards of us. It did not reach so far.[97] After all the artillery had left the Island we then followed, so we arrived home about one hour before sun this morning. It has been by far the hardest work since I have been in.

Wednesday we start on picket. I got no letter from you since I left. I feel like something is the matter at home as I asked you to write soon.

This is written badly. Don't let any one read it.

My love to you and the children.

Your Husband
James

Remember me to friends and Pa and Ma. I am feeling much better after sleeping.

———◦◦◦———

Leveretts, S.C.
April 18th, 1863

My Dear Wife:

It is with pleasure that I am able to write to you again. I received your letter a few days ago, which afforded me much pleasure to hear from you and our dear children. I would like to see you all very much.

Yesterday evening whilest I was on picket I lay down to take a nap

---

[97] On the night of April 10 Elliot retuned with his force and attempted to salvage weapons from the wreck. They found that the Federals had successfully removed a 24-pounder howitzer. Elliot succeeded in raising a 24-pounder howitzer but was forced to bury it on shore due to lack of transportation. Even though the Federals shelled them as they worked, Elliot's force suffered no casualties during the entire affair. Ibid.

whilest the men that were with me were watching. But do you think I slept? No, my mind wandered to home, thinking of you and the children, so you see I missed my nap. I have just gotten back off picket post. I have eaten my dinner and a hardy one at that, rice, bacon and molasses. We are drawing it now.

Now after dinner I am writing to you though I have nothing new to write to you, but will endeavor to fill up with something to satisfy you. I have attempted to write a letter even if it is a failure.

Mittie left for home this morning. She has been down some ten days. Elijah came after her. He came down to see us and says all is well at home. Sawyer brought Mittie down. He preached for us whilest he was down.

All seems to be quiet down here now. I don't know how long it will remain so. I hope the Yankees will evacuate the soil of South Carolina. Some think they will, but it is hard to know.

It is said that they are having Negro pickets on post.[98]

Henry did wrong in selling my peas at home as he told me he would go to Columbia for me and put a horse to my wagon. I told him to get all he could for my load. I heard that peas and corn were selling at three dollars a bushel before I got to camp.

I do not know how much cotton will be allowed planted to the hand. Some say one acre to the hand.[99]

If I had my watch chain I think I could sell it and watch for five hundred dollars. A man said if I had a fine chain, he believed he would give that to me for it. I have concluded not to sell the chain, so if William calls for it, tell him I have given up selling it.

How is the stand of corn? Have they replanted all? Write soon and give me all the news.

I hope I may be able to see you in two or three months, but I have no idea when furloughs will be given and so many that nave not been home in 6

---

[98] Union black troops had been serving along the South Carolina coast since late 1862.

[99] By 1863 the Confederate government had limited the amount of land that growers could devote to staple crops like cotton in order to encourage vegetable cultivation needed to feed the troops in the field.

months will want to go. I could have stayed one day longer at home, but I think it will be to my advantage.

Your True Husband,
J.M. Barr

P.S. Remember me to Pa and Ma and kindred that inquire after me.

———◦◦◦———

Editor's note: The following letter to Rebecca is from her brother William Preston Dowling, M.D. and D.D.S.

Bamberg, S.C.
April 22nd, 1863

Dear Sister:

Mother has received yours of April 18th and I write in the place of her. She thinks it likely she can't come again this Spring.

Sarah Rice has a seven pound girl, but is doing well.

John C. stated in a letter to some of his relatives that it is likely he will have to go back to Virginia.

Ellen and family are well.

I did not get to see the Colonel going to nor coming from camp. How does he look? Does he look like a soldier, planter, merchant or what? If he keeps on trying things or businesses, he will after awhile equal my course of life, but it does not pay to do so many things, but the last is praise worthy in any gentleman.[100]

Elijah went to the rear of the guns in Charleston Harbor just in time to be too late even to see the end of so beautiful a bombardment.[101] He seems

---

[100] During the war Barr had risen in the militia to the rank of colonel. Mc Daniel, *Correspondence*, 8.

[101] On April 7, 1863 Federal gunboats under the command of Rear Admiral Samuel F. Du Pont attacked the defenses of Charleston Harbor. The fleet attacked Forts Sumter and Moultrie and received brisk fire in return. In the end, Du Pont's force withdrew after suffering extensive damage, including five ships disabled.

to have given out going to war again for a while. He said as soon as Spring opened, he would turn to "soldiering" in good earnest. We are both here. I am trying to plant and be in the name of physician, while I feel myself in my duty. I do not think we both are.

I have tried my hand lately at cotton buying. I bought 25 bales at 20 cents and sold them afterwards at 33 cents less the commissions - pretty well that time if I had just stopped there, but did not. You know I am death on a thing when I once start, so I bought more at 30cents and cotton went down, but I hauled it off and sold it for 30cents, losing the labor of hauling only thereby. I have now quit the cotton business.

I bought a little girl to nurse our fat babe, which cost me the round sum of two thousand dollars, $2000. 00. Don't you think I am crazy?

In my older days I have concluded like yourself to quit the weaving for Mother's place, but I find little or nothing else for the women to do, so I just let 3 or 4 of them spin.

I am nearly done crop plowing corn and it is not yet visible when riding the road, but I think it will come up some day.

Mother's health is good. My wife, babe and myself suffer severly with colds just now. It seems to me, "Sis," we can beat the world in "gal" babies for size, sense and eyes.

The health of this country is good at present and may we be in better spirits now as the Yankees confess a whipping at Charleston. May God send them away every where soon that our homes may be as they were once and better.

Sis, Elijah forgot the ink from home and this was made at home and does not write well, so you will excuse this whole letter.

Tell us again soon of the boy babies.
Yours Affectionately
W. Preston Dowling

CHAPTER TWO
MY DEAR, CAMP IS A LAZY PLACE

In April 1863 General General P.G.T. Beauregard, commander of the Department of South Carolina, Georgia and Florida, detached various companies of the 5th South Carolina Cavalry to picket the approaches to Charleston. Company I was ordered to McClellanville and remained in the vicinity through the fall of 1863.[103] Barr and his wife continued to correspond during the period as he maintained an active role in the management of his farm. The Barrs focused on their farm and livelihood as the war continued to invade every aspect of their lives.

Wednesday Night
Pocataligo, S.C.
April 22, 1863

My Dear Wife:

I received your letters. I received yours of the 18th tonight as I came in off picket.

We have marching orders. We leave tomorrow, Thursday morning, at ten

---

102 Knudsen, "5th SC," 64-84.

o'clock for Charleston. I will write you where to direct your letters as soon as we reach our destination or place where we will be stationed.

I am well. I was glad you all were getting on so well. I will have to close this letter as I must pack up, Hope we may get where the sand flies will not use us so bad for they are miserable. My hands and face are spotted by their bites. I hope you will get on well.

Your ever dear Husband,
J.M. Barr

You asked me several questions that I cannot answer tonight. You can ask them again in your next letter.

———⊰⊱———

Mount Pleasant, S.C.
April 29, 1863

Dear Wife:

We have arrived at Mount Pleasant after a dusty and tiresome march. We passed the city yesterday and took the boat for this place. It is supposed that we will go to McClellanville, some thirty-six miles from the city.

I have a severe cold. I got hurt a little Sunday evening by my horse falling down with me.

We camped Sunday night with in sight of the Company Joe Guess is in. He is well.

Charlie is at the hotel with his wife. We met him in town.

I will write soon as I can. I don't know where to tell you to write. I hope you and the children are well. I would like to see you. Nothing more from your dear husband at present.

J.M. Barr

McClellanville, S.C.
April 30, 1863

My Dear Wife:

It is with pleasure that I embrace this opportunity to write you, my dear one, who is now so far from me.

We arrived here yesterday at sun down after a hard days ride of thirty miles. We were on the road six days and a half of slow marching. I don't like the place that we are at. Looks too sickly. The surrounding country is so low.

When we arrived at Mt. Pleasant from Charleston, we stayed there nearly a day. We got over in the evening and left at one o'clock Tuesday evening.

I have to write in a hurry as someone is going to carry the mail.

I trust, dear Rebecca, that these few lines will find you and our dear little children well. I feel very, very tired. I feel much wasted from the march. This rest will do me good. I will have to borrow a stamp to send this off. You can direct your letters to

McClellanville
By way of Charleston
Care of Capt. Tyler

My pants are worn out at the seat. I do not have a whole pair. I don't know how you can send me a pair. I have not worn the summer ones yet. Write soon and let me know all the news.

Your dear Husband,
J.M. Barr

———◦◦◦———

McClellanville, S.C.
May 1, 1863

My Dear Wife:

You perhaps may think that I am writing often, but as my mind is so confused, being nearly half of the time mad, I think it best to empty my mind by writing.

Looking around at the place where we are is enough to make anyone have a long face and I assure you there is many a long face here. I understand Major Morgan had his choice of coming here or staying at Charleston. He chose this place, I suppose so he would command the post. Nearly every man wants to get away from here. We will have it very hard here on picket every third day, but if our men get sick, of course, we will have to go oftener. Besides picketing, a camp guard is kept up, which makes it so hard. This camp guard is not worth a cent. It only fatigues the men, giving them work to do all the time.

When we were in Charleston we thought our company would be stationed at Mt. Pleasant. If we could have stayed there I would have got a house for you and Sallie, as Sam and I thought of renting a house. Elijah said he would bring you and Sallie if we stayed at Mt. Pleasant and that your Mother would take care of Jimmie and Johnny.

I wish I could see you all. I would like to spend the summer at home. I would put a substitute in if I could get one, though I am not so tired of the service yet. I would do it on account of being at home with you and the children.

At Mt. Pleasant the men had quite a jolly time drinking and getting drunk. I got tired of the place till order was kept. Unfortunately, no order was kept till we left the place. The Major in command of our Company Officers kept things straight. Capt. Tyler, I think will always keep it too, but he is entirely too easy. He will suffer himself rather than impose on his company.

I cannot write as the sand flies are constantly biting. They are very bad here. I was in hopes that we had left them in Pocataligo, that we would not be bothered with the nasty things. I would like to go back again, but I would rather stay about Charleston.

I saw this morning a nice gang of goslings and young chickens belonging to the soldiers. One Company of Artillery is stationed here.

I will draw my pay in a few days. Capt. Tyler has drawn his Company for two months. We were mustered yesterday for our pay for March and April, so it will be a month before we get that.

Our horses are not looking good. There is nothing to feed them but a little rice, only one bundle at a feed. The sand flies are enough to worry the life out of our horses. If we want to sleep, we have to cover our heads and ears up with a blanket and then they will creep through and go up our sleeves and pants.

Charlie Plat, perhaps you know him as Charlie - John C. knew him so well, says I can get my pants patched in his Company as they have a tailor in it.

Sam and John C. have just got in off of picket. He sent fifteen men a day. They brought in some eggs, which gave fifty cents per dozen. Sam says he can get most anything we need. Perhaps we will like the place better after we stay a few days. I hope we may become satisfied.

I am writing on my knee, constantly stopping to rub the nasty sand flies off. Camp is a miserable place where sand flies stay.

If I can get salt hauled to Charleston from here I will buy some. I don't know how much. I can get it at some four or five dollars per bushel. It is selling from twelve to fifteen in town. I don't know whether I can get hauling done or not.

I don't know how you can send me any clothing. Ance doesn't need any now.

Ask Pa if I must or does he want me to purchase five bushels of salt for him at five dollars a bushel. I will buy five for myself and if Pa wishes it, I will try and get him that much.

I am getting in a much better humor. I am beginning to like the place better. I think that when I get a letter from you it will revive me, especially if you write me a long letter.

Your Dear Husband
J.M. Barr

James M. Barr
McClellanville
Camp Parmer, S.C.
Care of Capt. Tyler

I drew my money: 86 dollars

———————

McClellanville, S.C.
South Santee
May 6, 1863

My Dear Wife:

By the goodness of God, I am permitted again to write to you a few lines
to let you know how I am getting on, and how I am pleased with the place
that we are now stationed, and how we are faring.

Thank God I am enjoying a reasonable portion of health. My bowels
have been somewhat out of order. The change of water I think is the cause as
a great many of our men complain in the same way. I still have a cold. We are
not well fixed. We are sleeping on the damp ground, but I am doing duty. You
must not think that I am sick to render you uneasy about me, for if I did not
feel able to do duty, I assure you I would not do it. I was for three or four days
not doing any duty on account of getting a little hurt by a fall from my horse
or by my horse falling with me.

I am now getting very well pleased with the place. We are faring very
well ourselves. We are getting plenty of fine beef, which you know I am very
fond of. This is the finest range, I ever saw for cattle. Our horses are not
doing so well. We do not get corn enough for them. We get twenty ears of
corn a day and a little rice.

I am not pleased with some of the officers. The Major is very tight on us.
He shows his authority over us. I could tell you all, but I do not wish to write
it. I don't think he will stay with us long. I heard yesterday that he was going

to resign in June. Officers are generally unpopular and are hard to please everybody. Privates, I believe, see the happiest time. There is nothing but their duty to bother them. Officers will be accused of using profanity.

We bought some eggs since we have been here, paid fifty cents a dozen. I got two chickens, twelve and a half cents a lb. Pork is about twenty-five cents a lb. and up. From the whole we cannot complain. The worst thing is that the railroad is so far from us when you get a furlough to go. We can get two furloughs at the same time. So you see only those two can be gone at once. The Captain will make mine that I hired count, so you see I cannot get home in a long time, but I will do all I can to get home in July.

The mail will soon close, so I will have to hurry my letter. I have just received a letter from William. He says he will be up in a few days as he wants to see Crout to settle up my note. He says he had paid my state tax. He says the war tax will be awful high. I have heard that it will be awful - too high for soldiers who are not home to make arrangements to meet it.

I have just got the paper giving us the good news of the victory in Virginia. I hope we can whip them at every point, then I think the war would soon close. I do not think the war will last longer than this Summer.

I don't think we will ever see a Yankee down here.

I suppose we will spend the Summer down here. We get a good sea breeze, but sand flies are bad.

My love to Pa and Ma and all the kindred.

Your True Husband,
James M. Barr
No letter from you yet.
direct to:
James M. Barr
McClellanville, S. C.
South Santee
Care of Capt. Tyler

McClellanville, S.C.
South Santee
May 12, 1863

My Dear Rebecca:

I received your very interesting letter last Saturday, but as we only have two mail days, Wednesdays and Saturdays, you see I could not possibly answer it till now. I was delighted to hear that you all were well. I hope and trust you may continue in good health.

As for McClellanville, I don't know what to say about the place. We get almost a constant sea breeze, rather too cold for me. I generally want two blankets to cover with and then feel rather cold. After the sun gets up, it is very warm and I think standing exposed so much and riding in the hot sun is enough to make one take fever.

On picket duty it is not hard as it was at Pocataligo. If we had a rail road from here to Charleston we all would be much better satisfied, yet, we have not that convenience. We are thirty-five miles from Mt. Pleasant by land. Mt. Pleasant to Charleston by the boat is said to be five miles. So you see when we left the city, we took a boat for Mt. Pleasant. The boat carried over some one hundred and fifty troops at once. I got in the center of the boat and could not see. I then got on my horse, which by being on him, gave me a chance of seeing Sumter, Moultrie, and other fortifications about the city.

We camped at Mt. Pleasant. As I have told you, a good many of our soldiers got drunk. Yet, I do not blame the men so much as the Major was drunk and rather invited the privates to drink.

Rebecca, some of our men, or most of our men, want to go back to Charleston. Captain Skinner wants to come here, but it seems as though Captain Tyler will not consent to make the change on some account.[103] I would rather be in town. Then you could send me boxes and more than that you could come to see your dear beloved. This would be a pleasure, but on the

---

[103] Captain Richard M. Skinner of Paxville, South Carolina, commanded Company H, 5th South Carolina Cavalry until being killed in action on June 24, 1864 at Nance's Shop, Virginia. Knudsen, "5th SC," 80.

other hand, this may be a healthy place. We can buy chickens at 12 1/2cents per lb., 25 cents for eggs and 50 cents for butter. I don't know what it will cost us, but Sam has some engaged.

If we get a box from home I think it will take a long time and the best chance is through the country. We are beyond Charleston from you or about ninety miles from the Orangeburg, Court House.

Wash Hanbery came through, but it is too far to ride our horses if we could get a furlough.[104] In speaking of a furlough, my thoughts go back to home, thinking of you and my dear little ones. Oh, if I could leave here for a thirty or sixty day furlough to spend that time with you, the one I love so well and with our dear little fellows.

My dear, camp is a lazy place. I was lazy enough before I came in camp, but now I am worse. Men get lazy doing what you might say nothing, lying about at one place, watching the coast for a boat.

I am sorry to hear of such luck in not getting a stand of corn. Corn that I have seen is nearly knee high.

A very poor yield of wool. Bill I expect got it stole last year.

Can't you have the hogs that eat your chickens shut up or make the little negroes dog them off?

Your True Husband,
James M. Barr

McClellanville, S.C.
South Santee
May 13th, 1863

My Dear Rebecca:

It appears that I cannot write you a good letter. I can't get one to suit me.

104 Washington Aaron Hanberry of Barnwell enlisted in Company I, 5th South Carolina Cavalry. Knudsen, "5th SC," 26.

It was a great misfortune in losing General Jackson. I understand we gained a victory in Tennessee. I will get the paper today.[105]

Down here would be a great place for making salt and I think the boilers could be rented.

I don't think William ought to have called on you for the money that you had. However, if you need money you must get it from him.

Did Henry pay Dr. Addy? Did he take up the note that I gave to Swygert's estate? Did he give it to you?

I would like to know where to direct a letter to Thomas.

I trust this will find you all well. I will write again Saturday if I can. Sam and Charlie have both been sick with colds. I think we will all get better of our colds as we now have beds fixed up. We are again very well fixed. We are as well fixed as anyone in camp, but we will miss our boxes from home. We get good beef here, but before we came here we got bad meat.

I suppose you let Mrs. Mitchell know where to direct letters to me. Dan, I suppose, is home sick. I think the Confederate Government treats all soldiers alike.

Your True Husband,
James M. Barr

Rebecca, don't keep my letters. They are generally written in a hurry and on my knee.

Your Dear One,
J.M.B.

---

[105] Although it is unclear to what "victory" in Tennessee Barr was referring, news of the death of General Thomas J. "Stonewall" Jackson on May 10, 1863, after the Battle of Chancellorsville, stunned the South.

McClellanville, S.C.
May 15, 1863

My Dear Rebecca:

It is a pleasure for me to write to you and tell you how I am getting on. But on the other hand, oh, what pleasure to hear from you and to read your long and interesting letters. It is a pleasure for me to receive a letter from you, my dear, one who tries to write me all the good news. But I must acknowledge that I was a little disappointed when I received Phillip C. Spann's letter. Why? Because you directed it. I felt a little uneasy until I saw who it was from. Why? Because it was such a little letter without much writing. So short a letter, I thought some of the family was sick.

Phillip wrote to me about coming here in the service. I told him he could get in and how to come. To come to Orangeburg Court House, then to Pineville, then to McClellanville, which I am told is some eighty or ninety miles from Orangeburg Court House.

If I was at home as some are, I would take a wagon and team and come here after salt. I believe it would pay to haul it from here at six dollars a bushel. The difficulty here is getting it hauled to Charleston. However, I am trying to make an arrangement to get some ten bushels and get it to town. Some few have purchased for five dollars a bushel, but they, the salt boilers, are asking now six dollars per bushel. I wish Walter Quattlebaum could come here and look around a few days and see if we could rent some salt boilers. I think we could get them. I would like for him to boil. I would hire a hand or two and put in with him. Wood can be got at a dollar a cord. A hand could make a bushel of salt a day or more.

How are the Negroes getting on with the crops? I suppose very well as it is so dry. I hope that you have had rain before this. Tell Bill if he can't get a stand of corn to replant the last of this month with peas and to plant them with hoes and I want every hill planted. How many bushels of peas did you keep? Let me know in your next letter.

I would like to know if any one is getting paid for the Negroes for the

time they worked in Charleston. They are due me for two months work. William I know got his.

One of our men, Hug W Zeigler, got shot through the hand this morning in his tent.[106] The way he got shot is this. He was sleeping on the ground in the tent with the gun beside him on the side of the tent. He caught hold of the muzzle to push it out of his way and as he made a push, the rifle fired. He happened to suffer a great deal as being shot so close I think caused it to burn so much.

We have purchased some stock chickens again. We have three hens and a rooster for five dollars. We want to get about eight hens. We pay one dollar a piece for hens. That is the cheapest way to get eggs.

Charlie and Sam, I think, will go on duty tomorrow. I have not been well, suffering from cold, but I feel better. The Dr. gave me some cough medicine, which helped me, I will be on picket to-morrow. However, if I can keep off, I will.

As it is our mail day today, I expect a letter from you.

---

[106] Probably H.M. Ziegler, who served as a private in Company I, 5th South Carolina Cavalry. Knudsen, "5th SC," 61.

I only wish you could have some of the rains that we get here. It is now raining.

If I were Phillip, I would stay at home if I could. I don't think Phillip would stand camp very well. I find that a great many men would now hire substitutes, if they had a chance. If I knew I had to go to Tennessee, I would try and get one.

I think the Yankees will again attack Charleston. They are now working on Folley Island and will be able to shell our men at some points. We are also expecting an attack at Pocataligo. I believe I like it here better than I did at Pocataligo.

Somehow I do not think the war will last longer than this year. Yet, it may last for several years.

Bacon here is very high, one dollar and fifty cents per lb. Butter I hear is selling at two dollars a lb., so you see if we can buy it, we will have to pay a high price.

Though we live on very little, I am now as fleshy as I was when I was at home.

I hope that I may get home in some six or eight weeks at any rate if we stay here, but it is uncertain how long we can stay. Yet it is probable that we may stay here this summer. I think my time for going home will roll around in the time above specified, as two can get off at a time on furlough and some go on detached service and some get off on account of a Father or Mother being sick by the Dr. sending or writing to the Captain that they are sick. All this helps the men to get off faster. Charlie has not got off yet, but I think he will in three or four weeks.

From this place I can get to Mt. Pleasant by twelve o'clock, take the boat and in one hour be in the city and then take the car for Columbia and get there by day. Hence to Leesville by three o'clock if I could ride with the Mail boy on that route. Just telling you how I could get home if I could get a furlough, but the best and only plan is to wait patiently till I can get off. I want to get off about Peach and Watermellon time. I think I could enjoy them so well.

How do you think the bacon will hold out? You must make allowance so it will last till December. How is the corn holding out? Will we have fodder for sale? I want Bill to tell you how much we can sell. I told him I wanted to sell fodder. The spotted cow that I bought at Swygert's sale, I want killed for the negroes when she gets fat. She will save some bacon for four weeks and I want her hide sent to Fulmers. Have you got the leather from Fulmers yet? If not, tell Henry to ask Jim when he can get it, two hides. Put it in the store under the counter.

Tell Henry I wish he would have me a wool hat made, 6 3/4" is my size. William can tell him how much wool to take and how to fix it and go with him. You can have one made for Jimmie and Johnny too. I want a nice hat.

No more at present.

Your Devoted Husband,
James M. Barr

Tell Henry to pay Fulmer for tanning the leather. I will get four hides. I sent him 2 hides, but the last is not ready.

McClellanville, S. C.
Saturday, May the 16th, 1863

My Dear One:

Sam is up knocking about, but he is not well. Sam is looking badly. He has no appetite. However, there is nothing here to give anyone an appetite, only beef. John C. is off on picket. He will be in today. I am not put on any duty more than sweeping up yet, so Ance can do my work.

I understand that the authorities have held a meeting in Charleston to see whether to give up the city or not. I understand that they have decided to try and hold her at all hazard. I think if our authorities give up Charleston and the Sea Coast that they might as well go back in the Union. Why? Because it would strengthen old Lincoln and his Government so much and on the other hand, weaken us so much. I believe in holding till we cannot hold her any longer and then leave her in one solitary black of fire on one heap of ashes. Let everything be burned, so it cannot do the nasty low lived Yankees any good. Oh, for the day of peace when we can have it fair and honorable, but there is no honor or justice about the Yankees. If they cannot take off, they will burn up. It would be better for us to destroy our property than for them to do it for us.

After today, we will have a daily mail to this place, which will be a great advantage to us in getting news. We can then get our paper every mail.

I would not close this letter until I received one from you, but as the mail will be daily I can write any day.

I am getting very tired of the War, but if I could feel well and enjoy myself as well as I did when I first came in, I would be much better satisfied; but let one be about half sick and I assure you camp life does not suit him. I hope this will not be long the case. If I could only feel well. I hope I may improve and feel well.

Your Dear
J.M. Barr

You must not be uneasy for me when I get the blues. Please do not be uneasy.

McClellanville, S. C.
May 20th, 1863

My Dear Wife:

I received your truly welcome letter, which came safely to hand on the 16th instant. I am sorry to hear that you are suffering from colds, but hope by this time that you are all better. Dearest one, you can't imagine the pleasure It gives me to receive a letter from the one I love so well and to hear how you are getting on.

Dearest, I am just in from off picket. I spent the last twenty-four hours out. It is now an every-days work. We send out about ten men every day, so you see it will hit me about every third day.

I am feeling much better this morning. I hope I may continue to improve. I have a cough, but I think if I could get shed of It that I would feel greatly relieved. However, I am feeling about as well as usual. I feel like doing my own work. Rebecca, the duty here Is not hard. It is not half as hard as it was at Pocataligo.

I am very sorry to hear of Jasper's liver affliction and I trust when I hear from him again that he will be better. He has suffered a great deal. He may not stand his disease long.

I am very surprised at Mr. Crout not taking Confederate money.[107] I did not think that he would get afraid of our Confederacy. If our Confederate money is not good, I think we might as well quit fighting. I think the Legislature made Confederate money lawful. I told William to see Crout himself. I am sorry he sent the money instead of going. I think that he will know how to use the money.

I think the tale about the authorities meeting to see whether to hold Charleston or not to be a hoax for it is reasonable that we will hold her as long as possible.

I don't know when I can get home. I will get off whenever I can. I think my clothing will last me till I get home. I have not worn my summer pants yet. I have just drawn a pair of shoes. I wish I had them at home. They are very common Negro shoes.

I have not gotten any salt yet. I have found no one to haul it. I can buy it for six dollars and I could buy it for anyone, but the chance of sending it away is bad. It would be better for Walter or Smith to come here. Ask Walter if he would not come on when he can.

Your True Husband,
James M. Barr

P.S. I have One Hundred Dollars.
J.M.B.

---

[107] David Crout was a local farmer in his sixties, who ran a mill. By this point in the war Confederate currency had lost most of its value. Many Southerners resorted to the barter system or used Union currency. *1860 Census*, Lexington District, South Carolina.

───✦───

McClellanville, S. C.
Sunday Morning
May 24th, 1863

My Dear Rebecca:

I received your truly welcome letter of the 17th, which afforded me great pleasure. My Dear, it was worth receiving and I know a pleasure to me to hear how you were getting on and to hear how the Negroes were getting on with my crop. Corn down here is nearly waist high. I expect it is much better than up the country.

You wrote me about my clothing and appear very anxious for me to get them. I am not needing them bad yet. I hope I may get home before I need them - that is if we stay here. I don't think I would like to be in Charleston.

I may write you to send me a box. We are needing something from home, but we get plenty of good beef, but I am tired of it. I have to throw away some of it at times to keep it from spoiling. You know we miss all the little treats that we used to get at home. We are out of bacon and lard. We have a little flour yet. I can't buy anything unless I pay the highest kind of a price. We do get some eggs occasionally for fifty cents per dozen, but anything else we can't get here. We did buy one dollars worth of butter, which was one pound, but it seems we can't get any more. It is rather too near Charleston to get anything at a fair price. I heard that eggs sell at two dollars a dozen and chickens from four to five dollars apiece. John C. has written home for a box. We will see if we can get that before we try for any mope [more].

I do not like to trouble Mr. Quattlebaum now as it is a very busy season for a farmer and he can't spare a horse from the farm now. If he were to come, it would be better to come by private conveyance by Orangeburg via Pineville and hence to McClellanville with a good wagon, four horses, and get a load of salt. Major Morgan asked me yesterday if Walter would not be down before long on a visit. I told him I thought he would come as soon as he could spare the horse plowers. When he comes, if he does, he must let me know two weeks before hand. I would put in one mule.

I am sorry you have not yet had a stand of corn replanted. I cannot make any thing this late. They may have set out and made corn if Bill had worked right. I want all the middles ploughed out. If it is not done good a crop can't be made. I am glad to hear that you are getting a good stand of potatoes and cotton. Tell Bill to keep dirt to the cotton. If he lets it fall down it will die.

Bill stops too long at Noon. I think one hour and a half plenty time, longer than they stopped when I was at home. Then they lose about two hours and a half from the time they stop till they get to work. If Elijah loses one hour in a day, it is the same as one hand was out eight hours. Bill must notice this.

How many seed peas are saved? I would like to know so I may know how to direct and how to plant them.

You said Henry had paid the Swygert note and the Doctor bill. How much was it? Did he give you the note or did he destroy it?

I wrote you when I left Pocataligo, or intended to do it, that I received your letter the evening before I left with bill enclosed of the sale of bacon and peas. I think Henry let them cheat him in weighing the bacon.

I am glad to hear that Jasper Sawyer is fast recovering from the attack of hemorrhaging. I hope I may be able to see him again.

Mr. Warren ought to pay one dollar a bushel for potato slips. I have paid $1.50 for slips since I have been in the service to eat. I think you would have done better to have paid Mrs. Warren the money for weaving. If you can have your wool spun at a reasonable price and can be satisfied that it will be safe, you would better hire it done.[108]

I was truly glad to hear from Thomas and to hear that he was well.

I intended to gather some Palmettoes to send home if I had stayed at Pocataligo. They would be rather hard to get from here.

I am pleased that Mr. Spann is taking an interest for you in my absence for that is the time to find out who cares for you.

I am glad to hear also of Phillips being permitted to stay at home for the Army is not fit for any one that does not enjoy good health. As for Phillip, I don't believe he would stand it long in the service, with his complaint. No one can be favored in the service. He has either got to be on the sick list or do

108 Probably J. F. Warren and his wife Ellen, who were neighbors of the Barrs. Ibid.

duty, and I would always try to do duty if half sick rather than be under the Doctor.

I am glad to know that our baby is doing so well. I would like very much to see the little fellow. I hope Johnny will be talking plainly till I get home. Ask Jimmie if he is a good boy. Tell him he promised Pa to be a good boy. I hope I may see you all soon.

I am glad to know that Denis thinks of me. When I write home I want to know how all are, meaning the blacks as well as the rest.

My Dear, I constantly pray to my Father in Heaven that he may spare my life, yours, and the little ones so that we may meet on earth again and that we may be permitted to live together here on earth and that we may live happier than we did before the War. I feel as if we ought constantly to pray to our Maker and pray to Him to stop this unholy War. Oh, that He would put a stop to it and permit sons to return home to their Fathers and Mothers and permit Husbands and Fathers to return home to their dear and loving Wives and little ones. This is the constant prayer of your ever dear Husband.

James M. Barr

Remember me to Pa and Ma and all kindred and friends. Ask Jimmie how the colt is getting on.

<hr/>

McClellanville, S.C.
Friday, May 29th, 1863

My Dear Rebecca:

I received your letter of the 21st instant, which afforded me much pleasure in hearing from you and the children and all the rest. I am sorry to hear of Pa's suffering for I know so well how much he has suffered from his complaint.

The writing I marked in the letter to you, which you spoke of, I did not wish you to notice for I believe it better for one to buy his salt than to bother for a few bushels. I can buy as much salt here as I want at six dollars per bushel, but I cannot get it hauled to Charleston. Major Morgan says he will allow two bushels to a man to be sent. I will get my salt and Pa's if nothing happens, but it will put me to a good deal of trouble. Some four of us will try and get a wagon and send forty bushels off. So you know that will be ten bushels to a man.

If I succeed in sending the salt, the wagon can haul a load of fodder to Columbia. With the money that Henry gets for the load of fodder, I think you would better have him to buy sugar with it. I expect you are now about out of sugar.

You had better get Walter Quattlebaum to rob the bees. I don't want him to wait too late for fear they will not fill up by Fall.

If the cows keep coming back. I would let them stay at home.

Perhaps the finest sheep is missing. As soon as Bill sees them he must salt them. I want them salted at least once every two weeks. I want them driven home when salted and that will learn them to come home after it. Have them put in pasture for one or two days and then turn them out. I think in this way they will come up better. I don't want to lose my sheep.

How many hogs have we in all - little and big?

We have been trying to get a small shoat. They ask us twenty-five dollars for one, so no chance to get one.[109]

Do you know what William did with the money, whether he put it out or not? You need not put your self to any trouble to find out.

I am surprised at Henry for wanting you to find him a horse to look after the stock. I know he can or does stop one of his or Pa's when he wants to send to old Sanfords. I told Henry when I first left home that I had three mules and three horses and that I would not need them constantly and that he could get Jim 's horse to ride to look after the stock, but What did he do? He sold a mule. Now I don't think he ought to look after my stock and he can find his own horse. Does Henry ever look after my Negroes to see how they work? I suppose not as I have not heard you say anything about his looking after anything.

---

[109] A shoat is a young hog.

I wrote Wesley last week saying I heard he had a fine daughter. I also wrote Tom telling him he had a fine daughter and saying to them both that I thought they ought to have got boy babies instead of girl babies.

I do not know what I am writing as John C. and Milford Rice are here in the tent teasing each other and you know how it bothers one in writing. Sam says Sallie will be along after awhile.[110]

I do not think the Yankees will try Charleston soon. I think the few hours they were at it satisfied them. However, if they fail to take Vicksburg, which I think they will, they may then try Charleston again.

I am still enjoying pretty good health or at least for the last week or two. Trust that I may continue in good health. Our family is now all well, I mean our own mess tent full of men. Yet, Ance is not much better, but I think he is improving some. I hope he will be up in two or three days.

You must not think that I am needing my clothing so bad. I can do very well without them yet awhile.

I do not want to trouble Walter to come here. I know he cannot leave at this time on account of his wheat. When will my wheat be ready to cut? When will the rye do? I expect it is nearly ripe. Nothing more now.

Remember me to all, Pa and Ma. I remain as ever your

Dear Husband,
James M. Barr

---

[110] Probably Second Lieutenant M. J. Rice, Company I, 5th South Carolina Cavalry, from Barnwell District. Knudsen, "5th SC," 46.

McClellanville, S.C.
May 30th, 1863

My Dear Rebecca:

This place is a great place for fish and yet I have not fished. I brought four or five fish hooks from home, but did not bring any line.

Mr. Crum was fishing today. He has caught a fine mess. There are six men in his mess, so you may. know he caught several. He gave me a fine one for supper. I will have it stewed as we have no lard or bacon. He caught different kinds of fish, cat, trout, sheep head and whiting. Sheep head is a very fine fish, looks in shape somewhat like the bream fish. They have teeth like a sheep and he had to cut off the hooks. When the tide is coming up or going down is the best time for fishing. If Ance was well he could keep us in fish. He could catch the whitings. They are small or if he could get shrimp, he could catch any kind.

See how well we could live if we only had what we wanted or needed. Although I expect we would soon get tired of fish. If we had plenty of lard and flour without butter we could live well.

Ance told me the other day that the officers' Negroes told him we lived much better than the officers. The Captain's boy said the other day that he wanted to stay with us till the Captain got back, but he did not apply for admittance.

There are only three of us together till Charlie comes back. I don't think Sam will hire himself a substitute. He says he is liking the place very well.

We drill twice a day. That is the men who are off of picket.

Your loving Husband,
James M. Barr

I think Ance is gettting better.

South Santee, S.C.
June 2nd, 1863

My Dear Wife:

I received your letter last Saturday and was glad to hear from you although your letter did not contain much good news. As for Cate losing her young one, it is no more than I expected. Yet, they all told me they would take care and not tote anything heavy. If she did it purposely, it would be enough to hang her for, but laziness I should guess to be the cause. She ought not to have washed at the spring. I do not think you ought to worry yourself so much as to be losing so much sleep on account of what she brought on herself. It is a great wonder she did not die too. I hope the rest have learned better sense and will take warning.

John C. got a letter from home this week saying all was well. Aggie has a fine child boy I think.

Eight men from our company will get furloughs and twelve from Capt. Caughman's Company are to go home to cut their wheat. The men that will go are those who have no help at home. Their furloughs have been sent off for approval. If they are approved, which I think they will, they will get off about Friday next.

I want my <u>wheat</u> saved and I want it well <u>shocked</u>. I want the big wheat, the Watson wheat, not to be mixed with the other wheat. Ask Mr. Spann if we can thrash at his thrasher or will he thrash it. After it is thrashed, put it in boxes or barrels in the store house till it can be hauled off. I want the big wheat thrashed first. Ask Spann to see if they cut it right. If Jerry can't cut the wheat, rye, and oats you must ask Pa and Spann to help us to cut it. When it is cut I want it shocked well. I want it ground at Quattlebaums or Steadman's Mill.[111]

Tell Henry not to trouble himself about having me a hat made for it appears that it will be a great deal of trouble for him. If I cannot get a hat made by a good hat maker I would rather not have it done. His "tolerable" hat maker does not suit me. It appears to me that he don't wish to go and get me one made. Tell him to let it alone. I have come to the conclusion that there is not much accomodation about anyone at home.

I will write you when I send my salt. I had a barrel made and will have it filled as soon as I can and send it off. I cannot send for anyone else as we are only allowed to send for our own use. I will try and have seven bushels in the barrel.

Ance is better I think. He is looking very badly and he is poor. He don't want anything to eat. He will eat a little milk and mush, which is some trouble to get.

I understand that they are now taking all the men up to forty years old and making a pretty clean sweep. I don't know how the crops will be cultivated and gathered, but I presume as well as the younger men did.

I do not know when I can get home unless some of the family should get sick and the Doctor sends a certificate to the Captain if such is the case. I will have to wait sometime for a furlough, at least two months or more, unless I get home by the Doctor's certificate. If I cannot get home till all the company gets off, it will be a long time.

I hope this will find you enjoying good health and find the children well. I also hope it finds Pa and Ma well and all the kindred.

I am doing pretty well. We got a little bacon, but on the account of Ance being sick we cannot do as well as we might if he was well.

---

[111] Barr's instructions regarding his wheat reveal much about the processes involved in cultivating that grain. Most wheat fields were sown with a mixture of varieties alternating by sections. The reason was simple economics. Particular breeds of wheat might be resistant to specific pests (Hessian Fly), disease (smuts), or might do best during particular growing seasons (winter versus summer wheat). By having several varieties grown in the same field, a particular blight or climate issue would not necessarily destroy the whole crop. The key to successfully farming wheat in this manner was that it was vital to segregate the varieties during the harvesting and threshing operation. Careful sorting, as indicated, was important. Shocking involved putting a dozen tied bundles (cradles) of cut wheat into upright piles allowing the grain heads to dry properly. See S. C. Salmon and J. W. Taylor, *Growing Wheat in the Eastern United States* (Washington: United State department of Agriculture, Farmers Bulletin No. 1817, 1939), pp. 36-37.

Ellen sent John C. a couple cakes the other day. The Captain brought some for Charlie. Mittie is in town with Charlie.

I will close. Nothing more this evening from

Your Beloved
James M. Barr

———

McClellanville, S.C.
June 5, 1863

My Dear Rebecca:

I am writing you today as tomorrow will be mail day and I know how you like to receive letters, and I especially like to receive them from you, the one I love so well.

My Dear One, how delighted I would be to take you by surprise! Oh, My Dear One, I would rather get home in the evening to see you and the little fellows wide awake and enjoying good health. I can't see yet how I may get off, although the Captain told me the other day that he would not hold me back on account of my going in March. Yet, it will be some time before I can get off because there are several men who have not been home in six months. Of course, these men will all get furloughs before I get one unless by sickness of some of the family with a certificate from the Doctor to the Captain saying such is the fact. But I hope all may stay well. I think I will get off about peach and watermellon time. Don't you think I would be just fixed? I could not be better pleased than to be at home with you and the children enjoying such fine fruit as we had last year. I would like to spend a few days with you even if I could not stay long. Ten days is the length of furloughs given. I think if I could get home with you for a few days it would remind me of the first few days after our happy union.

I understand that Preston is trying to hire himself a substitute.

It would not surprise me much if the War continues long. It looks like it

will be that Preachers of the Gospel, Doctors and every man that is able to do duty will be called out. It is thought that before long the men that have substitutes in the War will be called out. Did you ever hear whether the patriotic Emanuel Quattlebuam has yet gone in the service or not? I guess not. A man can talk and act brave when he is at home.

My Dear, I think Anderson is improving very little. He came out of the house and sat for a while under the shade of a tree. Typhoid fever is what has been the matter with him. He is now taking gum arabic, spirits of turpentine, laudanum and a Tea (Tody) of snake root. He is very anxious to get home. I may start him off in a few days. I wish someone could have come for him. I think I can get him to Columbia if I could let you know soon enough to send after him. I told him this morning he had better wait and go home with me.

Do you loan the buggy anymore? You know I would never loan my buggy unless it was to some one that could and would return the same favor. If the harness gets broken up, you know we cannot replace them. If the buggy gets broken, it cannot be mended to look as well. Tell all if you loan to one, more will be expecting it and it would be better not to run it only when you have to go in it. I think every body ought to have their own conveyances if they wish to go any where, especially when things are so high.

Nothing more this evening. I wish for you a happy night.

James M. Barr

McClellanville, S.C.
June 6, 1863

My Dear Wife:

I received your dear letter and hasten to answer.

Don't trouble any of the low boxes of bees. I wrote you last week to have them robbed soon.

I will start a barrel of salt home about the 18th. If Henry comes, he must first let me know that I may see how much salt he can get and what time he can get it.

I have written you every mail I think.

Ance is still mending.

I am not needing any clothing now. I have plenty. More than I could carry off if we should have to leave.

I do not know the cause of you not getting my letters.

You must not be uneasy for me. I will take the best of care of myself, as far as I can, anyway.

Your lover,
James M. Barr

———✦———

McClellanville, S.C.
June 9th, 1863

My Dear Wife:

I expect by the time this reaches you, that you will be looking for a letter from me. But, Dear One, I have no news to write you.

We are still here in camp getting along the best we can. Three of us here in our mess. Sam, John C. and myself. We spend three dollars a week for butter, but as for buying any thing else, it is a bad chance. We get beef a plenty, but we are tired of it. Can't have it prepared for table or to eat as well as we could at home. We get bacon on Sunday, beef the balance of the week. Several of our men are complaining and not able to do duty. Yet, they are not down sick.

We sent off two of our men this morning, Edd Neely and W.W. Hair.[112] Edd on a thirty day furlough and Hair on a sixty day furlough. I would like very much to have a sixty day furlough. I know you would be as pleased as I would be, but I cannot get more than ten days, and ten days is hardly worth going home on. It would just make you happy to see me and then make you unhappy to see me have to leave again. Though, my Dear One, considering all these things, if I can get a ten day furlough, I am coming home. You may look for me if I can get a furlough. I am rather getting anxious for one, but don't think I can get one till the last of July or first of August. It will not take long for a month to pass.

I want to see our baby to see how much he has grown. I have not found any name for him. I wish you to select a name. Write and tell me the name that you may select. I want you to name him.[113]

Yesterday morning was very cool like Winter. Over coats were worn to some extent.

---

[112] Ed P. Neeley and W. W. Hair served as privates in Company I, 5th South Carolina Cavalry. Hair was wounded on October 27, 1864 at Burgess' Mill, North Carolina. Ibid., 26, 42.

[113] Charlie Dacania Barr was born March 17, 1863. McDaniel, *Correspondence*, 12. Not naming a baby until several weeks or months after birth was common practice in that day due to the high instance of infant mortality.

Ance is now up and I think out of danger if he does not relapse. He wants to be rather too pert. He was very anxious to start home this morning. I told him he could not go, but as soon as he got strong enough he might go. I will let him go and stay till I get home and perhaps leave him home altogether.

I think Bill ought to commence planting peas soon. I don't know why he did not commence sooner for now it will be late till he gets it done. I want them planted like I had them planted last year. My wheat I want it cut when it is ready for cutting. It must not be put off. I have a good deal to cut and if put off till too ripe, it can't be saved as well. Bill must look at it and if it will do, it must be cut. I want it saved well and shocked well. Last year it was not half shocked.

Your True Husband,
James M. Barr

McClellanville, S.C.
June 10, 1863

My Dear One:

Your mother sent us by Charlie Plat a bag of potatoes, a ham and a shoulder of meat. Quite a treat.

Wash Turner yesterday evening was cleaning a pistol and the pistol went off, shooting him through his big toe.[114] The ball was as large as the one I gave Jimmie, so I suppose Wash will get a furlough for thirty days.

I am complaining some, though you need not be uneasy about me. I will write you by Saturdays mail.

I expect to send a barrel of salt home soon. Salt can be bought at six dollars and some at five dollars, not so nice. After crops is laid by I think salt will get higher on account of wagons hauling so much.

---

[114] George Washington "Wash" Turner joined Company I, 5th South Carolina Cavalry as a hired substitute for W. L. Zorn. Knudsen, "5th SC," 55.

I got a letter from Tom today. He is well, but he is a bad boy.

Your True Husband,
James M. Barr

———————

McClellanville, S.C.
June 13th, 1863

My Dear Rebecca:

It is with pleasure that I again attempt to write you. Your very interesting letter came safely to hand last Wednesday, which afforded me much pleasure to hear how you were all getting on. My Dear One, nothing gives me more pleasure than to receive your very kind letters and to hear that you all are getting on so well.

I received a letter from Thomas a few days ago. He would like to get in our Company. He says if he was with us, he could keep us all out of the blues. I wrote him to try and get a transfer to our Company. I think if Abb will favor it, that he will have no trouble. Thomas appears to be in fine spirits. I wish he could get with us.

Sam is not getting on so well. He has been for several days complaining. He has the asthma. He is bothered a good deal at night, frequently has to get up and sit up.

Ance has now gotten up. He is improving fast. He has taken charge of my horse, but still looks poor. I think I will try and send him home next week if any one goes from here home. He has had a pretty tough time of it.

I wrote to Wesley sometime ago, but have heard nothing from him. It is true that paper is high and postage pretty tight, so you see persons out of the service don't like to do much correspondence.

Do you ever hear anything from Daniel Mitchell? I would like to know where he is and where to direct a letter to him.

I am afraid this is a sickly place. Several of our men are at home now on sick furloughs. One of our men died here yesterday morning. His name was Frank Conally.[115] The poor fellow was not sick more than four or five days. He would cuss after he got out of his head. He was a very clever fellow, always tending to his own business.

I believe I told you that Wash Turner got shot accidentally while cleaning a pistol. He hit his big toe about the middle. He has gone home. He left yesterday as the wagon had to go to Charleston with the bodie of Conally.

I expect by the time this reaches you that you can write back how they are getting on with the wheat. I am afraid they will not save it well and not shock it well. I know Bill so well. He is apt to say it is all right when really the rain can run in and sprout the wheat.

Our wagon will leave for Charleston to-morrow morning. I will send a barrel of salt in it to be shipped to Columbia. It will be about eight bushels, but you need not tell how much. It is closely packed in six bushel barrel. When I get the receipt for it, I will send it home and then you can get someone to go after it. Without the receipt they cannot get it.

I think peas ought to have been planted instead of replanting with corn for I know it will not make. It is too late for replanting corn to do anything.

How does the cotton look? Will it make three bales or not?

Will we have much fruit? I hope to get home in fruit time.

Your mother sent us a bag of fine potatoes and some bacon. We have been having beans and squash. Have you had any yet?

We have a quantity of fleas. They are a great deal worse than bed bugs in a house that has not been scalded for a year. It is nothing new to see six or eight at a time in one sock. My ankles are spotted by their bites and thousands of sand flies. Hundreds get in the buckets of drinking water, the nasty things.

Lt. Guess and I with two butchermen from the German Artillery, took a boat and went out fishing Thursday. We went out about four miles, I had a pleasant ride as I did not oar any. We caught about sixty fish, trout, sailor choice, jacks, croakers, whiting and a few other kind.[116]

---

[115] Frank J. Connelly, Company I, 5th South Carolina Cavalry, died of disease on June 12, 1863 at McClellanville, South Carolina. Ibid., 14.

[116] Barr's company was stationed near two companies of the German Artillery at the time, Company A under Captain F. W. Wagener and Company B under Captain Frank Melchers. *OR* Vol. 28, Pt. 2, p. 159.

You must not look for such long letters from me.

Your Dear Husband,
James M. Barr

————◦◦◦————

McClellanville, S.C.
June 16th, 1863

My Dear Wife:

I again this Tuesday evening make an attempt to write to you, knowing that nothing can please you better than to hear from your absent one, who is far from you. Yet, My Dear One, we are not so far apart as a good many are. We may be yet farther apart than we are now before this unholy War closes. However, I hope to remain here this Summer and Winter and within the State till the War ends.

We have been faring sumptuously for a few days, having plenty to eat except bread. Our meal was so musty we could not make use of it, though we have rice a plenty. We have had bacon, potatoes, beans, squash, beef a plenty, and a few messes of venison. The boys kill a deer every week or two. We are getting pretty tired of beef. I think if I was at home and had such beef as we get here fried well. I would then like it.

We are getting on pretty well at this time. Sam will go on duty tomorrow. Charlie has not gotten back from Charleston yet. I think he will be back soon.

Mr. Crum has his wife down here and also Mr. W. Johnson from Blackville has his.[117] They board their wives about three quarters of a mile from our camp. They pay thirty dollars per month. Sam intended bringing Sallie, but cannot on account of whooping caugh. Jimmie I believe has it.

---

[117] J. W. Crum and William M. Johnson served as privates in Company I, 5th South Carolina Cavalry. Ibid., 16, 32.

Mr. Hilliard Jackson arrived back to camp last night.[118] He did not bring any bundle for me. I have not talked with him yet. I heard he said he started with a load and the horse would not pull, so he had to hire a man to haul them back for him. I am doing very well without my clothing and can do so till I get off to come home. It is true that I would like to have Summer pants, but can make out tolerable well without them.

I received a letter from Wesley the other day telling me what a change of vegatables Sallie had and what other good things they have had. He said he would be down soon to see me, but said he ought not to tell me of all these good things that they have as it would bring home too vividly to mind. I wrote him, rather urging him to come down the first of July, saying when I saw him I hoped to get a box with a few onions in it.

He is coming down to buy salt. I told him he had better see Walter and come with him or meet Walter here. Salt is selling at six dollars a bushel. Yet, some two or three are selling for five dollars. Wagons are beginning to come in and haul off. I think they had better come as early as they can for fear it may get higher. If the salt men should not have any, in two or three days one man could make enough to load a wagon. Tell Walter if he cannot get bags to get barrels and if he thinks boxes will do, he could get ours that had potatoes in them. I would like for him to bring me a couple of barrels if he has not too much of a load. Those vinegar barrels or molasses barrels are well hooped. Tell them to bring corn enough to feed the horses for staying four or five days. If salt can be had a plenty and I can get the wagon to stay a few days, I will get Walter to haul me fifty or sixty bushels to a boat landing some fifteen miles from here, provided I can get something to put it in. I can buy as much as I want now, but I cannot take it away. I have shipped one barrel of salt to Columbia. I wish Henry to go to Columbia after it. The salt I got was rather wet, but it will dry. I got it so as it packs well. It is eight and pine half bushels packed well. I want Henry to go after it as soon as he can. He can take a load of fodder and sell it and then buy the sugar.

Ance is doing well and mending up finely. I promised him I would send him home and perhaps will next week. I will send him home the first chance I get to stay a couple of weeks.

---

[118] Hilliard Jackson from the Lexington District served in Company F, 5th South Carolina Cavalry. Ibid., 31.

Today is a warm day, the warmest that we have had yet, but tonight will be cool. Yes, we sleep under two blankets every night.

Oh, the fleas! There are thousands of them here biting all the time.

I want to send a barrel of rice home if I can.

If Walter comes before I get off home, tell him to bring me three hundred dollars if he can get it. I think he can get it from J.W. Barr. I know in reason he will come before I get off if he comes at all for I do not expect to get off till August although I may get off sooner. If he should come here and I am gone, Sam will be here, that is if nothing turns up unexpectedly.

I thought Henry did not want to trouble himself about getting my hat made, so that caused me to write what I did.

I have almost got in the notion to move down here after the War if I am so fortunate to live through it. It is rather too much out of the world though.

I feel more like writing today than I have since I have been down here.

I think Ance will leave tomorrow evening. If he does, he will get home before you get this letter or by that time.

Kiss the children for me. Tell Jimmie Pa is sorry to hear he is a bad boy.

Your Ever Dear Husband,
James M. Barr.

McClellanville, S.C.
June 19th, 1863

My Dear Rebecca:

According to my usual habit, I again attempt to write you a few lines to let you know how I am getting on and try and give you any news that may be stirring here in camp. I am well and doing well, I mean as well as a soldier can do in the service.

Rebecca, John C. left this morning to go back to Virginia. His Captain, I think, would not sign his transfer. Therefore, you see he had to go back. Three other men in the Company had to go. Our Company is now four men less in number. John C. says in four or five weeks he will be back with us. I hope he may get back. He and Robert Baron want to make an exchange. Baron wants to go to Virginia and John C. wants to come back here. However, John C. will have to go on to his Company first. I expect your Mother will hate to hear of his going back as we were all here together. John C. left most of his clothing here. Charlie I think will be back in a few days. He saw Captain Tyler in town yesterday and told him he was coming back in a few days.

You wrote me asking how much of the gold wheat I wanted for seed. I want it threshed when they can and put in the store house and then you can let me know how many bushels it is. Then I will write back how much to save for seed. The keg wheat is the old wheat. I want about five or six bushels saved for seed. The balance you can have ground. I think you will have barrels enough to keep all of the fine flour in. The No. 1 family flour you can put in the box, but put a strip of cloth on the top to keep the dust out. Dust falls in when the lid is lifted up. I thought of keeping about ten bushels of wheat for seed, three bushels of rye and seven or eight bushels of Oats.[119]

Is the grass any account near the house? If not, have the field planted in peas. I think it will pay better to plant it in peas. I hardly know what ought to be done unless I was there to see.

Ance I think can farm and help Bill on for three weeks as Walter will not come down before the first Monday in July. I don't expect he will start down till about the tenth.

Mr. McClellan says his salt will be dry. However, any will leak. Mine I sent home was rather wet, but it was a damp rainy time when we got it. Has Henry been to see after it? I want to know if it went safe.

I want Walter to bring me about five pounds of four penny nails as we need them to nail the hoops on barrels. I want a few for sure so don't forget them as they are worth one dollar and one-forth in town.

Rebecca, inquire if any one will sell ten or twelve yards of Jane's cloth or if they will sell seven and at what price. I promised Dr. Baker to see if I could get him a few yards. So write and see if any can be had.

---

[119] Barr here is referring to harvesting and storage issues regarding his wheat. Some of his past crops had been sealed in kegs for later use. Gold and Red wheat mentioned in his letters were the two most common varieties of this crop. Red tended to be favored for winter crops, Gold for summer. See S. C. Salmon and J. W. Taylor, *Growing Wheat in the Eastern United States* (Washington: United State department of Agriculture, Farmers Bulletin No. 1817, 1939).

I would have sent the flour bag by Ance, but was off on picket when he started.

When you send me a box, warm the lard and put it in a jug. One gallon will be a plenty. Send thirty pounds of flour. I think that was as much as I brought at first. Send bacon, two or three hams or shoulders, but no butter as we get plenty.

Your Dear Husband,
James M. Barr

———◦◦◦◦———

McClellanville, S.C.
June 20, 1863

My Dear Rebecca:

I just received yours of the 17th.

Please send me a gallon of molasses and a little honey.

I am sorry to hear so much complaining among the Negroes.

I feel sad to hear of the death of Jasper Sawyer. Yet, we all have to die. Oh, that we may all be prepared for that solemn hour.

My hat brim will not suit me. I told William how I wanted it made. If too wide I can cut it narrow. Let it stay till I come home.

Did you get my last letter? I would like to see Walter and Henry.

Ance left last Wednesday evening and I suppose he is home by now.

Your letter was dated the 14th and mailed on the 17th. It lay in the office three days.

I find needles as scarce as hens teeth. I never see any unless I open my box to get one I brought from home.

I am glad to receive "howdy" from every one. I am glad to know they think of me.

Your Dear Husband
James M. Barr

McClellanville, S.C.
June 22nd, 1863

My Beloved Wife:

This morning having nothing to do, I have concluded to start a letter and write a few lines, knowing that tomorrow morning I will have to go off on picket and will not get in till Wednesday morning, the day of the mail. I thought at one time we would get a daily mail, but such is not the case. Our mail days are Wednesdays and Saturdays, though our papers come to us daily. Sometime we miss them as the couriers do not hit.

Speaking of the paper, we got encouraging news in Saturdays paper. It seems that our Generals have outsmarted the Yankees, It seems that they thought that General Lee would send his forces P.D.Q. to reinforce Pemberton at Vicksburg, but instead of that, Lee pushed his Army on and frightened the Yankees.[120]

I see the New York Times says Lee is marching North with 90, 000 troops. I hope he has so many, but fear he has not near so many. It seems that Lee is going to Pa. Lincoln has called for 100, 000 thousand Militia troops for six months. I hope we may continue to be successful and that we may out general the Yankees in all their plans.

Vicksburg I see is still safe, Grant cutting timbers behind him in the roads to prevent General Johnston's progress. If so, I do not think he can capture Vicksburg. No, not if he has to work before and behind. I think he is getting in rather a close place.

Rebecca, five negroes made their escape from here Saturday night, belonging to a Mr. McClelland and a Mr. Doar, three from the latter. I was off on picket duty the night they left. We have several boats here and we have to guard these boats constantly. A guard is kept there, but a man got one of the

---

[120] Barr seems to have been far better informed about the course of events during the war than many. During June 1863 Confederate General John C. Pemberton, under the direction of General Joseph E. Johnston, was attempting to hold off a Union siege of Vicksburg, Mississippi, led by Union General Ulysses S. Grant. At the same time General Robert E. Lee marched his Confederate army into Pennsylvania.

boats, as fine as one as we had here-worth at this time a thousand dollars, to go fishing. He left it on the opposite side of the river and did not bring it back as he ought to have done. He kept it locked for two or three nights, but on Saturday night he did not lock it. The Negroes got it and made their escape to the Yankees. Whilst the tide was high they could run out in a little creek behind the marshes away from our guard, they knowing every crook and turn where a boat could go.

Some men went in persuit of the boat to the Light House some ten miles off, knowing that if they could not see any boats, that the Negroes had now reached the Yankees. On they went for five or six miles and discovered two blockades. They knew the thing was out that they had already reached the Yankees. It was no fault of our men. It was the fault of the citizens in not returning the boat. Who will pay for the boat? I do not know. Major Morgan accounted for them. It was a boat from a vessel that ran ashore and one of the boats that the crew made their escape in.

The Negroes can give the Yankees a good deal of information concerning our force here.

Your Dear Husband,
James M. Barr

—————

McClellanville, S.C.
June 24th, 1863

My Dear Wife:

Imagine the pleasure it gives me to read one of your very interesting letters.
I have just got in off of picket with a fine chance of fine fish. Sheep head.
I got the line you sent me.
I can read your letters very well.
Did not write to Tom anything about a daughter.
Do you know how much wheat they expect me to make?

I hope my peas are all planted as it is high time that they were planted, as peas will not do much planted later than the twentieth of June.

You did not say whether you received any postage stamps or not. I sent some in letter.

Ance I suppose is home.

I have just got a letter from John C. Says if he had a chance, he could go to see you quite often as he is in Columbia.

Henry ought to say when he is coming, if at all, so I may engage the salt and how much. I suppose he has mine home.

I must close to put this in the mail. I am well and hope this finds you all well.

Sam sends his regards to you and all.

Your Devoted Husband
James M. Barr

P.S. I will not write till next week again.

CHAPTER THREE
BY UNFAIR MEANS I WAS DEFEATED

One of the greatest problems that plagued Union and Confederate armies during the war was the practice of permitting the enlisted men in each company the privilege of electing their junior officers. The popular custom dated back to the colonial militia and had a uniquely American democratic quality to it. But its drawbacks far outweighed any benefits. In all matters of military discipline volunteer soldiers naturally chose the path of least resistance and were far more inclined to elect incompetent officers who were socially popular and the least likely to enforce the strict discipline needed in combat. Many elected officers studied and learned their lessons on the job and became very capable leaders. Others, with little knowledge of drill, tactics, or logistics, would be responsible for the mistreatment and deaths of scores of soldiers.

Although James Barr had stated many times that he preferred the life of a private, in June 1863 he ran for the office of 2nd Lieutenant in Company I, 5th South Carolina Cavalry.

McClellanville, S.C.
Saturday morning
June 27th, 1863

My Beloved Wife:

In my last letter to you I said that I did not expect to write again this week, but My Dear, circumstances has altered the case and I think it due you to let you know.

I am now a candidate for Lieutenant in our Company. Became a candidate since I wrote my last letter to you. The election is next Tuesday the 30th of this month. Pretty hard electioneering for candidates. Sgt. M.J. Rice, Sgt. Mims, Abram Hartzog and myself.[121] The election now lies between Sgt. Rice and myself, Perhaps in my next letter I can tell you that I am now elected Lieutenant, if not, that I am defeated. I think my chance very good at this time, but what may be brought about by Tuesday, I know not. Something may be brought up to defeat me.

John C. Charlie and three other men, counting five, who would vote for me are now off on furloughs. I said five, but there are seven. Also Capt. Tyler is away and I think if he was here I would get his vote. So you see I will lose eight or ten votes. However, I will let you know in my next letter how the election goes.

I want three or four hundred dollars. Mr. Spann can tell William that I want it, so he can keep it for me or get it. I will tell you more about it in my next letter.

Rebecca, when the wagon comes, I want you to be sure and send me a chair. One of those chairs I had in the store house. When I saw them last, they were wrapped up in paper in sacking. I want one sent.

A shoe maker here has just made me a pair of boots.

Have you got the salt yet? I hope you have as I am very anxious to know if it went safe.

Lt. Guess resigned on account of his eyes.

---

[121] Sergeant M. J. Rice and Private A. N. W. Hartzog served in Company I, 5th South Carolina Cavalry. Mims was most likely First Sergeant Robert Minus. Knudsen, "5th SC," 27, 39, 46.

Rebecca, I think it best for you to set down on piece of paper what I want so you can refer to it.

Tell Henry to bring me a couple of good barrels, four if he can get them well hooped with good heads, if the salt has got home, it can be emptied in a box and he can bring that barrel back.

A Mr. Dreher of Captain Caughman's Company is very low. I think he will not live till night.[122]

It is warm down here now.

Sam says if there is any prospect of an increase, it is more than he knows. He says he don't want any more till the War ends.

Ask Ance did he carry Alewines' money safe.[123]

Your kind letter is at hand. Sorry to hear of Johnny's illness. I hope and trust he was not sick long.

Trust this will find you all well.

Can't board too many children. I think Crout can board. He was not very accomodating when I wanted to pay him that money.

You can grind wheat whenever you wish. I was only joking about grinding my wheat. I was telling the boys that I wanted a furlough to go home and grind wheat.

I am well. I expect to get home before long. My love to all.

Your devoted Husband
James M. Barr

---

[122] John H. Dreher, a private in Company I, 5th South Carolina Cavalry, died of disease on July 5, 1863 at McClellanville, South Carolina. Knudsen, "5th SC," 18.

[123] Probably David Alewine of the Lexington District. He enlisted as a substitute in Company F, 5th South Carolina Cavalry. Ibid., 5.

McClellanville, S.C.
July 1st, 1863

My Beloved Wife:

It is a pleasure to me that I am permitted again to write you a few lines. Though, my Dear One, I have nothing much to write about.

Charlie is again with us. He arrived here Saturday night. He says you must tell Major Walter Quattlebaum if he can have his watch fixed that he would be glad for him to bring it with him when he comes.

My Dear One, I have been defeated in my election. Five of my men were sent off on sick furloughs. Sgt. M.J. Rice was elected. I was next to him. He beat me eleven votes. We had six candidates. If the election could have come off last Friday or Saturday I would have been elected. Or if the other candidates had withdrawn, I would have been safe. Rice's party worked very hard for him, used what influence they could. Rice 26 votes, Barr 15 votes, Sgt. Mims 6 votes, Sgt. Boylston 3 votes, J.C. Stepp 5, Abram Hartzig 2, and if these men had not run, I would have got their votes.[124]

My friends all let the election go on quietly. Charlie did not electioneer. Sam did very little. Sam I think if he had tried could have turned a good many votes, but he was so sure that I was safe that he did not try or use his influence much. However, my Dear One, I am perfectly satisfied. Rice is a splendid fellow and will do his best for the men, but I hate being beat on account of two or three men.

Curtiss Fast was against me. I don't think he would have had me elected for five hundred dollars.[125] He ran once and got five votes and as he could not be elected, it is reasonable that he did not want me elected.

We are having a quantity of rain, raining nearly every day and night for

---

[124] Samuel Reed Boylston was the first sergeant of Company I, 5th South Carolina Cavalry. He was wounded during the Battle of Trevilian Station, Virginia, June 11-12, 1864. He died in Richmond on June 20, 1864. J.C. Stepp from Georgia also served in Company I. Ibid., 9, 53.

[125] Most likely C.C. Foust from Barnwell. Foust had been reduced from the rank of sergeant to private in Company I, 5th South Carolina Cavalry. Ibid., 21.

the last week. I expect my wheat will ruin if it rains so much at home.

Your letter of the 25th of June is at hand. Glad to hear that Johnny is better. Sorry to hear of the sty on your eye, hope it will soon be well.

Anxious to know if Henry got my salt.

I think Pa would better let Henry move back to his old place. It is a scandal for Anna to treat Ma the way she does.[126]

I think the wheat would better be hauled out the fields. If it is damp when it is threshed, it must be sunned.

Rice, I am tired of it as we have it three times a day.

My Dear, I am well and getting on finely, hope you and all are enjoying good health. I can't say yet by what time I will get off. My love to all. I remain

Your True Husband
James M. Barr

———

South Santee, S.C.
July 6th, 1863

My Dear Beloved Wife:

I received your very truly and welcome letter last Saturday. You can imagine the pleasure it gave me to hear from you and the children. The pleasure it gave me to hear that you all were quite well. Yes, My Dear One, if I am not permitted to see you, we are blessed with the privilege of corresponding with each other every week, to hear and know how each other are getting on.

It seems that you are getting along pretty well, weighing one hundred and forty-two pounds, which is a source of pleasure to me to know that you are not grieving yourself so much for me. I know that you ought to know that I am filling a position that all men ought to fill who are able, yet I know there are many that will never come in service if they can be cleared by any state

---

[126] Anna Barr was Henry Barr's wife.

law or anything that will keep them out. I feel as if I ought to be here or have someone else to replace me, but it is not like one filling his own place.

I am truly sorry to hear that my crop is so much in the grass and above all don't like to hear that the peas are not planted. The peas ought all to have been planted by the twentieth of June and if Bill had of commenced planting on the twentieth of May, he surely could have finished by the twenieth of June. Peas planted after that time among corn, can't make a crop. So you see my pea crop is bound to fall short. Last year I made a good pea crop by planting early, by commencing the middle of May and if they could not plough corn, they could have hoed it and kept the grass and weeds down, like I had them to do the field on the other side of the pond last year. It is much easier for them to tell you how they work than it is for them to do it. However, I am here and they are there, if they don't make a crop for me someone else must work them another year.

I think you ought to go to the Church whenever, you can. It is a place that all ought to go whenever they can. We have preaching sometimes in camp. Rev. DuPre preached twice for us since we have been here. He will preach next Sunday. I did not get to hear him but once. I was on guard last time he preached and may be on guard or picket next Sunday. He is a Methodist Minister, some eighty years old and reads without specks.

I received a letter from Thomas and Wesley Saturday. Also one from John C. They were all well. Wesley said he would be here on the 15th of this month. Would bring me some vegetables. Said he would see Walter and get him to come with wagon. I want Ance to come. I am needing him very bad. Can't get along very well without him. We can't get our meals regular and can't have anything taken care of like Ance did.

The boy that was attending to my horse, Lt. Brookers Sampson got drowned last Friday. He was swimming a horse and got thrown off and drowned.[127]

It is twice that John C. is in Columbia jail. I received a letter from him Saturday. He says he is doing first rate. Will take the jail for the War. Says he has received a box from home. Wish I had some of the good things. Said he had heard his old Regiment was in Maryland. He appeared to be in fine spir-

---

[127] Sampson was likely a slave, who may have belonged to Lieutenant E. Booker. See note 64.

its. They can't hurt John C. as a Confederate Doctor recommended a transfer for him and General Walker received him. Captain Tyler received him after receiving a note from General Walker. Captain Tyler gave John C. a certificate showing he was enlisted in his Company and was here doing service.[128]

Who is Dr. Mason?[129] Where is he from and where is he located?

I hope Henry divided the salt right and did not give me all the wet salt. If any choice, I should have had it. He ought to have done as I said to, empty it in a box in the store, measuring all, then measure for Pa out of the freight. You wrote me Pa would pay the expenses here. I had to pay to boat it over to Charleston and the dray to the Depot, which was three or four dollars.

The young man I wrote you was so low in Caughman's Company, Mr. Dreher, died yesterday evening.

My Dear One, we have been living pretty well for a few days. Last Saturday we had a fine turkey for dinner. It did not cost us anything. We bought five and sold four for the money and had one to eat ourselves. We had a chicken for breakfast every morning. We have some ten chickens yet. We have had for dinner for the last few days, collards, squash, tomatoes and beans. We are now out of bacon and flour. Would like to have a box.

Can't say by what time that I can get home. Would like to see you and the little ones.

Yankee rebels are in sight and have been for the last few days. Would not be surprised if they do not come out soon and give us a little fight. We are keeping a sharp look out for them. I do not think they can gain much to come out here only to get Negroes. They may be after getting recruits.

We are all getting on pretty well. Hope to see you in August. Charlie and Sam send their love.

Your True Husband
James M. Barr

---

[128] Evidently Confederate authorities arrested Dowling for deserting from his unit in Virginia. His company listed him as being absent without leave from November 11, 1862 through the end of June 1863. Salley, *South Carolina Troops*, np.

[129] Most likely this was Dr. R. C. Mason of Edgefield. *1860 Census*, Edgefield District, South Carolina.

McClellanville, S.C.
July 8th, 1863

My Dear Wife:

I seat myself again this Wednesday morning to write you how I am getting on. I am quite well and getting on tolerably well, considering that I have no Negro to wait on me.

My reason for wanting three hundred dollars is this. When we left Pocataligo John C. bought him a horse and I borrowed two hundred dollars for him, taking his note and giving mine. I would like for Walter or Henry to bring me the money so I can take up the note. I would like to have it paid up, and I thought whilst the wagon was down I would get them to haul me a load of salt to Charleston on it if they brought me the barrels (some five).

I want Walter to make me a box to keep my clothes in, 2 1/2 feet long and 12 inches wide and ten or twelve inches deep with hinges and clasp so I can keep it locked. I want a good box if he can make it. I prefer to send my valice home. I have a lock for the box.

You need not send me the chair as others constantly would have it.

Be sure and send the last taxes.

I have engaged about sixty bushels of salt at six dollars or whatever others are selling at when the wagon gets here.

It has been rumored that we will be sent to North Carolina. I don't think that we will be sent as other troops would have to come here.

We have been receiving good news from Lee's army. Hope it will hasten the day of peace when we can return to our dear families.[130]

I look for Wesley on the 16th.

No furloughs are granted now though. I think they will begin in a few days. Trust so and hope I may get one before long.

Twelve o'clock, very much disappointed in not receiving a letter today.

Your Devoted Husband,
James M. Barr

South Santee, S.C.
July 12th, 1863

My Dear Wife:

As I did not have an opportunity of writing to you yesterday and will have an opportunity of sending this by hand to Charleston in a day or two if the Yankees do not succeed in taking the City. My Dear One, I hope the Yankees will not succeed. If they should succeed, I think it will be useless to keep us here. I think we will hold the City though we don't know. Three o'clock. As I write I hear the cannons belching forth.[131]

My Dear One, the Captain is now in our mess. We are pretty well fixed.

---

[130] By July 8, 1863, Lee's defeated army was returning to Virginia after its defeat at Gettysburg.

[131] On July 10, 1863 Federal forces under Major General Quincy Adams Gilmore began an assault on the Charleston defenses with an amphibious attack against Battery Wagner on Morris Island.

If I only had Ance we could do well. We have been living well having squash, okra, tomatoes cucumbers and butter a plenty. Though it takes money to get along well. Today we had a fine dinner. Can you guess what we had. A fine turkey (wild) squash, cucumbers, rice, tomatoes. Don't you think we are faring well.

Captain Tyler killed the turkey yesterday evening and shot a buck but did not get him, though they kill one or two a week. A great many deer down here. One of the men told me last Friday that they saw about ten in one day. An old Lady said she could sit in her piazer and see the deer feeding in the woods.[132]

I am glad that Jane did so well. If only Mariah will do well.

I am sorry Jimmy was so much disappointed in not seeing me. I know the little fellow thought sure of seeing me after his dream.

My dear one, some of our men was sent after some deserters. If I had gone, I could have staid five nights at home. The men was at Dave Shealys. They had their horses shod there. Shealy charged them $1.25 cts. for shoeing their horses and charged them for feeding their horses. I wish they had gone to my house for dinner and had their horses fed. Three men from our Company and three from Captain Caughman's Company. The three from our Company was David Sourgounner, Bed F. Esterling and William Stokes.[133] All very clever men and friends of mine. Would have voted for me if they had been here.

Elijah wrote to Captain Tyler yesterday saying if he came to our company would he receive him. So I will not be surprised if he comes. If so, we will have five in our mess.

I don't think John C. will get back. The young man that promised to swap places with him is ruptured and I think he will be discharged. I do not think they can hurt John C. for if General Walker had not received him he would have gone back to his company. As for putting him in jail, was for the purpose of carrying him back to Virginia.

I would like for Jimmie to come with the wagon if I knew they would

---

[132] Perhaps Barr was referring to piazza, another term for a veranda or porch.

[133] D. E. Sojourner and W. E. Stokes, both privates in Company I, 5th South Carolina Cavalry. Stokes was later captured on June 11, 1864 at Louisa Court House, Virginia. There is no record of Bed F. Esterling. Knudsen, "5th SC," 52.

take good care of him, though I fear he would get hurt. If he could be here in camp, he could tell you a many thing after getting back.

Charlie is a bugler, has an easy time.

My Dear One I can't tell you when I can get home at the shortest time. Not till September or October unless I should get sick and be sent home on a sick furlough or unless someone was sick at home and the Dr. stated the fact to me or the Captain. If Pa is or should get bad off, either Pa or Ma, you must let me know. I hope we may all stay well, but would like to get home on some terms or other.

I am afraid they will injure the corn by ploughing, also afraid the wheat will spoil and we have musty flour.

If I had known Henry would not have come down, I don't believe I would have let him have the salt. Though if no one comes, I will try and send enough for another year home.

Hope to see Wesley and Q. soon.

You said in your letter that Henry had got back from Columbia. You did not say whether he got the salt or not. Was my reason for wanting to know and another thing, I did not get a receipt for it, and did not know whether I would ever get it or not. Glad to know it went safe.

I close. My love to you and all.

Your Devoted Husband,
James M. Barr

Have you named the baby yet? Can't you find a name for him?

———⋙◈⋘———

McClellanville, S. C
July 15th, 1863

My Dear Wife:

Thinking perhaps you may be uneasy about me, knowing that I am not very far from Charleston, I want you to know we are still here at McClellanville, but do not know how soon we may leave here. Yet we may not be ordered away from here. Two companies of our Regiment have been sent to North Carolina.

I see from the papers that the reserves for six months service have been ordered to Charleston on today, the 15th, instead of the 1st of August.

Wesley wrote me he would be here on the 16th, but I am afraid he will not come. I will be disappointed if no one comes for I wanted ten bushels of salt for myself. If the Yankees should succeed in taking Charleston, salt will be hard to get and very high prices. Salt now in Charleston is selling at 16 dollars per bushel. Henry deceived me in not coming. I think it would have been well for Pa to have sent and got a load.

I do not know what to say about the news as we are not getting any from Charleston and very little from General Lee's army. I get a daily paper, but do not get much news. When your paper is out, get someone to send after the Carolinian, Try Weekly.

I think Walter ought to stay at home with his family as long as he can. If they call for all the Reserve Forces from forty to fifty, then it would be time enough for him to go. He ought to recollect that he has a house full of children depending on him and when he goes who will look after them? It is best not to expect anybody to look after ones affairs.

Tell Spann I wish he would tell William to again offer Crout the money in the presence of some one. I think he ought to have taken my money, and if not, to lose the interest. Some person wanted me to give his name to the Editor at Charleston, but I do not feel willing to do it. I hope he will take the money.

I do not like to ask Dr. Baker what he will pay for cloth. I think Mary ought to set a price and then see whether he will give it or not.

The potato patch may be ruined by working at this time.

My crop is not large. I expect to have to buy corn.

I don't want Bill to let the hogs get poor. I want to fatten about forty head. I want to kill the ones that eat the chickens. They ought to have been spayed before turning in the field.

Have the sheep put in stubble field and your milk cows.

I am well, hope you are all as well as ever. Kiss the children for me. I would like to see them and you, but do not think that I will be blest with that privilege soon, but hope and trust it may not be long.

Your True Husband,
James M. Barr

———⊰∘⊱———

McClellanville, S.C.
July 17th, 1863

My Dear Rebecca:

It is with pleasure that I embrace this opportunity of writing you a few lines to let you know that I am well and hope you and our dear little children are well.

I must acknowlege that I have been very much disappointed in no one coming down. I expected them, but the excitement in the city may have caused them not to come. Yet, it ought to have hurried them off to get a supply of salt. If the city should fall, I guess it will sell at high prices. Fearing that the city might fall was my reason for wanting to get enough salt for two years. I have heard of one man here raising his salt up to ten dollars per bushel. Have not heard of any others.

My Dear One, I would like very much to send some of my clothing home. I have entirely too many here for if we should move, it would be impossible for me to carry them unless the wagon would haul them. I have four pair of pants, four coats, four shirts and three flanel shirts (one is a red flanel) five pairs of draws, three pair of socks, one cap and two hats. Though the hat I drew is not worth much, about such a hat as I sold for fifty cents. We drew our clothing yesterday. If anyone comes I don't want you to send me but one pair of pants. I drew a pair of shoes some three weeks ago and swapped them off for an allegator's hide, but if the wagon don't come it will be lost to me. I had my boots fixed since I have been here, so I have a pair of boots and a pair of shoes.

Charlie received a box from home yesterday containing bacon, dried peaches and potatoes but the potatoes were all rotten as the box laid over in the City for fifteen days.

You said in your letter that you were sorry that I was beaten in the election. We cannot help these things. If everything had worked on fairly I would have been elected, but by unfair means I was defeated. However, I believe the Company is sorry I was defeated. If so many had not run, I could and would have been elected. We are all getting on as well pleased as we were before the election, all perfectly friendly.

I have not heard from John C. since he left Columbia. I am expecting a letter from him, would like to hear from him, how he is getting on.

We are all in fine spirits considering the fighting at Charleston. I expect you get the same news from there as I get. We get very little as Bourigard will not publish or let be published the news.[134]

We are still faring pretty well in the eating line, squashy tomatoes and venison. The Captain was out driving yesterday and one of the boys killed a fine buck, so we have venison.[135]

Your True Husband,
James M. Barr

---

[134] General Pierre Gustave Toutant Beauregard.

[135] Driving is a nineteenth century term for hunting. Game would be driven from cover into the sights of a waiting shooter.

———◦◦◦◦———

McClellanville, S. C.
July 18th, 1863

My Dear Rebecca:

My Dear One, I have just received two letters from you. I am truly sorry to see that you are fretting yourself so much for me. We must put our trust in the Lord. He is able to shield us from the enemy's balls, if he sees fit, and if we never meet on earth, let us meet in Heaven where parting will be no more.

I was mad to hear of Cates' disobedience.

Charlie and I rode out the other day to Mrs. Guardners, about seven miles from here. The old lady gave us a very fine watermelon, as much as we could eat.

I don't think we will be ordered to Charleston. I think the Yankees will hold Morris Island. I have my doubts of Charleston falling. I did not get any papers yesterday. Hope you are more reconciled.

My love to all.

Your Husband,
James M. Barr

Seed Wheat: 5 bushels Gale wheat
               5 bushels Red wheat

You overlooked the wheat I wrote you about.

———◦◦◦◦———

McClellanville, S.C.
July 21st, 1863

My Dear Wife:

It is with pleasure that I again embrace another opportunity of writing
you a few lines to let you know how I am getting on. My Dear One, I am well
and faring exceedingly well in the eating line, considering I am so far from
home and my loved ones. Yes, My Dear, far from you but I hope it will not be
long before I get to see you and our dear little ones. But my dear, I don't know
when furloughs will be given. Not till after the excitement is over in the city.
It seems to me that the Yankees suffered so severly, as reported in yesterdays
paper, from the fight Saturday and Saturday night, that they surely will give
up for a bad job.[136] However, they are so determined and have so much
hatred for the city because our Convention met there and it was there that
the ordinance was prepared. They say they want to take the hot bed of secession, meaning the city of Charleston. Oh, I suppose the paper represents the
Yankees. Their losses have been fifteen hundred or two thousand. Our losses
are comparatively small, not exceeding one hundred. Quite likely we lost
more, but do not know.

Our losses in Virginia were pretty heavy or I should have said at
Gettysburg, in Virginia. I guess you have seen the casualties or at least some
of them. I do not know what to think of Lee's movements. Think he had better stayed in Virginia. I see the names of several of the Lexington boys among
the wounded. I see that Lt. Bouknight received a slight wound.

Oh, if this cruel War would only stop that sons might return to their
fathers and mothers and that husbands might return to their wives. When
we hear of a victory gained, how thankful we ought to be to our Maker, who
is able to see us safe through this struggle if we will only put our trust in

---

[136] On July 18, 1863 Federal forces under General Gilmore were repulsed after a desperate frontal assault
on Battery Wagner, which guarded Charleston Harbor. In the attack, Union forces suffered 1,515 casualties
in comparison to 174 Confederates losses. The Union casualties included Colonel Robert Gould Shaw and
many of the black soldiers of his 54th Massachusetts Infantry. In the aftermath of the disaster Federal
forces began a slow siege of the fortification.

him. Oh, my Dear One, how many prayers do you suppose was offered up to the Throne of Grace for our cause on last Sabbath. I suppose many a one. Yet, I suppose there are many at home wishing the War would stop for fear they will have to go in and yet never thinking or praying to God for it. Oh, how wicked our people are and I do not think the War will stop whilst so much wickedness is around. All are thinking how they can make money. That, I guess, is the chief object of their study.

Yesterday evening we received the good news from Charleston that our men were victorious in the fight on Morris Island Saturday night and some of our boys were fiddling and dancing. It seems to liven them up for some reason or other.

Mr. Guess and Mr. Graham sent their wagons down after fifty three bushels of salt. They left this evening. They got salt at six dollars per bushel, but the salt boilers now refuse to engage to anyone, looking up for higher prices. Several have raised to ten dollars and other to seven. I hardly know how low it could be bought as wagons are hauling off pretty fast and the men say they can sell as fast as they make so they will not engage to anyone.

Sallie sent Sam a lots of good things, cabbage, beans, squash, irish potatoes, a box of very nice apples and some dried peaches. Was wanting to send ripe peaches, but too ripe I guess. She also sent ham, lard and a bottle of ketchup, as fine as I ever ate. It had a few onions cut fine in it. If only it had been a gallon instead of a bottle.

I sent my black jean coat, two flannel shirts and flannel draws back with the wagon to Sams and my Crewel scarf.[137] If I need them, I think I can get them from there, but I want Henry to get what I sent to Charlies when he goes down to Barnwell, also my saddle.

Your Husband,
James M. Barr

---

[137] Crewel is worsted yarn, slackly twisted, and used for fancy work.

McClellanville, S.C.
July 22nd, 1863

My Dear Rebecca:

Twenty three wagons came in last evening for salt.

I am detailed for picket today, but am waiting for the mail and to get a good dinner. I did not get a letter. We only have two mail days, Wednesday and Saturdays and if you don't send by proper mail days, I get both your letters on the same day. In writing two letters a week, you should send off by Fridays mail for me to get it on Wednesday. Wednesday's mail for me to get it by Saturday.

Your Devoted Husband,
James M. Barr

McClellanville, S. C,
July 26, 1863

My Dear Wife:

I have just received your letter and have not time to answer. I am well, glad to hear you and the children are well. Sorry to hear of Pa and Ma's illness.

Would like to have Ance very much, but he could not get through Charleston as they would take him and put him at work.

The meat must hold out. Tell the Negroes I said that whole plantations of Negroes are not getting any bacon and the soldiers very little. When we get it, it is about 1 lb. Ance knows. Sorry you did not get in the Beef Club.

Note: in the original letter about seven lines were torn off the bottom of the letter at this place in the letter.

It would not do for Jimmy to come down as the roads are too bad if anyone should come. I do not look for anyone as they put off the day too long.

I will get off home as soon as I can though no furloughs are being given here. I don't know why unless it is that we are held in readiness to march at a short notice.

I will write Wednesday. I just got in off picket, wet as a rat.

I heard from Tom. He is in hospital, I guess at Richmond.

Your Husband,
James

————◦◦◦————

McClellanville, S. C.
South Santee
Tuesday Evening, July 28th, 1863

My Beloved Wife:

Again this evening I seat myself to answer yours of the 19th of July, knowing that my Dear Wife is ever anxious to hear from me and always ready to receive a letter from me. Yet, My Dear One, I have no news to write you.

The booming of cannons is till distinctly heard here. It appears from what I can hear that we have a battery erected on James Island and they, our men, are shelling the enemy on Morris Island from it. I suppose with fifteen inch shells. Hope and trust that they may be successful in driving the enemy away. I do not think the Yankees will succeed in taking Charleston this Summer if they take it at all. It may be next Winter, but I trust that they may be foiled in all their undertakings and that we may never lose the City.

No chance for furloughs as long as the Yankees are trying to take Charleston. I am very anxious to get a furlough to go home and see you and our dear little boys. I am now more anxious to get home than I have been since I have been in the service. None get off unless by sick furloughs or by their families being sick.

I am glad to hear that the corn is holding out so well and if Bill will do right, he can save a good deal more by feeding the grass that he could not kill. He ought to feed the horses on grass constantly and when corn is ripe enough, feed corn tops.

I would like to be home to select out my killing hogs for another year, or at least the ones I want killed this Fall. Bill and Henry will have to select them out the last of August if I don't get off.

Our eating doings is getting scarce as Sam's box has about given out. Sallie did not send any flour.

Ance can't come unless someone would come with him. They might take him and put him at work on some of the fortifications. I am not willing to send him there any more. They kept Ance two months and have not paid me anything and I think others can now send. I need Ance here and I need Jerry at home. Therefore, I can't send any hands. Men that own more and who are at home ought to send.

When you write me again, say how many bushels of salt you think you have in all. I would not have bothered with putting the salt in jars. It would have done in a barrel. You must take care of it for if the Yankees succeed in taking Charleston, which I don't believe they will, salt will be a tremendous price.

I said we were getting scarce of eatables, I forgot our chickens. We have a pen full, some thirty two head. I expect more than you have at home. We bought them here.

Sam is doing very well. Charlie is grunting a little, but nothing serious. I have not been feeling so well for a day or two, being fatigued so much on picket every other day. Today I am in camp though detailed to haul off manure. Tomorrow I will be on Camp duty and will finish this after the mail comes.

Your Dear Husband,
James

McClellanville, S. C.
July 29th, 1863

My Dear Rebecca:

The mail has arrived, but no letter from you, my Dear One. I am somewhat disappointed in not receiving one of your ever dear letters.

I received a letter from John C. today. He is near Richmond and still in the Guard Tent. He says he does not know his sentence, says he is well and from his writing, he appears to be quite lively.

I would send you some stamps, but have them all on the envelopes. I will enclose you a couple envelopes ready backed. You can put the stamps on the letters.

Your Dear Husband,
James

McClellanville, S. C,
August 1st, 1863

My Beloved Wife:

It is with pleasure that I embrace this opportunity to writing you a few lines to let you know how I am and how long I will remain here at McClellanville. My Dear One, I am getting along very well. I am enjoying pretty good health. Have been complaining some with my back, but feel better.

My Dear One, I expect we will soon strike tents to be ready for leaving here. We have been looking for marching orders. I expect we will get orders today and we will leave tomorrow morning for Charleston. It is said that we will be stationed in the City. I know that we cannot get so well fixed up as we are here, that we will have to make our beds down on the ground. However, we are soldiers here to defend our Country and I must try to do it under any circumstances.

Yesterday Capt. Tyler and a couple of our men brought in three men. They claimed to be North Carolinians. Said they had been taken prisoners and were on a block aiding vessel near Charleston and had made their escape from a small boat whilst out after wood. They were questioned and searched. On the first two they found nothing, but the last one had a letter showing he belonged to a Regiment now in Charleston. He owned the whole truth after they found the letter, and said they were on their way home, but appeared anxious to be sent back to their Company. They said if they got back soon they did not think they would be punished much. They left Friday. They were sent back today.

Has Henry sold my fodder yet?

I have just received your very interesting letter. As I was reading it, a Company came up to relieve us. We will be certain to leave for Charleston. I will write to you when we get there. We will miss all our good things.

I am sorry Mittie did not send our pair of blankets home as it was such a good chance.

Have our wheat ground where you please. I expect it would be better to have it ground at Quattlebaums.

I wanted my fodder sold whilst fodder was bringing a good price.

Think it no use to hoe corn this time of the year.

I was glad to hear from you and the children. Sorry to hear Johnny and Baby being sick though. The Doctor would have to send a certificate for me to get a furlough. C.C. Hartzog received a certificate that his mother was sick and anxious to see him, so I think he will get off soon.

I am confused as we will have to move so I can't write. I would much rather stay here. We will miss several good things by leaving. Perhaps we may stop at Mt. Pleasant. I don't know when I can get off.

I will have my likeness taken as soon as I can.

Hope Walters will be elected and hope Harte may be defeated.

Your True Husband,
James

James Michael Barr was thirty-four years old when this photo was made, most likely in Charleston. Although a private in the 5th South Carolina Cavalry, he continued to be called "Major," his pre-war militia rank. He had been at war for eight months and wrote frequently to his twenty-two year old wife Rebecca, at home with three small children.

Courtesy of Raymond McDaniel, Abilene, Texas

Editor's note: While J.M. Barr was home on furlough, his messmate and brother-in-law Charleigh T. Dowling wrote to his sister Rebecca.

McClellanville, S. C.
August 12, 1863

Dear Sissie:

I received yours of the 7th today. I am glad to hear that Maj. Barr is not worse off, I expected to hear that he was very ill. The Doctor thought he was going to have a very severe spell. I am sorry that you all are unwell so much so that you cannot enjoy the peaches and watermelons you have on hand. I wish I were there. I would be sure to slay a few.

Tell the Major I don't think we will leave here under a month. C.C. Faust is just from Charleston.[138] He says Kitt told him that it would be a month or six weeks before the Cavalry Company will be organized and probably never. Sissie, this is my place for the War if I am allowed.

I received a letter from Mitty today, She says Aaron is better than he has been. He has had an attack of Typhoid fever.

Old Mr. Walker is to marry on the 27th to Dick Rices' widow, Janie Rice.[139]

You asked me if I did not wish to get sick to go home to see Mitty. Yes, I wish I could get home, but I am like Barr. I want a well furlough but, Sissie, I don't know if I don't get home soon. I have something like unto rheumatism in my left knee. Our Doctor would recommend a furlough now, but I don't want the boys to think I am playing sick. Otherwise, I am as hearty as I ever was.

I have no news worth writing. I am tenting by myself. Tell Barr I have moved in a house where there is a fire place with a good bedstead.

My love to the baby and the boys.
C.T. Dowling

Good news, Major. Cortez is now with the Company answering to his name night and morning.[140] He is awfully put out. He looks like he would get sick now if he could. I think he is going to try to get into our mess and I am going to kick against it.

C.T. Dowling

---

138 C.C. Faust served in Company I, 5th South Carolina Cavalry. Knudsen, "5th SC," 21.

139 Mr. Walker was probably R.W. Walker, a substantial widower, who farmed in Barnwell. *1860 Census*, Barnwell District, South Carolina.

140 There is no record of Cortez in the 5th South Carolina Cavalry.

McClellanville, S.C.
September 3rd, 1863

My Dear Rebecca:

I take this present opportunity of writing you a few lines, knowing that you are ever anxious to hear from your absent one who is seperated by this War far from you. yet, My Dear One, I am looking forward to the time through God's blessings that I may be permitted to return home to my dear Wife and little ones. Yes my Dear One, I hope and pray that the day is not far distant when Peace shall spread her wings over our land and we all be permitted to return home and enjoy the comforts of home and the pleasure of each others company again.

Under the circumstances I am as well satisfied as I can be, knowing that it is the duty of every man to battle for his rights and our Independance. Our forefathers fought for the privileges they enjoyed and the time is now here for us to fight for our liberty. We ask nothing of the Yankees, only to be let alone. From what I can hear, the dawn of day is still shining on us and if we only, as a Nation, would put our trust in God as we should, I don't think the time would be long before we would have peace.

I hear that Gen. Lee is pressing on Meade, that Meade is falling back toward his fortifications near Washington, and that the Yankees in the West are rather in a critical position, though they will fall back.

Thomas wrote me that they were picketing within Thirty yards of each other, nothing but a creek between them. Quite close picketing, yet they do not shoot each other. Yet, if they intended to have a fight then they would begin to fire. Thomas says he is well and from the tone of his letter he is in fine spirits. He says John C. is well and asked if you received a letter from him.

I am glad to hear that your Mother intends to pay you a visit for really it seemed as none cared for you. However, I know that your Ma is excusable as she cannot have her own way.

My Dear Rebecca, I am now a stronger Methodist than ever being associated as I am with other men who will try and hold up their denomination and run down others. I have no confidence in the World in any man's Religion who obtained it and can't tell when he obtained it. God's work is not a secret work nor is he a partial God, for if we go to him as we should, he is willing and able to bless any of us. Some men will almost resort to anything to carry a point. Yes, lie to carry them. Curtis says we have two disciplines in our Church and other things that he cannot prove and others siding with him makes me have no confidence in their Religion. I think our prayer meetings will go down if arguing is not let alone. For it will not do to pray one hour and then lie another, for some do lie.

My Dear One, let me not influence you to join my Church by saying that I was a stronger Methodist than I ever was. I only spoke as I felt. Prejudice has a good deal to do with it. I hope all I hear will not make me so. Yet, I believe some here think that their Church is the only way to Heaven. God pity them and help them to do better than some of them are doing.

Your Husband,
James M. Barr

McClellanville, S. C.
September 4th, 1863

My Dear Rebecca:

Charlie has gone fishing today so you see we intend to have a stew or a bake. We had potatoes baked for breakfast yesterday morning, but at dinner we got some beef. Some man, I don't know his name, gave us a couple of loads of potatoes. They were quite a treat to our men as our rations are slim. We do not get any more Sugar, but we still drink muddy water without the sugar.

Captain Tyler is going home on a ten day furlough. He will be back next Wednesday. Charlie I think will get off on furlough next week as it is his time. Next we can send three men at a time, but men going to see their sick families throw others back a good deal.

I have not heard from George Hartzog in a day or two.[141] I expect he is dead as he was very low when I heard. Nick got his furlough extended and is at home yet.[142]

We had a better turn out at prayer meeting last night than usual. I think we will get along better as they see and know it wont do. Our head or leading men are Mr. Asque and Mr. Smith, former a Baptist and the latter a Methodist. He is from Lexington near Sandy Run, but I think he will be sent to the Hospital in Columbia as he is not fit for service. He has sore legs.[143]

Some think the War will end by March. Oh, if it only will be so what a happy people we would be. It is thought the Yankees will give up the Seige at Charleston, but I think they will try every effort before they do.

How are the Negroes getting on sowing wheat? Tell them to do good ploughing. How does the rye look? Do you think our corn will do us for another year? How many seed peas has Bill? Tell him he must save enough for seed. I don't care if you kill the red Swygert cow too if she can get fat, but do as you please about it.

Just received your letter. Henry ought not to have taken my mare to Columbia. If they take her from me, Henry and Pa must only pay me for her. I would not have her taken for several loads of flour. Tell him what I say. I think she could have ploughed.

Our wagon will get back today or tomorrow.

This leaves me well.

I wrote to Joe Leaphart last week about the money.

Your True Husband,
James M. Barr

[141] In all probability G. F. Hartzog, who had originally served in Company A, 1st (Hagood's) South Carolina Infantry prior to transferring to Company I, 5th South Carolina Cavalry in May 1862. One record notes that Hartzog died of disease on November 9 1862 at McPhersonville, South Carolina, while Barr gives his date of death as November 16, 1863, at McClellanville, South Carolina. Salley, *South Carolina Troops*, np; Knudsen, "5th SC," 27.

[142] Almost certainly C. C. Hartzog, as both Barr's letters and the muster roll record the death of Hartzog as a result of being wounded during the Battle of Haw's Shop, Virginia, on May 28, 1864. Knudsen, "5th SC," 27.

[143] Probably George N. Askew, who served as a private in Company I, 5th South Carolina Cavalry until transferring to Company B, 2nd South Carolina Artillery in 1863. Smith possibly could be J. E. Smith, who served as a private in Company I, 5th South Carolina Cavalry. Ibid., 6, 51.

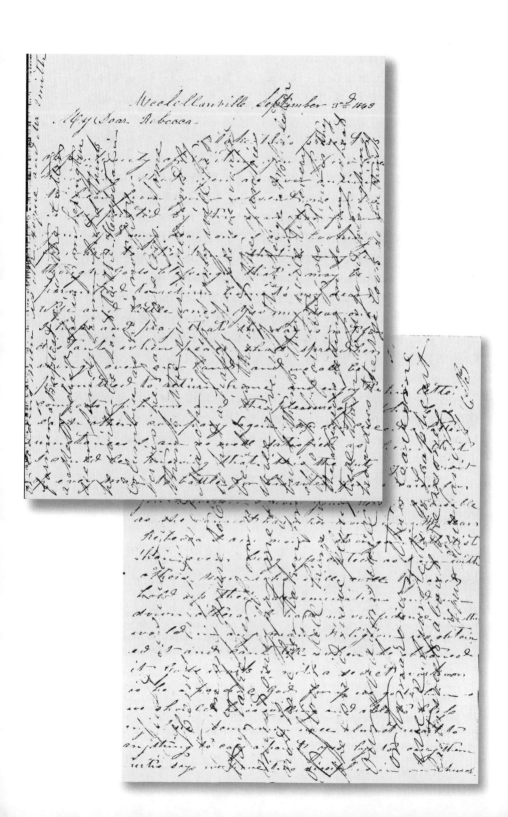

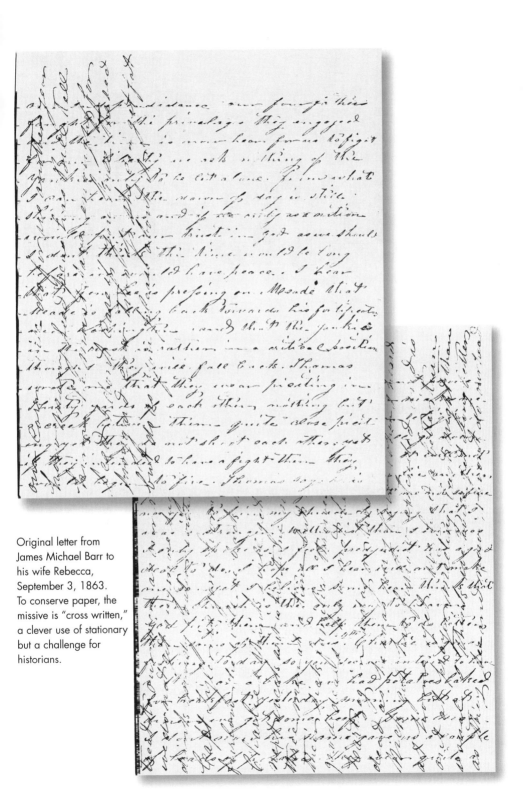

Original letter from
James Michael Barr to
his wife Rebecca,
September 3, 1863.
To conserve paper, the
missive is "cross written,"
a clever use of stationary
but a challenge for
historians.

McClellanville, S. C.
September 9th, 1863

My Beloved Wife:

I arrived safely here in camp yesterday about eleven o'clock. I secured a pass in Columbia, which brought me through, meeting with a friend in the Passport Office. He said he would not ask me for my papers. I told him very good for I had none, but did have a furlough, but got it lost. He said all right as he knew me.

I came over from Charleston to Mt. Pleasant about Twelve o'clock Monday. Stayed till five o'clock, found our horses, had Ance to saddle them. We came fifteen miles and put up for the night.

I find our Company much larger than when I left. Several recruits, Jacob Rawl from Lexington, is here.[144] He got here Sunday night. Sam is here, but I have not seen him as he is off on picket. Charlie is well and as lively as ever.

---

[144] J. E. Rawl from the Lexington District served as a corporal in Company I. Ibid., 45.

We are having a fine time now as we have a large room to stay in.

My box came safe.

I see that the Reserves are ordered out. That Walter Quattlebaum will go to Pocataligo.

I do not know how long we will stay here and don't believe anyone else knows.

The Yankees have Morris Island. Our forces left Sunday night. We were shelling them as I crossed over. I do not know what to think about Charleston, but a many hard lick yet before they get it. Morris Island is some six miles from the City.[145]

Captain Tyler will be here today. He has been home.

I hope this will find you all well. I trust our little baby is well by this. I found Ma quite unwell as I left. Trust she is better.

My horse is looking badly. He will not eat hearty.

The men all appeared proud to see me.

Be sure to burn this.

I am quite well.

Your Husband,

James

I don't know how to direct John C. letters nor Thomas.

McClellanville, S.C.
September 12th, 1863

My Beloved Wife:

It is again that I am permitted to write you a few lines to let you know how I am getting on. I am now enjoying very good health, feel nearly or quite

---

[145] The Union siege operation against the Confederate fortifications on Morris Island had finally made the position untenable for the Southerners. On the night of September 6, 1863 General Beauregard ordered the evacuation of Battery Wagner and Battery Gregg, leaving the crumbling Fort Sumter to guard Charleston Harbor.

as strong as I ever did. I now feel that I am able to do the duty of a soldier. Yet, I have not been put on duty but one day since I have been back. Then I was detailed for picket duty. It is not as hard as it was before I went home.

Our men are holding up extremely well. Very little sickness now. James Gant is sick. I expect he will get a furlough. All the men said I had improved so much. Our Company has several new members though we have four or five men home now on sick furloughs. Charlie has been trying to get off, but has failed to do so.

I trust when this reaches you that it will find you all well. I hope our dear little baby is well by this. I hope Ma is up again.

Some of our men stayed over their furloughs and when they got back, they were put in the Guard Tent for eight days and then made sweep the Camps for several days.

I hope you got along fine making molasses. I expect you will be done by the time you receive this. If not, be sure and have the juice strained well and skim well in boiling. Don't let them skim over the kettle.

I want the seed taken good care of. I told Henry what to have done with them. Send me word what Able said about selling them (The Seed). When I get the word, I will write back how to do. I want the Rye threshed and measured up also the Oats. I want to know the number of bushels of each, particularly the Rye. I will sow Rye in the grass field where the calves are kept. It must be broken up first. I want it sown the last of this month. I want it sown soon so it can be pastured by the lambs if we have the luck to have any.

Bill must haul straw at every chance and make manure. Keep the stables always full. Jerry must cut all the hay he can. I expect Pa would let him cut in old Princes Patch if Prince don't want to cut it himself. Tell Bill to take good care of his hogs. They ought to fatten fast if he feeds them well. Ask him if he got Smith to spay them yet and if he has not, tell him I said to get it done.

We are having plenty to eat. My box and contents are all here except a little honey. Sam just got a box, or at least a wagon has one for him, flour and potatoes, etc. Charlie and Ance have gone to the wagon after it.

The Captain and some of the boys went out driving. They brought back two deer.

My Dear One, I hope you were not so lonesome after I left home. The children ought to be company for you if you can stand their fuss, but I know it is pretty hard to stand. Jimmy was so bad when I was at home. Yet, he is a smart boy not withstanding all his badness.

My Dear One, I left this space to write you after the mail, but as I failed to get a letter from you, I will close as I have no news. I have not seen a paper since last Tuesday.

Your Devoted Husband,
James

⟫◦◦◦⟪

McClellanville, S.C.
October 16th, 1863

My Dear Wife:

Again at old McClellanville, seated to write you a few lines. I arrived in due time safely and sound though somewhat fatigued, though I can rest a day or two.

I did not have a very lonesome trip as I overtook one of our men Tuesday about Noon. Had company in the forenoon. We overtook Joe Corbett before we got to Camp.[146] Both had stayed some four days over their time. I expect they will be put in the Guard Tent, but they both say they were sick.

Nick and Crumb have not gotten back. They will be sent after in a day or two.[147] I was the only man out of six that reported back in time. I got along fine and fared well on the way.

You would hardly know Charlie he has gotten so fat, He says it is the molasses (millet) he supposes that caused him to fatten so.

I received a letter from John C. He says he is well, says it was not my fault in not getting my letters, but was yours.

---

[146] Probably Private J. M. Corbett from Company I. Ibid., 14.

[147] Most likely J. W. Crum, who served as a private in Company I, and C. C. "Nick" Hartzog, who was also a private in Company I, 5th South Carolina Cavalry. Ibid., 16, 27.

I got my fine pipe. It is a beautiful one, the finest Pipe in Camp. How I delight in smoking it.

A vessel is now here. Ran in here a few days ago loaded with Turk Island Salt. They ask forty dollars per bushel. I expect the Government will take it all.

We have prayer meeting now every night in our room. Commenced about two weeks ago.

Don't let Smith forget the shoes at Sams.

Sugar Cane must have plenty of dirt on it when it turns cold (no use of scaffold) but when it turns cold cover it about eight or ten inches deep in dirt.

Send me a box as soon as you can, mostly bacon, middling, shoulder and molasses. Send by express. Henry can send as William did.

Your Husband,
James

Send the box by express, directed to J.M. Barr, Charleston

5th Reg. Cavlry
Care of Capt. E.C. Green[148]

McClellanville, S.C.
October 21st, 1863

My Beloved Wife:

It is again with much pleasure that I embrace this opportunity of writing you a few lines to inform you that I am well and getting on pretty well. Hope and trust that you and the children are enjoying the same blessing.

---

[148] Ellis C. Green from Charleston joined the 5th South Carolina Cavalry at age 25 as a second lieutenant. He was promoted to captain and then to regimental and later brigade quartermaster. Ibid., 25.

My duty has not been hard since I have been back, only on picket now some twice a week. Out one night and in three, drill once a day, so you see one ought to fatten doing such light duty if he can get plenty to eat. We had a fine mess of fish yesterday. Our beef is not as good as it was before I left for home.

Our horses are not going so well. We are getting no fodder for them and do not get our corn regular in consequence of hauling so far.

I told William to sell some of our flour to Howard if he could get (50) fifty dollars per barrel of one hundred and ninety six lbs. (196).

I wrote today to John C. and Walter Quattlebaum in answer to theirs. They were both well.

Ance says keep his money for him, but if Jane has not got the quarter from her Uncle Daniel, to pay her a quarter.

I wrote you the other day to send me a box. I want it to get to Charleston by the last of this month. Send to James M. Barr, Care of Capt. E. C. Green, Quarter Master 5th Regt. Cavalry, Charleston, to be forwarded to McClellanville. Henry will take it to Columbia and send it off. Send some bacon and molasses. Don't send a large box for fear it be lost.

I enclose 20 dollars.

Your Ever Dear One,
J.M. Barr

McClellanville, S.C.
October 23rd, 1863

My Dear Wife:

I did not think that I would write today, but on account of my wheat being sown, I thought it best to write as my next letter would get home too late. I want my wheat sown as we will sow it in poor land. Therefore, it ought to be sown early. The Blue Stone is in the Store House in a box on shelf. I have enough for two years, so don't use but half this year. Have them to commence as early as you can to sow. Old Prince will sow it as Pa promised me when I was at home. Sow the white wheat first, then the red. Let all soak one night, enough to sow in a day.

Tell them to be careful with Sam and the Colt if they plough her, that she must not get hurt. Has Henry hauled off my wheat and potatoes yet? I don't want the Colt walked to Columbia. How has Sam's eyes gotten? Does Jerry bathe them three times a day or not? I ordered him to do it.

I think I left the gun caps in the Secretary, if not on the Piano.

I can't loan Sam to anyone as I will need four horses to work.

If you have not started my box, put in about 1 1/2 dozen last tacks and 1 dozen awls.

We are all well.

Our wagon goes to town twice monthly. Last and middle of month.

Tell Henry to take the direction and A. Lee can tell him how to direct to me.

Your Husband,
J.M. Barr

Hope this will find you all well. Wrote this in a hurry as the mail will leave soon.

Our Company numbers near 100 men.

I will write on Wednesday.

Your True Husband
J.M.B.

McClellanville, S.C.
October 27th, 1863

My Dear Wife:

It is again with much pleasure that I again embrace this favorable opportunity of writing you a few lines to inform you that I am well and getting on pretty well. Though our rations are not as good as they have been yet we are faring tolerably as we get venison occasionally, but we have no bacon.

My Dear One, I stood the trip here very well, had a pleasant time the last day. The 15th we had some rain on us, but did not get wet on account of having leggins and an oil cloth. I found plenty of stopping places on the way and fared very well.

Our Company is now large, numbering about one hundred men and health very good, but we are having cold weather here and this will be a very cold place this Winter. Wood is scarce here and litewood we can't get any way or means. We have to treat all our wood and burn green pine at that, so you can see that we will not keep big fires.

We have a good room to stay in. We have prayer meeting in our room every night. Some night the room is crowded and then again not many.

I drew a woolen shirt and another pair of drawers, though the drawers are not so good. I sent after my black woolen jeans coat. I expect I will get it in a few days. When you get my cloth woven, let me know before you make them so I can tell you how to have them made up. I have clothing plenty to last me awhile. I have pants a plenty, but they are not so warm. However, I can make out for two months.

I want you go get Mary Waters to weave the cloth as I want it woven with four treadles. I think you ought to have Jane to weave as soon as you can and not put in a large piece at a time.

Let me know how they are getting on <u>sowing wheat</u>? I want three Pecks (3) of the white wheat sown to the acre and (2) two Pecks of the red to the acre. Tell Henry if he has not hauled off the wheat yet to weigh it. I wish he would haul off the wheat, fodder, potatoes, rye, as soon as he can, what I am due the Government.

You had better have the cow killed for the Negroes. Tell Bill to take good care of the hide and not let it spoil. I don't know yet who I will get to tan it.

You must have the cane covered well with dirt. I believe I wrote to you how to have it done.

Did Bill haul the millet seed that I got from Henry to Williams? I hope he has.

How are the hogs getting on? Are they getting fat? Tell Bill not to let his woods hogs die from the want of care.

Did you receive the money I sent in letter?

I was sorry to hear of the death of James Wolf, a brother of Jacob Wolf.

Your Husband,
J.M. Barr

McClellanville, S. C.
Wednesday Morning
October 28th, 1863

My Dear Rebecca:

Yours of the 22nd at hand. Glad to hear that you are all well.

Mr. Asque is our head man with the assistance of some man from Capt. Kitt's Company. They have not called on me yet. If they do, I shant back John Faning, Edd Neely, Smith, Johnson and several others.[149]

It is now cold here and if you have such weather, you must have the Sugar Cane covered about ten or twelve inches deep with dirt and have the shed taken down so it can rain on it. They say if I keep it covered that it will take a dry rot.

---

[149] John C. Fanning enlisted at age 28 from the Orangeburg District. He became the first sergeant of Company I, 5th South Carolina Cavalry. Johnson could possibly be William M. Johnson, who was as a private in Company I. Ibid., 20, 42.

Sam is complaining a little with a cold. Charlie is well and gets fatter every day. Sam says that Capt. Tyler is making a man out of him and if the War ends and he gets home, Mittie will have a man yet.

Kiss all the little fellows for me.

Did they work the Colt? How did he do?

Tell Jimmy to be a good boy. Tell him Pa says he must be a good boy.

Your Loving Husband,
James M. Barr

—————◦◦◦◦—————

Editor's note: Rebecca Barr's brother John Caldwell Calhoun Dowling enlisted at age 18 as a private in Co. A, 1st South Carolina Infantry under Colonel Franklin W. Kilpatrick in Micah Jenkins' Brigade. This letter appears to be misdated; Jenkins' Brigade arrived at Chattanooga around September 22, 1863 and remained there until November 5, 1863. The correct date is most likely between September and November 1863.

Camp Near Chattanooga, Tennessee
Feb. 5, 1863[150]

My Dear Sister:

After waiting this long to see what we are doing or going to do, I gain nothing. I thought I had just as well give you a few lines. I received your message and was quite glad to hear from you and to know that you are well and others. I am still surrounded by the blessings of God and many friends; a few I will mention: F.W. Rice, J.M. Smith, Wilks Sawyer, Henry Zorn, T.D. Barr

---

[150] This letter appears to be misdated; Jenkins' Brigade arrived at Chattanooga around September 22, 1863 and remained there until November 5, 1863. The correct date is most likely around November 5, 1863.

and others which would be too tedious to mention their names.[151]

I must tell you too, I called to see Mother as our Brigade passed through Barnwell and I can assume I experienced more pure pleasure than ever before in so short a time, and more still, I felt at home once more. W.P.D. and I joked and it seemed to offer Mother so much pleasure.[152] Now if E.H.D. could only do just that, we would be one united family again and peace and pleasure would once more be realized and what would poor mother do? She would be over come with joy. [153]

I understand E. H. D. sent me word when I was in Charleston jail that he would speak with me. His object, no doubt, was good, but probably he intended or had some other object beside the object of affection. He might have been like the Yankees - if they had a good excuse, they would recognize the South. I say this might have been his object. He knew I, or thought that I was in distress and would come when thinking I would have to recognize him in any shape and then after that, if we should fail to agree, he could fall back to that aim, and say, "I never should have made those advancements, but you were in prison and could not help yourself." If I had not had those notions, I should have given his message some attention, but' when will we ever understand each other; probably not till death and after. I hope we may be able to comprehend each other and forgive and forget the disagreements.

How are you getting along with your farm? Will you make plenty? I hope you will. I miss Major Barr and C.T.D. very much indeed.[154] Rebecca, Major Barr made himself, in my estimation. You know I have said in your presence, "Camp is the place to fine out a man." I found him to be, as W.P.D. says, "The fine stuff."

I must close as the night is creeping on. Oh, I expect next news you hear

---

[151] Most likely J. W. Rice, who served in Company A, 1st South Carolina Infantry. He was reduced from fifth sergeant on August 1, 1863 for an unspecified infraction. He was wounded on September 30, 1864 and later furloughed. J. C. Dowling's brother-in-law Thomas Daniel Barr also served in Jenkins' Brigade as a member of the Palmetto Sharpshooters. J.M. Smith enlisted at James's Island on July 6, 1862 ,and after spending some time in and out of hospitals, he was elected second lieutenant in June 1863. Wilkes Sawyer enlisted at James's Island on June 20, 1862 and was present until the unit surrendered at Appomattox. Salley, *South Carolina Troops*, np; Brock, *Appomattox Roster*.

[152] William Preston Dowling was one of John C. C. Dowling's brothers. McDaniel, *Correspondence*, 274.

[153] Elijah Henry Dowling was John C.C. Dowling's older brother. Ibid.

[154] Charleigh Thaddeus Dowling.

will be that we are shelling Chattanooga. Those were the orders. They told us to accommodate ourselves the best we could, as they expect the Yankees to return the fire, or probably you will hear that even before this reaches you.[155]

We are pretty well and healthy. Hoping to hear from you, I will remain as your Brother til death part us.

J. C. Dowling

Kiss Jimmy and tell him to be a good boy and teach him to know God, the only possible chance.

Via Atlanta, Georgia
Company A. Kilpatricks Regiment[156]
General Ken's [Jenkin's] Brigade
Via Atlanta, Georgia

———⊲∘∘∘⊳———

Camp Near Chattanooga, Tenn.
October 27th, 1863

Dear Sister:

I received your kind letter and it afforded me much pleasure to hear from you and to know that you are well, but did not like the message I had to deliver to Tom. He is quite well, but denys having reported that I was in love with Miss Ann Barr.[157] He rather accuses Henry Barr of making that tale. I am glad that you contradicted it, as I am really not acquainted with her. There is no doubt but that she is a very nice young lady. Yet, I dislike false reports to be afloat about me.

---

[155] By the end of October 1863, Confederate General Braxton Bragg's siege of Chattanooga had begun to fall apart. Grant had reopened the supply lines to the city and was daily being reinforced.

[156] Colonel Franklin W. Kilpatrick.

[157] Miss Ann Barr may have been one of J. M. Barr's many nieces.

Was glad to hear that the Major had just paid you a visit, if it was but a short stay. I have just received a letter from him and Charlie. They complain of being quite well. The Major thinks there is no chance for Tom and I to get in his Company. That would be too good a pleasure to realize. It would seem almost as if the War had closed with us, but with you all at home.

Tom is very anxious to get a recruit in order to get a furlough. Brag is granting 10 days to any and all who will furnish one except Commissioned Officers. They are not allowed any showing at all.

We received orders to prepare 3 days rations and hold ourselves in readiness to march at a moments warning. It is supposed that we will go to Bridgeport, Ala., some sixty or seventy miles distance. That will not agree with my feelings as I have not done any marching in some time.[158]

Rebecca, this is a most abominable Country. It is as slippery as all get out and boggy according.

I am surprised at the folks at home for they don't write to me either. They are becoming too independent I guess.

I wish I was home. I would certainly go up to see you and enjoy that fine syrup. That and Sweet Potatoes seem to trouble me more than all the other luxeries.

I believe you said something about a distant peace. Yes, I think I am fearful that it is very distant though I hope for it soon. Would that I could realize the sweet feeling once more. I would be more than happy if possible, but alas I am afraid there will be many lives lost before any Americans can see it.

Tell Henry I would like to get him to cut my hair in the same place he did last year. Give him and Mr. Smith my regards. Also Mr. and Mrs. Spann and Mr. and Mrs. Barr.

I saw Fletcher this evening. He is well. Also Tom and J.M.S. are well. J.M.S. has never taken command as a Lieut.[159] I think they are treating him badly, but from all that we can learn, it is not his fault as he passed a good examination.

---

[158] Dowling's regiment did move out on November 5, 1863 as part of Lieutenant General James Longstreet's advance on Knoxville, Tennessee. Noting the tension between Longstreet and Bragg, Confederate President Jefferson Davis split Bragg's army around Chattanooga into two separate commands, essentially dooming both to failure.

[159] J. M. Smith joined Company A, 1st South Carolina Infantry, on July 6, 1862 on James's Island. In June 1863 the men elected him second lieutenant. Salley, *South Carolina Troops*, np.

There is a good deal of sickness in this part of the Army. I am not so well myself, don't infer that there is anything much the matter as I acknowledge that I am simply feeling badly.

Tell Jimmy to be a good boy and if I kill a Yankee I will bring home something or sent it. Tell him to grow fast and come out here to beat the drum for us.

As the Ordely is ready to carry the mail off, I will have to close. Give my regards to all inquiring friends.

As Ever your True Brother,
J.C. Dowling

Write soon and give me all the news. I want you to be sure and not forget me in your prayers. I try to pray myself.

———⊃∘∘⊂———

Editor's note: Rebecca Barr's brother Charleigh Dowling wrote this letter for Barr's slave Ance while James Barr was home on furlough.

McClellanville, S.C.
October 30, 1863

Dear Sissie:

Anderson asked me to write you for him. He says you will please let me know how Mary is. "I am well and hope you are the same." (meaning Mary). He encloses $7.50 Seven Dollars and fifty Cents for the use of his wife. Whenever she needs anything she can come to you and get the money.

He says you will tell Major Barr to bring him a blanket if he has it and can bring it under his saddle and if not, he will try and get one some way.

He says will you ask Jane if her Uncle Daniel has paid her the 30 cts. he owed her and if not she can have a quarter of this.

He says you must read this to his Father and that he would like to hear from them as soon as possible.

He says to tell Jane to look stuck up in the kitchen on the right hand side of the window in a crack for some leather. He had cut it out for a pocketbook and give it to Major Barr to bring if he can.

I have wrirten this in great haste, but hope you can read it.

We are doing well, getting on as usual, pretty well for soldiers.

C. T. Dowling

Sissie. I heard the other day that Aunt Rebecca Zorn was married to Herb Milhouse, that Set Drunkard. She has driven her geese to bad market, I think.[160] I also heard that Sallie Barnes had come back home pennyless almost.

Nothing more. Kiss the babies and young Soldiers of the Southern Confederacy.

C.T. Dowling

<hr>

McClellanville, S.C.
November 9th, 1863

My Beloved Wife:

I received your very interesting letter last Saturday. Was glad to hear that you were all well.

I received my box in due time. It came safely to hand last Wednesday and I do assure you its contents were duly appreciated.

I am glad to know that the wagon got safe back home for I was very uneasy about Lady Gray. Afraid she would be pressed as her color suits the fancy of most officers.

I am glad the flour is sold, but flour is quoted in the Charleston paper at

---

[160] Possibly H. W. Millhouse, a Barnwell farmer then living in Lexington. *1860 Census*, Lexington District, South Carolina.

One Hundred Dollars per barrel. Glad to hear that William has paid up Joseph Leaphart. I wrote to him sometime ago that I wanted him to take the money as I wanted to pay my debts. He did not write to me but suppose he did write to William. I want now to raise money to pay Elijah the money I borrowed when I went to merchandising. If you and William can raise five hundred dollars and with the two notes on Charlie and John C. I can pay it. Then William can get Henry to go down and pay it.

The doctor is now staying at Charlies.

If I could send it safe, I would send Eighty Dollars home. I have sent you forty dollars three or four bills in the first letter and a twenty dollar bill in the last letter. I expect I have lost the last twenty by your not getting it.

I have been offered One Thousand Dollars for my watch, but I do not think I will take it.

I am sorry to learn that Walter and Amanda have lost their little one, but My Dear One, it is better off for our Saviour said, Suffer little children to come unto me and forbid them not for such is the Kingdom of Heaven. My Dear One, if we expect to be saved, we must put our trust in him who is able to shield us from all harm. I was out to Church yesterday, Mr. Coner preached a good sermon. He, I think is a cousin of the Coner that stayed with us.

I am glad to know that Walter Quattlebaum is standing Camp so well. Hope me may get through his time of service and get back to his family without mishap or sickness.

My Dear One, I expect your mother is now with you. I hope she will spend sometime with you.

I know in reason that Mittie did not go up for I know she is looking for Charlie. I think Charlie will get off by Wednesday on a ten day furlough. I am anxous for him toget off.

What has become of my Tobacco? Has Bill put it away or not? Has the seed been gathered? I want them taken good care of for I want a good patch planted another year.

Has Bill fenced off the patch? I told him to do it for my Sugar Cane. If he has not, tell him he did not obey my orders.

I expect Prince will sow my wheat right as he ought to know better than me as he has sown so much. My reason for wanting him was because I knew he would do it as it ought to be done.

I do not want Lady Gray worked but very little as she is too young for hard work. I want her kept fat, expect I will have to bring her in service yet as Jim don't suit me.

I think you ought to make Jane weave.

Bill, Jerry, Mariah and Jess could have ploughed under the wheat.

I will write you and Henry a few lines and enclose them in this letter concerning the carelessness of the Negroes getting out. Tell them that I have written Henry about it.

Will the hogs get fat enough to kill by the last of this month?

Did the corn fill the crib full?

Don't let the sheep or calves go in the cotton patch, where the trees are.

Capt. Gilliard invited me to take dinner with him last Friday. Had a fine wild gobbler. The next morning I was on picket and had racoon for breakfast. Faring fine, don't you think?

Kiss the boys for me.
Your Loved One,
J.M. Barr

McClellanville, S. C.
November 10th, 1863

My Dear One:

I received a letter from John C. and also from Thomas. They were both well. John C. says in his letter that perhaps it was better that he was sent off, that being exposed to danger has caused him to reflect.

My Dear One, in your letter a week ago you said I need not be uneasy as everything was satisfactory to you. Glad to hear it unless we could of had things to have suited us.

Our baby is too young to wean. I would like to have a daughter, but am very willing to wait till the War is over for one. Would like to see our dear children, but expect it will be a long time unless sickness should throw us together. I do not think a furlough can possibly reach me in ten months.

Charlie's furlough has been disapproved, but I think when the Captain gets back that he will make another effort.

I am sending a fine comb enclosed in this letter. Anderson makes Jimmy a present of it. He gave two dollars and fifty cents for it, so don't let Jimmy break it up.

We are all well and enjoying ourselves very well. It is now very cold here.

Your True Husband
James M. Barr

McClellanville, S.C.
Nov. 16, 1863

My Beloved Wife:

I received your very dear letter of the 10th instant last Saturday, which afforded me much pleasure to hear from you and our dear little ones, but sorry to hear our baby is not doing so well. Hope he is now well. My Dear, it is a pleasure to me to receive long letters from you.

I received the bill for the flour. Did you keep plenty to do you. I hope you did.

I received a letter from William, also one from Leaphart. William says he wants to raise enough money to give Crout another trial. Says he thinks he can succeed next time. I wrote to him about the note Elijah has against me. I told him you had two notes, one on Charlie for 160 dollars and one on C. and J. C. for 140 dollars making 300 dollars and that Smith owed me (50) fifty dollars, for money loaned Mr. Fink to buy him salt last August the 4th and that you could let him have one hundred dollars which would make 450 dollars, so he would not like but (250) two hundred and fifty dollars to take up the note with all. I have mentioned the note calls for Seven Hundred dollars. I sent fifty dollars by Charlie to pay the interest. I told William to get Henry to go down and pay it by Christmas. Don't let your State money go. You can let him have one hundred of Confederate money if you have that much and I will try and send you more, but you have not said whether you received the other (20) twenty dollars or not. I would like to know. You said you had received (20) but I sent twice in different letters (20) making (40) forty dollars.

Potatoes, you ought to have dug sooner. They will rot. Can't keep if they are frost bitten.

You can sow the oats over where you spoke of. Pa will let you have the ground and if you have not oats enough sow rye.

I am allowed twenty bushels of peas before the Government can get any, but if four bushels are my seed, I think it miserable.

I don't think I shall buy any corn if they have not made enough. They must only eat the less. Corn in Barnwell is selling at two dollars per bushel. Milford Rice has sold 400 bushels at that price or Jack did it for him.

William wrote me about the Millet seed. I had with what I got from Pa fifteen bushels.

Henry knows I won't give him part of the W[illegible]. I have just as good a right to the seed as he had to his sugar cane. I told him that I claimed the seed as he did his money for this sugar cane. I wrote to William to let me know when it was ready and I would write to you to send after it. Whenever you send for it, be careful to keep the bung up and put it away in a safe place till I get home and if I see cause to let Henry have a gallon or two, then I can do it, but he must wait my notion. He thinks you will give it to him, but I want him mistaken for once.

I am sorry your Mother did not get up to see you, but hope she will go yet and spend some time with you.

Our Prayer meeting is going on yet. Quit arguing. Last night was the first night we missed on account of an alarm given by some of Captain Kitt's pickets. We were ready for a fight, but no Yankees made their appearance, so we are all straight again this morning.

George Hartzog died this morning. A week ago he appeared willing and was in his senses till his death, gave his watch to his youngest sister, give his

Mare to his brother Nick and a filly and sent a Negro to his mother on Saturday before he died. He told them not to fret that he would not die today nor tomorrow, but he died early the next morning, Monday. My Dear One, may we be prepared for death at any hour for we know not the day nor the hour. I am well.

Your Devoted,
James

———∘∞∘———

McClellanville, S.C.
November 17, 1863

My Beloved Wife:

I am not feeling very well this evening, but am not sick enough to report sick. Hope I will feel better by morning. Pains in my breasts, sides and back. Don't feel uneasy about me for I am doing duty and you know if I was bad off I would not be up and doing duty.

Ask Henry what he will take for his little gray horse and ask him if I was to buy him would he bring him down to me or would I have to send for him. Tell him to let me know soon for if I get him I would like to trade with Sam.

Is Noah Shealy coming to this Company?[161] If he comes and I buy Henry's horse he could bring him if Henry don't come. I think Henry asked me five hundred when I was home.

You would better get my leather from Fulmers if it is ready.

Ance bought him a tolerable good pair of shoes for twenty dollars. Did Smith get the shoes from Sams for Georgiana or not? If he did not, you ought to try and get them as soon as you can.

I sent two red flannel shirts and two pair of drawers to Sams. If anyone goes down send after them or if anyone comes up, write to them to bring

---

[161] Noah Shealy was a close neighbor of the Barrs'. Shealy was in his thirties during the war and worked a small farm with his wife and children. *1860 Census*, Lexington District, South Carolina).

them. You may need them for the children. I will not need them as I will have my white flanel shirts and drawers when Charlie gets back. He will get back next Monday, had a furlough for ten days.

Also send for my Allegator hide if you can. It is at old Mrs. Guesses.

Did you get the comb that Ance sent to Jimmy?

Heard a splendid Sermon last night by the Rev. Mr. Whilden. He left this morning. Hope he will come back soon and preach for us. He is a Missionary preacher travelling about and preaching to the soldiers.

Remember me to all inquiring friends. Trust this will find you and children well. Would like to see you but cannot for the present. Give the Negroes that inquire after me howdy for me.

Remaining as ever your True and devoted Husband.

My love to Pa and Ma and relatives.

James

———◦◦◦◦———

McClellanville, S.C.
November 20th, 1863

My Dear Rebecca:

For fear of your being uneasy about me I have concluded to write again this week. I am as well as usual, doing very well, but think I could do much better if this cruel War could only stop. But it does not seem as if there is any stopping place. The cloud of War hangs heavy over us. Peace seems to be a long way off, but one thing we do know that the end is nearer than when the War began, but we do not know whether we will live to see the War close or not, but we can only put our trust in the Good One and trust in him to carry us through safely that we may be permitted to again live happy together.

This thing of being separated from you and the children is bad, but when our Country calls we must obey for if the Yankees were to overrun us we would be an awful people, our property all taken from us but hope and pray that this never will be so. Yet, it seems that some will stay at home, sitting up to their tables and sleeping on good beds and thinking how they can make money, hardly thinking of the poor soldiers, unless thinking how they can make money off of them. My Dear, those that are blest with the privilege of staying at home ought to do all that lays in their power for the soldiers who are sacrificing their lives and everything that is dear to them. But is this the case? I fear not. Too much speculating, buying and selling. Can our cause prosper when so much of this is done. They ought to put every such man in the service.

I will enclose twenty dollars in this letter. It will be mailed either at Charleston or Grahams T.A. on account of not hearing of a twenty I sent, think it best not to send any more from here.

Very heavy firing at Charleston last night and this morning.[162] Did not get any news yesterday. Would like to hear. Hear the Yankees intend to make an attack about Ashapoo and get in rear of the City.[163] I expect we will have bloody works if they attempt it.

Sam will go to town after Charlie, starts tonight. Charlie will come down Sunday night. Our men are still getting off home three at a time on regular furloughs and others on account of certificates of sickness at home, but at this rate it will take a long time to reach me.

Hope this will find you and the children well.

Your True Husband,
J.M. Barr

---

[162] On Friday, November 20, 1863 the Federals fired 1,344 rounds into the defenses of Charleston.

[163] Ashepoo River.

CHAPTER FOUR
CAVALRY SERVICE IS A HARD DUTY

In November 1863 Barr's company was reassigned to picket James Island, South Carolina. Here Union and Confederate troops faced each other across the James Island wetlands as Federal Major General Q. A. Gillmore's artillery continued to shell Fort Sumter and the civilian population of Charleston.

McClellanville, S. C
Tuesday, Nov. 24th, 1863

My Dear Wife:

Tomorrow we bid adieu to old McClellanville. We all hate to leave the place. We are busy packing up. We will commence the march tomorrow for Charleston, thence to James Island. Our Company may be stationed in the City. Yet, it may stay on the Island.

You will direct your letters to Charleston, I will write whenever I can. It may be several days before I can write.

Charlie is back. Arrived this morning. Sam was sent after him with horses. Had three days. He run the blockade home, he had quite a short stay, eh.

Elijah says he don't want me to pay him any money. He did not want to take what I sent by Charlie. Says he is going to give each one of the children one thousand dollars as soon as he can, so if he does that, the debt will be paid. If you have a chance, tell William not to send him any money and you must keep Charlie's and John C. notes.

My love to all, Kiss our dear little boys for me.

Your Devoted Husband,
J.M. Barr

James Island
November 27th, 1863

My Dear Wife:

We have just landed on arrived on this Island. We took the boat at Mt. Pleasant at 8:00 o'clock last night, landed in the City something before ten, stayed in the City the balance of the night.

We are now without tents, but think we will get some soon. No one has a tent in our Camp, but I think we will have a nice place after we get fixed up if we don't have to leave.

I am well and in fine spirits. All appear to be satisfied to any move. We might as well be. We cannot fare as well here as we did at McClellanville in getting something to eat.

Mail will leave early. We have been here about one hour.

Your Devoted Husband,
J.M. Barr

James Island, S.C.
Dec. 2nd, 1863

My Beloved Wife:

It is with much pleasure that I am again permitted to write you a few lines to let you know how I am getting on. I am well and faring very well. We still have some bacon. We think we will have plenty to last us till Christmas. The Capt. says he will send home after a box soon. Sam is making arrangements to get potatoes shipped. We bought two rutabaga turnips, fifty cents apiece. We will have them for dinner today.

Our camp is on the edge of the Island, just over the bridge near where we camped when on our way to McClellanville. Our duty will be some harder than we had at McClellanville. Our picket posts are about seven miles from our Camp at Battery Island and Long Island and not far from Johns Island.

We are in site of the Yankees whilst on picket post. Our posts in the day is about two hundred and fifty yards apart. In the night about forty yards, just a creek between us. A Yankee offered a man the other day a fine Cavalry pair of boots for a peck of potatoes. One came down near our post Tuesday morning, wanted to swap papers. He came in five steps, so I heard. I was on picket at the time, but had been relieved a short time before he came down. Our men are forbidden to talk with them. It is against orders, but I expect the orders are violated by some. However, I heard none of our men talked to them.

I went out on picket Monday Morning, came back Tuesday about Twelve o'clock. I will go out tomorrow, Thursday morning, Courier. We send fifteen men on picket on day and fifteen the next for Couriers, which I think is the worst duty as we have to ride more. I would rather be on picket, but I would not be exposed so much.

Our Camp is in the woods. All raft men know our place. I forget the bluff.

My Dear One, Monday night was the worst night I ever spent out, so awful cold, high wind all night, but we had five on the post and were relieved often. My Dear, I am not exposed to the weather in Camp as we got twenty

large new tents the same day we came over to the Island. In the Infantry they would be large enough for eight or ten men, but for Cavalry, five is enough if saddles are to be put in. We have four in our Tent now, Charlie, Sam, Jacob Rawl, and myself. I expect we will have to take someone else in.

I received your letter yesterday also received the one you sent to McClellanville. I am glad you received the money, Eighty-Five dollars (in all I sent).

Charlie will now go to duty as they won't keep but one bugler. I expect it will go hard with him as he has had it easy so long. Sam is out again playing Doctor. He was detailed the next day after we got here, has nothing to do but receive the medicine from the Doctor and give to the sick.

If I had been home, Bill would have had my hogs fat. I told him I wanted to kill early. I don't want you to let anyone have my Liverpool Salt. When you kill weigh the hogs particular as we will have to give a tenth in proportion meat to the Government in bacon.

Ask Spann can he let me have five or six bushels of peas. Tell him to set his price on the peas.

Give my love to all. My love to you and the Children.

Yours as Ever,
J.M. Barr

Direct in Care of
Capt. Tyler

James Island, S.C.
Yellow Bluff
Dec. 6th, 1863

My Beloved Wife:

Knowing that you are ever anxious to hear from me, I have come to the conclusion to write you a few lines this Holy Sabbath to let you know how I am getting on and how I am faring in general. My Dear One, I am getting on very well. I am enjoying very good health with the exception of a little cold.

Duty is not as hard here as I expected to find. I came here last Friday a week and have not been out but twice. I expect to go out on picket Tuesday again.

The Yankees are anxious to make swaps of something or other with our men, a pipe for a small piece of Tobacco. One of our men got a fine pipe thrown over to him the other day for a small piece of tobacco. I hear that they are always ready for swaps, but our men will be punished for talking with them if found out. Yet, I expect some talk to them.

I do not know the number of troops on this Island, some say Ten Thousand and some say Fifteen and some say Thirty. One thing I do know, we have a large number of troops here and well fortified if the Yankees make an attack here. Though I doubt very much if they make one. I think they are satisfied that they cannot take the City. I learn that they are doing no damage to the City by shelling as their shells fall harmless. Fort Sumter is said to be stronger than she ever was. I hope and pray that the Yankees may soon give up the seige. The news in the papers, I guess you have seen as much as I have. I get a paper every day.

We have fixed up our tent on poles, some five poles high, and fixed up our beds so you see we are comfortable fixed up. We bought a log cabin for twenty dollars and have had it hauled. We expect to put it up tomorrow. We will cook in one end and have one end to sit around the fire as we will have two chimneys.

Our beef allowance is small. The meal we draw is very course, have to make it very wet to stick together and after it is baked, it will crumble up. We still have bacon. I think enough to last us till Christmas.

Charlie received a letter yesterday saying he had a box on the way. Preacher Ray has it in his charge though Mr. Ray has not let Charlie know anything about it yet. Hope he will get it today. Capt. Tyler will soon send home after a box, says he wants some pudding and sausages. He has butchered part of his hogs. Sams says he will have potatoes this week.

I see several of the Negro boys down here that I know, Leaphart's Ned and I believe Morris. Mrs. Boyd's Dick. He is here waiting for me to write a letter for him home.[164]

My Dear One, I hardly know what to write you about things at home as I do not know how everything is getting on. Phillip wrote me that my wheat was up better than any he had seen. You said you did not know what you would feed the sheep. Meal will have to be ground for them. If Pa will gin my cotton, you then can feed them cotton seed with their meal, the best feed that I ever fed sheep on. Tell Bill to keep them clean. that if they get nasty and are let alone, they will die. If Pa will let Prince gin the cotton, haul it back after it is gined and pack it behind the Counter, but be sure and mind your lite if you go in the store after dark.

I want to plant the same piece of ground in Cotton again the next year. I want it well manured for I don't think it was half manured this year and Cotton where I had Millet. I want Millet planted down in that patch near the Church.

Whenever the hogs get fat enough, kill part of them, salt like I did last year.

How is Lady Gray? I hope she is looking fine. Do they keep her in good order or not? Do they rub and curry her regular? Did they ride her whilst she worked or not? I don't want her ridden. I don't want her swayback.

I took dinner Friday with Joe Belinger and DeCainey Guess. They had a possum for dinner. Major Turner has joined our Company. He came yesterday. I hear that they are making a clean sweep with overseers now. Hope they will strike Miller a hard blow and send him in service.[165]

---

[164] Confederate authorities impressed thousands of South Carolina slaves to work on Charleston fortifications.

[165] Possibly J.R. Turner, who served as a private in Company I, from the Barnwell District. He was later discharged. Knudsen, "5th SC," 55.

You will direct your letters to John C. as you did. Looked for a letter from you last night, did not get one. Hope this will find you and the children well and the Negroes. Give Pa and Ma my love. My love to you and the children.

Your Ever Dear Husband,
J.M. Barr

———⊰◦∘◦⊱———

James Island, S.C.
Dec. 8th, 1863

My Dear Wife:

We are all in a bustle, packing up to leave this Island. Don't know where we will stop. We will have to report to Gen. Wise.[166] We may go somewhere about Adams Run or to Johns Island.
Hope this will find you all well. This leaves me quite well.

Your True Husband,
James M. Barr

P.S. I will write again soon as we find a stopping place We had gotten pretty well fixed up but had no chimneys on our house.

J. M.B.

---

[166] Brigadier General Henry Alexander Wise. The former governor of Virginia spent much of the war defending the coast of South Carolina.

U.S. Naval Institute

James Island, S. C.
Dec. 8th, 1863

My Beloved Wife:

I wrote you this morning but did not know positively where we would go. But after report to Gen. Wise, we have learned where we will be posted. We will be stationed at Adams Run, so you can direct your letters to me at Adams Run. We will be some twenty-five or thirty miles from Charleston. I do not know how I will like the place, but I believe I am satisfied to go anywhere, but would rather stay in the State. James Island is not as bad a place as some represent it to be. Yet, it is a very confining place as soldiers cannot ramble about as they wish.

Cavalry service is a hard duty, always on the out Post duty. Infantry picketted on James Island, but we had to picket a mile in their advance where we could see the Yankees at any time. The old Pownee and two or three sailing Vessels close by our post at Battery Island.[167] The old Pownee shelled our pickets for two or three days. One shell hit the old house the picket stayed in when relieved. Some of our men say they don't know how they and the horses escaped. I happened to be on the post the day they shelled. The Yankees are rather too friendly on Post.

We will be some eight miles from the Railroad. I expect a bad chance to

---

[167] USS *Pawnee* was a heavily armed screw sloop carrying four IX-inch Dahlgren smoothbores in each broadside as well as a 100-pounder Parrott Rifle on a pivot. One hundred and fifty-one sailors served aboard the vessel, which was 233 feet long, 47 feet wide, and had a small draft for a ship its size.

get a box from home. Charlie did not get his box, has heard nothing more of it. If it started from Grahams, it is lost. Charlie will know, still he has not.

I think Sam will return to duty unless he is smart enough to work out. Joe Guess is well. I am quite anxious to hear from home. Tell Philip if he comes to come to Adams Run.

This leaves me well. We are five miles from Charleston.

Your Husband,
J.M. Barr

————⟨∘⟩————

Adams Run, S.C.
Dec. 14th, 1863

My Dear Rebecca:

It is a pleasure to me that I am permitted to write you to let you know how I am and how I am faring and how I like the place. I am well and still faring very well. We bought a pig the first night we got here. It weighed eighteen lbs. We paid sixteen dollars for it. The next day we got a possum for one dollar, bought some potatoes. We can get them here at four dollars per bushel, much cheaper than we could on James Island. They are twelve dollars per bushel in Charleston.

We are all quartered in log houses. Splendid new houses just built. Some of the cracks to chinse up yet. We have no chimney to our house. Some of the houses had chimneys just started up. Col. Aiken was having the houses built for his men, but they were ordered off to Green Pond.[168] Hence the houses were left vacant and our Company being on the ground occupied part of the houses. An Artillery Company has the balance of the houses. We have two streets. We have a good kitchen with chimney to cook in. We have good stalls for our horses to stand in if they had a chance to do it, but our duty js rather

---

[168] Colonel Hugh Aiken commanded the 6th South Carolina Cavalry. U. R. Brooks, *Butler and His Cavalry in the War of Secession, 1861-1865* (Camden, SC: J.J. Fox: 1989 reprint), 244-5.

too hard for man or horse to get much time to occupy their quarters. I am well pleased so far with the Place. I don't think the duty will be so hard after today.

I am just off of picket. Only sent out four men yesterday and four today, all the rest has been relieved by Infantry picketts and think they, the last four, will be relieved today. We then will only act as Couriers. We may have more riding to do, but we will not have to stand watching for the Yankees.

We brought our chickens from McClellanville. One of our hens has laid two eggs since we have been here. We have four hens and one rooster.

Where did you haul the Government supplies to? I wish you had all that they are to get from us. You must be careful in weighing the hogs as we will have to give bacon too.

I hope you get the cards you sent by Henry for. I sent over to Charleston the day before I left for a pair of wool cards, but the store was only opened for Ladies and children on that day. Fanning said he could have gotten them by waiting and getting some Lady to get them for him and at ten dollars. If I had gotten them, young Fanning was to take them up with him home.

Of course, get your shoes made and have your old-ones half soled. Ask Spann what sort of leather will do. It won't take very much.

I shall send my valice up to Sams the first chance I get with part of my goods as I have entirely too many things here to bother with. I do not need any clothing of any kind. I have just drawn a pair of pants, coat, socks and shoes. I gave Ance one of my coats and bought him a pair of pants for five dollars, so he needs none. I had him to sell the first pants I drew, told him I wanted twenty and all over it he might have. He got Thirty dollars for them. I don't expect to keep more than I can carry on my horse in camps, so when you get my cloth woven, don't make it up till I let you know. I have plenty of shirts, yet think I will send another home.

You must kill the hogs whenever it suits you. I would like to have Sausages and pudding, but do not know how to get them. Perhaps Wesley would come down. If you see him, ask him to come and bring me a box and Preach for us. Paul Derrick came down and preached, why not him. He then could kill two birds with one stone.

Write soon. I have been looking for a letter. Tell Jimmy Pa has an orange, but can't send it.

Your True Husband,
J.M. Barr

———————

Adams Run, S.C.
December 18th, 1863

My Dear Rebecca:

This is the third letter that I have written since I have left James Island, but have not received an answer from you. How is this? Have you not received any? Our Postmasters surely are very careless. They ought all to be sent in service and the Ladies act as Post Mistresses.

I think Congress will pass a law to bring in service all men who have hired substitutes. They are hammering hard at it and I do hope that they will pass such a law. They must do something to fill up our ranks and I do not know anything better to get men than to pass a law that all who have hired substitutes shall again shoulder their musketts and fight for their freedom. I know they pay good attention to what Congress is doing, but do they care for what the War is doing? Oh, pity to the Seventy-five or Eighty Thousand who have substitutes. Why they would make us a pretty large Army, could guard some place I think pretty well and perhaps turn the invading Yankees. May the time soon come when they will all have to come out for I think they, or at least a part, has made money enough to come on and mess with some that have been in a long time and receive rich boxes from home.[169]

I happened the other day to walk around on Second Street to the Gleaton mess.[170] They had just opened a large box that one of their Mess brought

---

[169] By 1863, Confederate authorities estimated, more than 50,000 Southerners had avoided service by hiring substitutes.

[170] Apparently five members of the Gleaton family who served in Company I, 5th South Carolina Cavalry. Knudsen, "5th SC," 24.

from home. Of course, I was invited in. It was bountifully filled with good things. I dined heartily.

I have just received a letter from you dated 13 of December. It was sent to Green Pond, carelessness of Postmasters.

Hall owed me and when I saw him he said it was all right. Bill ought not to have given him the money. I think I have his marked off of my Books. I think he owed me one dollar and 70 cts.

I am sorry Georgiana has no shoes. If I could send a pair home I have here, I would do it.

What does Dave Crout ask for his horse. Get Smith to see him and tell me what Smith thinks of the horse.

Charlie says he thinks I can get peas from your Mothers. The bushel of Oats you have you had better sow where the chickens pulled up. Henry ought to have let you have two pairs of cards as you sent after them or after 2 pairs. I think you had better kill the hogs before they eat up all of our corn, if they are fat and I think they ought to be fat. Bill told me no reason for the Sows losing their pigs. By his saying he told me makes me know he don't tend to them.

My Dear One, there is a chance for me a furlough if any one will work for me. If any one will get or send a young man from 16 to 18 years of age to me or to join our company I can then get a twenty day furlough. If I was at home and could get one or two or more between this age of 16 or 18 to come and join our Company I then could get 20 days for every one. I heard of a man this morning who had five, so you see he will get one hundred days. Can't you get some one to get some one to come. How old is Tom Warren? When will Henry Gable be old enough, but I don't expect he could get a horse unless the neighbors would help him if John and his wife will let him come. Get some one to start or draw up a heading for the list and you put down twenty dollars (but he must come here) if you put down. I think enough will subscribe to buy him a horse. Tom Warren might get a horse the same way, then let some one buy them horses. Keep it a secret for I don't want any one to know I wanted to get them in.

I have my valice packed. Will send it to Sams, if Henry don't go down soon ask Pa to let George go down for it. I send three shirts, one round coat, one orange, some soap and a lot of other trash that I have too much of. Ance sends Jimmy a little lock that he found, my pistol and led and some balls. Take good care of the balls and led.

A furlough is a long ways off if I can't get one the way I have written. Hope some one near about eighteen will come as they will have to go some where. They had better come here at once. The men that were home last March are just now getting furloughs, so if I wait my regular turn I will not get home in six months. My time is a long time off. Tell Henry to send some one here to join our Company.

We have just put us up a stove in our house, so we will fare better in the way of keeping some warmer.

The woolen shirts I send home, you can use for the children. I mean the flannel and one part wool that I have drawn since I have been in the service.

I have plenty socks, two good shirts, 3 pair pants, two coats besides my over coat. Plenty for Winter.

Your True Husband,
James M. Barr.

Little Briton, S.C.
Dec. 30th, 1863

My Dear Wife:

Little Briton is one of our picket posts. It is a small Island or at least so by being surrounded by tide water. The house that we picket in is a beautiful house, the prettiest house that I have seen on the Coast, but it is awfully abused by pickets who did duty here before we came. The house has twelve rooms, three piazzas, the upper one is for a lookout made to answer for a roof. On the top we stand in the day, we can see a long way off. An old blockade is always in view. Yesterday a steamer came to her. I suppose to give her wood or something of the sort. A river runs by the house, or it might be called a creek. I think its name is Toogaodoo.[171] From the upper piazza we can get on

the roof of the house, but don't get any better view than we can get from the second piazza. In the lower piazza we stand at night. We came here last Sunday morning, seven of us, and will be relieved next Sunday. We have two hours to stand in the day and two hours at night a piece, so you see it is not hard on us.

This week one goes to camp every day after he stands his turn, which is about eight miles. I was back Monday to answer Phillips' letter and expect to go back Friday. We do our cooking here or at least nearly all. Ance cooks my bread in camp and send it to me.

I look for Charlie here today. He wants to spend a night with us if the Captain will let him.

I am writing on an old bureau torn to pieces by the soldiers, sitting on a small door with one end on the banister railing the other where the drawer goes in. Up in the Second Piazza writing whilst I am on post.

We cut broom straw and put down on the floor and lie on it. Rawl and I sleep together.

This morning we took a possum hunt, but did not catch any.

If soldiers only could fare as well as some Negroes at home. If we could only get two lbs. of bacon we could do pretty well. My Negroes need not complain. What if they had to fare like some soldiers, bad beef and musty meal -

---

171 Tagodo Creek runs from just south of Adam's Run and flows into the North Editso River.

course at that. A week or so ago some damaged bacon was sold or offered for sale. I don't think any one bought for you may know when it gets too bad to give soldiers, it is not fit for dogs. Now, My Dear One, don't think for one moment that I am grumbling for I do assure you that I am doing tolerable well. As long as we can get potatoes we can do fine. Why a soldier or any one can do fine on potatoes. Since I have been in the service I have learned the good of potatoes. They will do for meat and bread. After dinner - what do you think we had for dinner? I know you think from reading the above that it was a sorry dinner, but I leave you to guess. I can say though that I dined heartily.

If we had a shotgun and shot and powder, we could kill ducks plenty or if we could stay here two weeks, we could catch patridges. Any quantity of ducks down here.

Now I will tell you what we had for dinner - a little bacon, rice out of part of the rice we made helping John, so you see we had a few peas, private property of Joe Zeigler, also bacon was not drawn.[172]

I would like to sell the cow if she was fat, but the hide I want tanned. Will Pa tan my beef hide or not? If be can't do it, let me know soon. I would just as leave kill some of my cattle as for the Government to take them. If I kill them, then I get the hides. If I could get one dollar and fifty cts. or two dollars a lb. I would sell three or four hogs, but that risk would be to run. Pork is selling at $1.50 a lb. in Orangeburg, I hear.

I am sorry to hear that my Sheep are looking badly for I always when home kept them looking well. I expect Bill looks to Jess to tend to them and then no one does it. I could not expect him to tend them. I do not think that I could trust Jess yet Bill will say, "Yes, Jess feeds them well." He may take the food and pour half of it on the ground instead of carefully putting it in the trough.

Have you had the cotton ginned? I guess you have by having seed to feed the sheep for those old seed in the crib were not fit for them to eat as rats had been over them so much. I know they won't eat them and if they do I don't know if they will do them any good. Tell Bill that I said the sheep don't like to eat shucks and straw. Have them changed from one fold to another every week or less time. Sheep do better to shift them about.

Did you salt all the meat with Ocean salt? Will we have the Liverpool

---

[172] Several Zieglers served in Company I, 5th South Carolina Cavalry, including J. I. Ziegler and J. M. Ziegler. Ibid., 61.

salt after salting our meat? I would like to buy a few bushels down here if I could get it away. I can get two bushels for ten dollars per bushel.

Now if the hogs heads leak, the meat will not keep good. Ask Pa how long you must leave it in salt and when you hang it up, don't smoke it so much for our meat this year was smoked or dried entirely too much I want it put down early in ashes before the flies lay their eggs on it.

I think we can pay the Governmet in salt pork. I don't know how much, but they take the hog round excepting the skull, so you see you must weigh two middlings, 2 hams, 2 shoulders, and one jole. This is the way even if they should take bacon, but I think they will take salt pork.

I am pretty sure Congress will bring every man in the field who has hired a substitute. It has already passed the House four to one. They intend to hold the substitutes too. The Senate I expect has passed the bill by this time.[173] Don't you think it will go hard with some, especially Henry and Anna. I expect a many one has been keeping up with the proceedings of Congress. Millers and Overseers I hear are not exempt, so Noah Shealy would better come on here and bring his exemption papers with him.

By bringing in those men who have hired substitutes we will have a larger Army in the field than we have ever had. President Davis says there are Eighty Thousand exemptions in Virginia. North Carolina. South Carolina and Georgia. In four States Eighty Thousand.

Tell Henry to come to this Company if he can for I expect he would like Cavalry service better than any other service.

Have you heard of Preston's fight? It is talked here in Camp freely that Dr. Bagot whipped him.[174] It is said they fought about corn. Preston was offering more than the Government and Bagot told him he was wrong, that it made Soldiers' families have to pay more for it. Speculation was the cause of it. He was buying to sell, which I have no room to doubt. We know that he was wrong.

Some bad reports about Aaron. I think if I was in his place I would come in the Service.

My Dear One, I would like to get home to see you and our dear children,

---

[173] On December 28, 1863 the Confederate Congress abolished substitution in military service.

[174] J. F. Baggot was an M.D. in his mid thirties in the Barnwell District. *1860 Census*, Barnwell District, South Carolina.

but I cannot cipher out any time that I may get off.

If Philip comes here I do not think Capt. Tyler would put himself to any trouble to get me off and I do not know whether I would be entitled to a furlough or not. If Shuler would have given Philip a certificate saying that I was entitled to a furlough, I then could have gotten it, but if furloughs continue and we stay here, I think I will get home in March.

Have the Negroes fixed up the fences?

Is the cane patch rich?

If I have to buy corn I will not make one cent on my place this year, for the money for the flour will have to go for corn, tax unpaid, Negroes to feed, nothing made, bad news. Bad news to me off in service with no corn at home.

You will I expect have to cut down the Negroes' allowance in meal as well as meat. Don't give them too much. Make out on as little as possible. How much do they take to the Mill a week?

Hope this will soon reach you and find all well.

Your Devoted Husband,
James M. Barr

Wednesday Evening.

I have just received another letter of Dec. 27,, which makes three for this week. Would like to know Crout's price for his horse. Would like to see all the boys here now. I know I would do all I can to get home. Henry need not say "if" he has to go in the Service for it is very certain that he will have to go. He might as well get ready for it. I think I better sell out than pay five dollars per bushel for corn.

I am glad you have gotten your cloth out. I know that I will like the mixed, but I don't like black. They say Jeans Cloth is worth One Hundred Dollars a yard in town. Hope all are better.

Your Dearest,
J.M. Barr

Adams Run, S.C.
January 5th, 1864

My Dear Rebecca:

I received three or four letters from you last week which afforded me much pleasure to hear from you and home. Sorry to hear that the Children and negroes were sick. Hope by this time that they are well. Colds have been very general, the weather so changeable. We have had some very cold nights. Last Thursday night was one of the coldest nights. I was then on picket at Twelve o'clock at night. Was up when 1863 passed away and when 1864 came in. Now we have commenced on another year of the War. Soon it will be one year since I have been in the Service.

My Dear One, as another New Year has begun, the year 1864, let us try to begin to live nearer to our God than we did the year that has just passed away and may we pray that this year Peace may spread her wings over our Confederacy when Sons may be permitted to return home to his Sisters, Fathers and Mothers and husbands to their dear little Children and Wife.

I received another letter yesterday from Philip saying he was going to see Shuler and try and get his time extended to the thirtieth. I am very sorry that he is going to get his time extended. Would have been glad for him to have come on by the twentieth as I had told Capt. Tyler he would be here by the Twentieth. If Phil comes and brings his proper papers and papers of exemption, I can get a twenty day furlough if it is not stopped before he comes. I am afraid he will put it off so long that there will be no chance for me to get off. Capt. Tyler told me the other day that I could go about the twenty second of this month, but if Phillip puts off coming my time may or will be put off twenty days longer on the account of others going. Hence I may be knocked out entirely. I will be very sorry if he does not report by the Twentieth, which I think he ought to do by all means as so many are trying to get here the Company is getting very large and Capt. Tyler may get orders not to receive any more men in his Company and he cannot put any man down until he comes. If he fools about he may not get in.

Aaron I hear will be here in a day or two. We are looking for him and Rice every day, the one that married Miss King.[175]

Mr. Crum has offered me two hundred bushels of corn at two dollars and fifty cents per bushel. Sam says I can have his at Government price and that is $2.40 cts per bushel. I got Charlie to write to Elijah to go up about Jordons and John Town to try and engage me two hundred bushels. If I can get it there, it will be much nearer. Wesley says in his neighborhood corn is $3.00 per bushel, scarce at that. Flour $85 per barrel, Bacon $3.00 a lb., Grass Pork $1.50 per lb. Milk cows from one hundred to five hundred. Cow peas five dollars per bushel. Penders 50 cts. per qt., awful prices How are poor people to live at these extravigant prices.

My Dear One, I would like to have a good pair of woolen gloves, thread not fine and have them mixed. Rodella knit Rawl a pair that I like better than any I have seen. If you can't get them easily don't trouble yourself about them.

When I get home I think I will let you make my mixed coat. I will have it cut by my over coat pattern or at least the length of it. I will need a pair of pants, but <u>don't want them lined</u>.

Ask Henry has he had my Saddle fixed as he promised to do.

We are living high. Our kitchen looks somewhat like a smoke house, backbones, ribs, sausages and hams. Sam got a box, it seems it is a feast or a famine with us. We caught patridges whilst on picket, lived well.

Hope this may soon reach you and find you all well. I enclose one for Phil. You can send it to him. I am well.

Your Husband,
J.M. Barr

---

[175] Probably B. G. Rice, who enlisted from the Barnwell District into Company I, 5th South Carolina Cavalry. Knudsen, "5th SC," 46.

———◦◦◦◦———

Adams Run, S.C.
Jan. 10th, 1864

My Dear Wife:

As it is so very cold this morning you must not look for a long letter for I assure you it is too cold to write, but as I have to go on picket tomorrow and be off for one week I think it best to write fearing I may not have an opportunity of doing so till I get back.

I received a letter from you Thursday. Was glad to hear from you. My Dear One, I know you are anxious for me to come home. I know you and the children would be delighted to see me. I am as anxious to come as you are anxious to want me to come, but cannot get off till I get a furlough and don't know when that time will come, so I must write as your mother did, "look for me when you see me" but I do assure you I will come as soon as I can get off. I think it very doubtful of my getting off when Philip comes.

Capt. Tyler advised me wrong how Phillip should proceed. If Philip had just come on here with his exemption papers and had not gone to an enrolling officer, my chance would have been good, but Capt. Tyler did not give me such instructions. Hence I did not write to Philip to do that way. I wrote him to go before an enrolling officer. Yet Capt. Tyler says he will try and get me off, but my chances are bad. I think Sam and Charlie will get off soon by reporting some one, though they may not.

Dr. Dowling says he will attend to my business as soon as he can and if he succeeds in buying my corn, I would like to come home and get four wagons to haul for me and get Jim Spann to go with the wagons.

The sheep will have to be fed meal as I have nothing else to feed them. I hope you did not take out the line loins and ribs of all the hogs as I will have to give the Government all. I think I can sell One Thousand lbs. of bacon at $3 dollars per lb. If I can, it will bring me Three thousand Dollars. Surely I can sell that much or at least I ought to do it.

I can kill two or three beefs next Summer and if the Negroes do not work better, they won't need any meat for if they don't work, I don't care whether

I feed them or not.

I intend to get Jim Spann or Jeter Mitchell to look to my business this year.

Well, what is Henry doing? Is he fixing to go in service or is he going to try and get an exemption on overseer or miller? I don't think either will do. I wrote him the other day about coming in the service. If he comes on, he will be a volunteer, but if he waits till he is called, then he is drafted and may not get to the place that he would wish to go. And more than that, if he was to come before he was compelled, it might benefit, me but I know he won't come till he is compelled.

Charlie says because he don't send his love to you, you must not think that he has forgotten you. Says you must kiss that little Charlie for him.

If I can get to come home, I would like to bring some eggs and butter back with me, particularly eggs. We have now very little flour. We have about two dozen eggs. Salt at McClellanville is selling at Seven Dollars per bushel. I would like to have twelve or fifteen bushels.

Just received your letter.

We have had awful bad weather.

Tell Bill I think it a bad chance to have hogs raised and nothing else hardly done and then can't get to eat the meat. I think his belly and company is most what he thinks about.

I think the material is beautiful, but you did not say how many yards of it you had. I want enough to make me a good coat when I get home. I would like to have a pair of pants not lined. I showed it to Capt. Tyler, I mean the scrap you sent, he says it is beautiful and told me to tell you that my wife was worth more than he thought she was. Tell him if he will give me a furlough that you think he is worth more.

I think Noah Shealy can come on without going to the enrolling office. I think Tyler will take him. If I knew of any one liable, I would report them to get a twenty day furlough.

Kiss all the children for me.
Your Dear Husband,
J.M. Barr

Ance sends a ring to Jimmy. Says if too large to give it to Jane and he will make him another.

━━━━━◦◦◦◦◦━━━━━

Youngs Island, S.C.
Simmons Bluff
Jan. 15th, 1864

My Dear Wife:

I received yours of the 8th January yesterday which you started to me by Philip. As he did not come, he got Sue to mail it for me. I was rather surprised to hear that he had started before the Twenty-fifth, but expect it was well he did it for now I guess he is a member of the Company. So many may join that it maybe difficult to get in after awhile.

I understand that Capt. Tyler enlisted five men in this Company whilst at home. He was only on a forty eight hour permit and if they join the Company that way, it won't take long to have it full. Now men who have substitutes and other exemptions can volunteer, but if they wait till they are called for, they will be conscrips and not allowed to choose their Company.

Henry will hate it very bad if he stays at home till he is obliged to go as he says. Then he might be put in the Infantry and sent to Tennessee or Virginia. He ought to know that he is now like a partridge under the trap and not yet taken out. Sallie says the poor fellows ought not to be laughed at, that they ought to be pitied. Says they hate to go in Service so bad. I pity them all, but hope to know soon that they are all in Service.

Rebecca, I don't know that I can get home soon, but wish I could. Your being so anxious to see me makes me more anxious for a furlough.

As for Wesley getting the Chaplaincy of this Regiment, I think there is no chance. I don't think Col. Dunavent ever thinks of appointing one and I think the men would rather hear a preacher who would come and volunteer

A native of Chester, South Carolina, Colonel John Dunovant had been a ferocious soldier for most of his thirty-six years. He fought in Mexico as a private with the Palmetto Regiment of volunteers, then served in the 10th U.S. infantry in the 1850s. An avid secessionist, he led the 1st South Carolina Regulars as their colonel and served in the defense of Charleston until being cashiered for drunkeness in late 1862. When the 5th South Carolina Cavalry organized a few months later, Dunovant returned to service as the new regiment's colonel. His new command had their reputation to make; he had his to regain.

V.R. Brooks, *Butler and His Cavalry*

to do services with them.[176] I cannot feel around as we have two Companies here.

I am glad to hear that the stock is standing it so well for I don't want to lose any whilst they are so high. As for the sows losing their pigs, Bill's doctoring won't do, but mine will. It was for the want of attention. Bill can't fool me if I am in the service I know they don't work as they ought. If they did, the fencing would have been repaired.

It is cold here, <u>but we have to go</u>. We are not allowed to go to a fire because it is cold, and more than that, some troops are about barefooted and badly clothed. When we are on post, it is for two hours at a time.

Now, when will they get the lands ready for planting? It will take three or four weeks to haul corn to do us. I want the ditches cleaned out well so they can make some corn this year.

Yes, you ought to have all the meat of the first hogs you killed hung up and have the last hung up as soon as it is killed long enough. I want it put in ashes this year soon in March.

---

[176] Colonel John Dunovant had been an enlisted man in Mexican war. After fighting in Mexico he was commissioned into the regular service as a captain. He began his Confederate service at Charleston Harbor during the attack on Fort Sumter and was later commissioned colonel of the 1st South Carolina Infantry (1st Regulars). While serving in Charleston in June 1862, he was dismissed for drunkenness. When he assumed command of the 5th South Carolina Cavalry, the commander of Company B, Captain A. B. Mulligan, wrote his mother that "Col. Dunovant is a brave man with much experience having been in the U.S. Army before the war. He has been unfortunate, having been addicted to drinking but he has entirely reformed it is said & I hope will make a good Col." Dunovant commanded the 5th South Carolina Cavalry until promoted to brigadier general in August 1864; he was killed at Vaughn Road, Virginia, on October 1, 1864. Knudsen, "5th SC," 19; Hutchinson, *My Dear Mother*, 82; Brooks, *Butler*, 479.

You did right in cropping the wings of the geese, but ought only to crop but very little, just to keep them from flying. You must have them fed. If you don't they will die and if they are not fed, they will not lay early.

I have six buttons for my coat. I got enough from Rawl. He wrote home to have them sent to Rodellas. If you can get them, clean them up nice till I get home and I will bring the six I have. They are beautiful buttons, just the buttons to put on such nice cloth. Every one who has seen the scrap says it is beautiful.

Hope to see you and the children soon, but may be disappointed. The fortunes of War are bad. I will be relieved Monday, then will spend 7 days in Camp, if I can't get a furlough, but don't think I can get one.

I will have to stop writing.

Your True Husband,
James M. Barr

Adams Run, S.C.
January 19th, 1864

My Dear Wife:

Your letter came too late for me to answer it and for it to get to you before Phillip left.

Aaron is here in Camp, had to come to make himself safe, I mean to get in this Company. He says he is sorry he could not stay and come down with Phillip, but says the place got too hot for him. Several who had expected to get in Capt. Tyler's Company were taken to Columbia, but I hope Phillip will be able to work his passage safe here. If he gets here, I think I will get a furlough. I have just had a talk with the Capt. and he says he will try and get me off on Phillip.

Charlie has gone home on a ten day furlough. Aaron came in and did not bring his horse and got a furlough for ten days, but was afraid to go back so soon. Afraid that some one might take him to the conscript Camp.

I have engaged one hundred bushels of corn, but do not know whether I can get it or not as writs are being served on persons not to sell their corn out of the neighborhood unless it is to the Government. If this is the case, I can't get any down in Barnwell, so you see you will have to take care of every grain of corn and try and make out with what we have.

I see that the men that furnished substitutes and the exempts are ordered to enroll by the first of February and then go to the camps of Instruction after having a ten days furlough from the time they enroll.

Henry, I think is caught. They will be allowed to pick their Company, but I think it will have to be Infantry in Bragg's old army. I hope Henry may get here, but I am afraid he can't.

Hope this will find you all well.

Your Devoted Husband,
J.M. Barr

I can't get peas down the country. I wish George could go down after my valise.

━━━◦◦◦━━━

Editor's note; Barr received a furlough at the end of January 1864. The following note commuted his rations during that period.

James M. Barr on Furlough from Jan. 27th to Feb 17, 1864
The Confederate States To private J. M. Barr

Co..I.5th Regiment S.C., Cavalry.

For commutation of rations while on furlough from the 27th January to the 17th February and from the 23rd February to the 14th March 1864, both inclusive.

40 days at $1.00 per day $40.00

1864
January 27th
To
February 17th
and from
February 23rd
To
March 14th

I certify that private J.M. Barr is entitled to commutation for rations while on furlough from the 27th January to 17th February and from 23rd Feburary to the 14th March 1864 and that he did not receive rations during that time.

Thos. W. Tyler
Capt.CO.I, Reg. Cav.

I certify that the above accounts is correct that the commutation was made by my order and was necessary for the public service is not being practiable to take rations In kind.

L.N. Shelden Corp. Comdr
Received the_day of_1864 of Capt.

acc $40.00 in full of the above

———⊶⊷⊶———

Editor's note: While Barr was home on leave, his brother-in-law Charliegh
Dowling sent him the following note from the company.

Feb. 28, 1864
Adams Run, S. C.

Col. James M. Barr

Dear Brother:

In accordance with my promise, I will write you a few lines.

We are all in a stir down here. An order is out for the reduction of the
Company. Those who have no horses and those who have sorry ones and not
able to replace them if they should die or be condemned, will be transferred
and after that, I do not know by what process they will take more. If the
Company is not reduced to the maximum number, it might be necessary to
take out some of the first class.

D.O. Hugh told me just now that he would swap horses with you if you
would give him three hundred (300) dollars difference.[177] Your judgement
must control your actions. I have not made any trade with him for you whatever, but I think, yes, I know if you will give him three hundred ($300) dol-
lars difference, he will trade, so if you think it fair, write me and I'll make the
trade for you and have Ance to take charge of the horse.

My love to Sissie. Kiss the babies for me and write soon to your Brother.

C.T. Dowling

---

[177] In all probability Private D. O. Hughes, Company I, 5th South Carolina Cavalry. Knudsen, "5th SC," 30.

———◦◦◦———

Editor's note: Barr returned to duty sometime after March 15, 1864.

Adams Run, S.C.
March 20th, 1864

My Dear Wife:

As I will be on picket next week I will write you a few lines to let you know how I am and how I am getting on, I am well and getting on finely.

We are drawing Salt Pork. The day I came in we drew some Hickory Shad. The boys say that they drew some splendid Shad. Now, don't you think Soldiers are doing well when they can get these good things to eat, but My Dear One, after getting all these things and expecting to receive a letter, I must confess that I have been sadly disappointed. I was very confident that I would get a letter today, but none came for me.

Rebecca, I don't want the Sheep put on the rye any more as I will want it to feed my horses on as corn is scarse.

How has my horse's back gotten? Does Smith come to see the horse? If he does not, send Dennis down for him to come and see the horse. I would like for him (Smith) to see him ever two days. After his back gets well enough to work and if he is in order to do it, they can plough him, but Bill must lead him and Jerry Plough him. I mean for Bill to lead him a few rounds till Jerry can manage him, but I want them to be very careful with him - not to let him run away and whilst they are breaking him, the colt can rest a few days. They must put good lines on him as I would not have him to run away and injure himself for anything.

Tell Bill to be careful with the corn, not to waste it but I don't want him to let the hogs die. Has he got that load of cow food from Pa's yet or not? If he has not, he would better go after it.

How much corn has he got planted? I expect by the time this reaches you, he will be done planting corn.

If you think you won't have potato slips enough, you would better bed some. Tell Bill to bed the patch next to the meeting house for millet after he gets the manure out for the cotton.

You will have to look at your hens every day that I set to know when they will hatch. I hope you may have better luck than you had last year. Ance has set two hens for us, so it seems as we think we will stay here for awhile.

At any rate, it is now thought that we will remain on the Coast this Summer or till the War ends. I believe it is the opinion generally that the War will end this year. It really seems to me that it will as we appear to have so much the advantage so far. Yet, it may not, but God grant that it may soon end.

I expect the children, as well as yourself, missed me a good deal when I left for camp. I don't know when I can get home again, but hope I may in three or four months. Would you not be delighted to hear that peace is made? No more so than I. Yet, as long as the Yankees invade, we will meet them.

Hope I may hear from you soon. Remaining as ever your

True and Loving Husband,
James M. Barr

—◦◦◦◦—

Editor's note: Rebecca Barr's brother J.C.C. Dowling wrote his sister the following.

Camp Near Bulls Gap
East Tennessee
March 20, 1864

My Dear Sister:

With much pleasure I take my pen in hand to acknowledge the receipt of your kind and interesting letter. It afforded me much pleasure although you had been suffering greatly with your foot. From what I inferred from a letter Preston's wife wrote me I was quite uneasy about you, but I received yours of the 8th instant, which relieved me a great deal. I was really afraid something serious had befallen you.

I know you could scarcely help getting well when you looked around and beheld the two dearest and nearest relatives on earth, Mother and Husband. The happiest hours since the War. I would like to have come upon you about the time they all got together, but it is possible that I may never behold either of you again, but let us all try to meet in that better World where there is no Wars or rumors of Wars nor separation but entire unity and peace.

Did you hear the Major say how he liked the pipe I sent him from Petersburg and did you hear Johnson say anything about a little gun I sent him. I captured it in a little skirmish with the enemy at Dandridge, Tenn. in Jan. last. I expect if Preston is not too tyranical with him, he will enjoy it, but I know Preston's disposition so well, I am afraid he will not be allowed to put his hands on it.

By the way, how does the Major's Colt do? I guess that it would command $2, 000, dollars by this time. I guess there is no chance for me to get with Charlie and the Major as Congress has passed an act to hold us as we are, and not only us, but the whole Army of the confederate States. Don't you think that too hard? I am getting a little despondent, but will try to hold out as long as anyone else does.

I see you have received a couple of letters from Urbana and you intimated she wrote only from or through selfish motives. Has she ever seen our Piano or has she only heard about it Did. you have Ellen Dowling to look at it or is it all hear say? What makes them want it? I think I can see the reason they are afraid that currency will not be worth anything and that it will be a good investment, but stand up for what you have decided. Don't let any of them have it and when you are tired of it, I will take it off your hands.

You said also that you had not selected me a Sweetheart and gave your reason, which I don't think was well founded, from the fact that I did not say anything about marrying. As you say, it is pleasant to have a Sweetheart while in camp and if she is the right sort of stock, we can tie the knot after the Cruel War ends. I therefore insist upon your making your selection known. I expect if I were to try I could guess in three tries, but I will not attempt it, hoping you will save me that trouble.

I suppose Jimmy is not so bad yet. I wish I could see the little fellow. If I get a furlough and should come up to see you, he would have to come back home with me and you too. I guess you would hate very much to leave home now, but old Uncle Jim or your driver, I don't remember if that is his name, can look after things.

Have you had your third child? I have not heard of it. I suppose you will have young Jimmy off to the War soon or the girls will have him. Sing him a song, The words are as follows:

Oh weep not Conscript, weep not, Old Jeff has called for Thee

A soldier Congress has made you, a Soldier you must be.

I am tiring your mind and mouth, so I will close. You said you would have written me ere this, but you did not know my address. I will give it to you so you will never be at a loss for it. It does not make any difference where we are or what State or Post Office, etc., if we are in Long Street's Corp and Jenkins Brig., that is all that you need to know. Until you receive different instructions, this will be our address.

This is all that is necessary, but I added a little more as you know we are here.

John C. Dowling
Co. A Haygoods Regt.
Jenkins Brig., Field Div.
Long Streets Corps
Bulls Gap, Tenn. Army East Tenn.
Via Petersburg, Va.[178]

P.S. Be sure you do not get me the wrong one (that is Sweetheart). I am going to send her an April Fool. I received a Valentine from Leesville, Lexington Co., Some think it is from Miss Smith. Did you hear anything of it? Would like to know if it was either of them or any of your neighbors. Write soon and tell me all the news. I wrote Walter Quattlebaum some time since. I am sorry to hear of his sickness in family. Has Henry Barr taken service yet? I have been looking for him for sometime out here.

I remain as ever your brother,
J.C.

---

[178] Dowling served in Company A, 1st South Carolina Infantry.

Chapter Five

I Will Try and Go Cheerfully

In comparison to other South Carolina units then serving in Tennessee and Virginia, Barr and his regiment had enjoyed relatively easy service during most of the war, patrolling the coast in South Carolina. Their relative comfort did not go unnoticed, and on March 18, 1864 Barr's 5th South Carolina Cavalry as well as the 4th and 6th were ordered to Virginia to exchange places with the 1st and 2nd South Carolina. These two regiments had been serving at the front since 1861. The 4th, 5th, and 6th South Carolina Cavalry were then to be organized into a new brigade under General Matthew C. Butler and ordered to join the Army of Northern Virginia.[179]

Many South Carolina soldiers then serving in Virginia had little respect for Barr and his comrades. Private Samuel Elias Mays, who had been fighting with Hampton's Legion (2nd South Carolina Cavalry), noted that "General Butler will have a new brigade entirely . . . among these are mostly men that have not as yet seen war." Mays also added, "It gives me great pleasure to see these gentlemen at last having to incur the fatigue and dangers of a war that they were so foremost in bringing on and which they have kept out of for nearly four

---

[179] "Special Orders No. 65," *OR*, vol. 33, p. 1232.

V.R. Brooks, *Butler and His Cavalry*

Brigadier General Mathew C. Butler was a native of Greenville, South Carolina and the eleventh of sixteen children. He spent part of his youth on the frontier near Fort Gibson, Indian Territory, where his father was Indian agent to the Cherokees. Young Mathew returned to Edgefield, South Carolina to finish his education in the local schools, where he studied law. He entered politics and was one of the legislators who led the state into secession. He served in the cavalry of Hampton's Legion until promoted to lead the 2nd South Carolina Cavalry as its colonel. Only twenty-seven years old, he had already proven a dashing and fearless leader, and had won high praise for his service in various raids and at Brandy Station, where he lost a leg. A favorite of General Wade Hampton, Butler earned the rank of brigadier general in late 1863. When Hampton's cavalry reorganized in early 1864, Butler learned that some untested newcomers from his home state, the 4th, 5th, and 6th South Carolina cavalries, would serve as his new command.

years."[180] *This comment reflected a general resentment that spread through the Confederacy in 1864.*

Adams Run, S.C.

March 23rd, 1864

My Dear Rebecca:

I expect you have heard by this from a letter from Philip that we are under marching orders to go to Virginia. Many will receive this news with a sad heart. I mean the wives of soldiers and a many one of our men have long faces. They are down in the mouth. Yet, why should they be so? We volunteered for the War and are liable to be sent any where and we are no better than other soldiers who have been on the trot ever since the War began.

I expect we will go by Columbia and if we do, I will try and get by home. Yet, there will be so many who will have the advantage over me. Why?

---

[180] S. E. Mays, Jr., comp., *Genealogical Notes on the Family of Mays and Reminiscences of the War Between the States* (Plant City, FL: Plant City Enterprise, 1927), 132-3.

Because I am just from home. That will give men who have been from home the longest the advantage.

Rebecca, if we go to Virginia I will not have the opportunity of sending you any money. You will have to sell some bacon and then you can have money to spend. Rebecca, I want you to sell and buy whatever you want.

Send the beef hide to Pa's. He said he would tan it for me. Joe wrote me that he would collect my money for Ance's work. I will write him to send it to you. If it is tens you will have to lose the percent on it.

I do not want to go to Virginia. I would rather stay in South Carolina, but if I have to go, I intend to try and go cheerfully.

I wrote to William to see if I could get John's horse. I have not received a letter from you yet. Remaining as ever

Your Husband,
J.M. Barr

Little Briton, S.C.
March 26th, 1864

My Dear Rebecca:

I received your letter of the 19th yesterday. It was mailed on the 23rd of March, a screw loose somewhere.

We are still under marching orders, don't know when we will go, but we evidently will go somewhere I guess to Virginia as two Regiments from there have been ordered to this State, their horses having broken down. And now two more regiments must fill their places.

Capt. Tyler has been notified to have frames to cover his wagons. Seems as a long journey is ahead. I would much rather stay here in this State, but if we have to go, I will try and go cheerfully though some of our men are awfully, put out.

I now wish I had my over coat and black coat here. The coats I left at

home. If I had them, I would send this coat, the last one you made, home. Tell Walter if you see him to come down if he can, but I don't suppose he can well leave home.

I wrote to William for John's horse, but don't expect he will let me have him. I offered to swap him Hughs for him. I am glad to know that his back is, mending so fast and if I have to go on the Gray horse, you would better get Mr. Spann to break the Hughs horse when he gets well enough to work. I am afraid my Negroes won't manage him well, but if Spann will come up and see him hitched up and charge them to be particular with him they will do it.

I may get home soon, but there are a hundred chances against one for me. I don't want to do anything that might cause me to suffer later.

Preston wrote me, Aaron and Charlie too. Now, if it was our desire or something of the sort for him to leave the place, said he could do better or something like that and could pay the Government Bacon, etc. I don't remember the exact words. Aaron wrote him to do as he pleased, but his farm would suffer by E.H.D. leaving. Charlie wrote him to leave if he wished. I wrote him that it was a matter for him to decide and said where a man's interest was, there he wanted to be also. I expect he will leave and move to his wife's place. I think it would be better for him to go and E.H.D. to stay with your Ma. Perhaps all would be better satisfied.

I am going up to Camp to-morrow if the Yankees don't catch me to-night and if I hear any more news, I will Write you. I expect to send Ance home if I go to Virginia. I will send him to stay.

We do not get any meat to eat, nothing but dry bread. We have some of our bacon yet, but if we did not, we would have to eat as the other soldiers.

I don't know what time we will leave. I will write the day we leave.

Your Devoted Husband,
James

———◦◦◦———

Adams Run, S.C.
March 27th, 1864

Dear Rebecca:

No letters today, but suppose you have received mine before this.

I will apply for leave to go by home. I told Capt. Tyler that I wanted to go by home anyway, but I had a child very sick which made me more anxious, perhaps he will try and get me off.

We will rendezvous at Columbia after we leave here, but we do not know positively whether we will go on or not. The order may be countermanded. Yet, I think we will go.

Rebecca, what do you think? Rebecca Millhouse has a baby.[181] It weighed ten lbs. pretty good for a six months child.

Radcliff Walker is dead. John C. is a master Mason.[182]

You must put up all the Negroes shoes.

Your Husband,
J.M. Barr

---

[181] Rebecca Milhouse appears to have been the wife of Samuel L. Milhouse, who served as a private in Company I, 5th South Carolina Cavalry. Knudsen, "5th SC," 39.

[182] While several Walkers served in the regiment there is no record of Radcliff.

———————◦◦◦◦◦———————

Editor's note: On March 27 James Barr received the following letter from his brother William Joseph Barr.

Barr's Mills, S.C.
March 27th, 1864

My Dear Brother James:

Doubtless you will be surprised to receive a note from me so soon.

As John's horse will not do for Cavalry Service and Jeff Davis like (his Presidential Highness) refuses to be subjugated and wear the name of plowhorse, I have concluded to offer him to you on one condition. That is for your filly. The matter now rests with you, to do or not to do.

I offer to you the <u>best young horse in the State and</u> one that I consider worth more than your filly. I cannot swap for your other horse, boot. I do not want, in other words, I don't want the money.

You may have scruples in reference to the raising of colts. These scruples can be overcome after the War is over better than now. And you spoke of carrying your filly in the service, is the cause of this offer.

If you decline this offer, I wish you to send this note to Joseph Guess. I have understood that Joe wanted Jeff Davis <u>for a friend</u>. If he can scare up anything in the shape of two mules, not too old or broke down, I will give him a fair trade.

As I said before, the money I don't want. I cannot use it. Now you are the only two men I intend shall know that Jeff Davis is on the tapis. For when known he will be off in a little while there are more wanting him constantly, but I would rather some friend or relative have him for I know that his equals are few, <u>his superiors</u> -there are none.

From Your Affectionate Brother,
W.J. Barr

Adams Run, S.C.
March 29, 1864

My Dear Rebecca:

I received a letter from you yesterday. I am sorry to hear that you all are complaining so much, but hope you and the children are better.

I do not know when we will leave here and it appears that nobody knows, but I think it is known by some of the officers and they are afraid to let the men know when we will leave, fearing the men will go by home. Some don't think we will go, but I think we will leave in less time than twenty days. If we go, it will take us thirty days to get there.

Capt. Tyler says if Henry will come to him any where on the march, he will take him now. If he can leave Anna to go to Virginia, he will have an opportunity. I will enclose him a few lines with this scribble.

I wrote you that I thought I would get home. It does not seem as though there is a chance now. Philip has sent up two permits and failed both times. Wish he could get off to see Fletcher, but it seems as he cannot.

I had a good time on picket, out every other night, had to walk two miles to the post. It rained two or three nights and was cold, but we did not mind the bad weather. Fared very well, but did not get any meat for four days.

Your Husband,
J.M. Barr

Smith promised me to see my horse every two days. Did you send for him? Does the horse mend any or not? Does Bill tend to the stock well? Write soon.

Yours,
J.M. Barr

———•◦◦◦•———

Adams Run, S.C.
April 1, 1864

Dear Rebecca:

I write you a few lines to let you know that we will march to-morrow, so you can't write me any more to Adams Run.

Phill says tell Jane not to write to him till she hears from him. We will go to the Four Mile House to meet the Regiment.

We are all well. Hope this will find you all well.

Your Devoted Husband,
James M. Barr

P.S. I received a letter from Brother William. Says he will give me his Jeff Davis horse for my Lady Gray. Tell Henry to watch out if he wants to go with us. We will go by Columbia, but don't know yet what day we will get there.

Your
James

———•◦◦◦•———

Adams Run, S.C.
April 2nd, 1864

My Dear Wife:

No doubt you will be surprised in receiving a letter from me so soon, but as we are busy packing up for the march and all hands can't pack at the same time and having the day before us, I will write you a few lines as I now know when we will march and to what point.

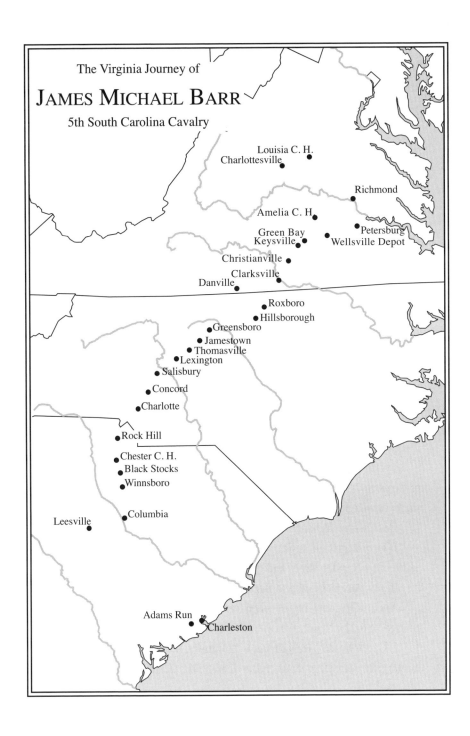

The Virginia Journey of

JAMES MICHAEL BARR

5th South Carolina Cavalry

Louisia C. H.
Charlottesville
Richmond
Amelia C. H.
Green Bay
Keysville
Petersburg
Wellsville Depot
Christianville
Clarksville
Danville
Roxboro
Hillsborough
Greensboro
Jamestown
Thomasville
Lexington
Salisbury
Concord
Charlotte
Rock Hill
Chester C. H.
Black Stocks
Winnsboro
Columbia
Leesville
Adams Run
Charleston

First, we will march from here to Charleston on tomorrow. We will leave here early to make the trip. We will rendezvous about the race course and stay there till our horses are all shod and we thoroughly equipped. I suppose we will be there about one week.

The officers think the men will be allowed to go home from Charleston, but I think after the Regiment gets together it will doubtful whether any get home or not. So, My Dear One, if I am not allowed to go home, we must console ourselves by saying that it has not been long since we have seen each other. But if we are not permitted to see each other here on Earth, let us pray that we may meet in a happier clime where we can enjoy each others presence forever more. Yet, My Dear One, I feel cheerful or try to feel so. I hope and pray to live to see this War at an end, when we can enjoy each others presence here on Earth. When we can once more live happy together as we have in days past and gone. I don't think this War can last much longer unless Lincoln is reelected. Sometimes I think it is better for us to go to Virginia. We will get good water and get rid of the aggravating sand flies.

I will make an effort to get home when we get to Charleston. Some of the boys I think will run the blockade, but I will not if I cannot get off with a leave. I will not leave. They might not trouble me and yet they might.

You had better get William to buy you five bushels of salt. You can sell the meat whenever you wish.

I want the hides off of the cattle you kill saved well, two steers and two or three cows. Smith said I could put old stray in his pasture. I am afraid if she is turned out I will lose her.

Has the raw hide been sent to Pa's?

If Jerry wants his shoes, you can let him have them. He told me he wanted them for Sunday shoes and would buy his winter shoes.

If any one goes down to Barnwell send after my bottles.

Ance will come home when we leave for Virginia. We cannot draw enough to feed a Negro. We can hire our work done.

I expect we will pass through Columbia, but don't know when. I hope we may see each other soon, but if we should not, let us pray for each other.

Your Devoted Husband,
J.M. Barr

———⊰∘⊱———

Editor's note: On April 9, 1864 Rebecca Barr's brother John C.C. Dowling wrote her the following from Tennessee.

Co. A 1st S.C.V.
Jenkins Brig., Field Div.
Long Street Corps

Camp Near
Zollicaffa, Tenn.
April the 9th, 1864

Dear Sister:

These few lines leave me rather on the grunting order, but hope it will reach you enjoying good health, also your little family.

If I were only married I could sympathize with you, but as I am not, I say you are in great trouble as it is thought that Tyler's Company will go to Virginia. I know that will not please A.D.D., C.G.D., J.M.B., nor S.D.G.[183] For their poor families' sake I hate it most.

I received a letter from C.T. and A.D., but not a word from the Major.

Aaron wrote as if he thought there was a strong feeling to divide the estate after the present crop is made and gathered. That will suit all who have a home to put what they get on or to work and make something out of it, but for me what, could I do? I can't get home to make any arrangements there. Don't you think I had best kick against it? I think when the War is ended, it will be time enough and the proper time, when all can be present and exercise some judgement. Mine I am afraid is always going to be limited as I did not cultivate my mind as I should.

If this War ends in our behalf, I will try to complete my course. I will be a good size school boy though.

You never have told me the girl you selected for me. Do I know her? Did

---

183 Aaron Decania Dowling, Charleigh Thaddeus Dowling, James Michael Barr and Samuel D. Guess.

you hear of any Valentine sent me from Leesville? I received one, very pretty one, from some one up there, or the envelope had the stamp that your letters always bear. If you can find who sent it, you will please send me her name and I will give her an April Fool in return.

Well, about the War. Are you in as good cheer as when you wrote before? I guess not and the reason is that the Major is going too far from you. But as to the War, it should not change your mind or everybodys thinking as it is on her last legs. I hope it is and will be so.

I see Tom every day or so. He is as fat as a buck. He has been very kind to me. He received a fine box from home and came to my company in the snow to get me to go around and help him enjoy it, accordingly I did so.

I must close. Give regards to all who inquire of me. I remain as ever your True and Affectionate Brother.

Calhoun
John Calhoun Dowling

———◦◦◦———

Editor's note: On April 13, 1864 James Barr received the following note from his brother William Barr.

Barr's Mills, S.C.
April 13th, 1864

Brother James:

In reference to Jefferson Davis, you can do just as you like until tomorrow.

I did not have him for sale, neither had I him for trade. If such had been the case, I would not be willing to recant, as it might injure the value of him.

If you conclude to send him back to-morrow, you can say to any inquiring mind, that might have penchant for hunting Yankees on horseback, that Jeff Davis can carry such a one, at a salary of Six Thousand Dollars, no questions to be asked, and term of office to last during pleasure.

Affectionately,
Your Brother William

This letter sent by Anderson

———◦◦◦———

Winnsboro, S.C.
April 16th, 1864

My Dear Wife:

The evening finds me thirty miles from Columbia. Our Regiment will leave to-morrow morning at five o'clock. A Lieutenant and fifteen men are here and I am one of that number. We are detailed with Capt. Green. Our Quartermaster to go ahead of the Regiment to look up forage.

I will try and get back with the others as I don't like to leave them, though I would fare better, but my horse will not. My horse will not stand me. How sorry I am that William came up to see me with his horse. I wish I had Jim. William may not take Lady Gray. He may keep him and work him but keep the mule. I don't know what he will do. He says he would rather keep the mule, but will keep the Mare till he wants the mule. I will send the horse home as soon as I can get another horse.

Frank Banks says I can send Ance back anytime with him if I have another horse to ride. If I had Jim I would be much better satisfied.

We will go today to Black Stock, sixteen miles from here. The boys from Virginia say that they were very healthy there. They are afraid of fever on the coast.

I think we will all be satisfied if we can get home in six months. I am well and hope this will find you all well.

Your Affectionate Husband,
J.M. Barr

I hope William will keep the Mare, but if he will take the mule, let him have her.

James

York District
Rock Hill, S.C.
April 19th, 1864

My Dear Rebecca:

As we are a long ways apart and as I know you are anxious to hear from me, I will write you.

We are here at Rock Hill, got here yesterday evening. We left Columbia Saturday morning, came to Winnsboro, stayed there that night and I wrote you a note from there. Sunday we got to Chester Court House, stayed there Sunday night, and yesterday we came here.

It rained very hard here last night and is raining some this morning. Our horses have been sheltered every night till last night, which was the worst night we have had. It rained some night before last, but yesterday was a good day.

We will remain here until to-morrow morning. Wednesday morning then we will go to Charlotte, N.C.

The Regiment is at Winnsboro or at least stayed there last night. To-night it will stay at Chester Court House and to-morrow night at this place. I know the boys fared bad last night.

We have had a house to stay in every night. We got shelter for our horses this morning. My horse looks better than he did at Winnsboro. Yet, I don't think he will stand me long in Virginia from the way the horses look that we have met.

The men say they only get a little corn for the horses and occasionally get a little wheat straw, but we will get there when we can get clover. We are getting an abundance of corn and fodder to feed on our march. When we get to Charlotte we will stay there till the Regiment comes up. The Regiment will stay there two days. On every hundred miles we will rest two days.

I have only one blanket with me and wish I had some of my clothing home. I have too many for my horse to tote. I have too many drawers. Will have to throw away some. I wish now I had my Gray Horse. Yes, Jeff Davis is too young for the trip and it is a pity to kill a young horse. Yet, he is no better than I am and I have to go. I wish William would take the Mare as he first wrote me. Yet he told me at Lexington Court House that he would ask me five hundred dollars to boot. I told him I wished I had his horse back home. I was foolish for ever trading. I won't give any boot between the Mare, but will swap even. If he wants the mule, he will have to have her as he has my note. I am sorry I gave my note, but if he holds me to the trade perhaps we can pay it sometime.

Tell Walter that he would better give you a note. Tell him to draw one so it will not draw any interest till called for and he can pay it whenever he pleases. In the meantime I don't want to take any money but the new.

Bacon was selling for $4.50 in Columbia.

You can write me at Greensboro, N. C. It will take us ten days to get there.

Your Devoted Husband,
James M. Barr

———※———

Charlotte, N. C.
April 21st, 1864

My Dear Wife:

I am now in Charlotte, Came in yesterday evening and will stay till the Regiment comes up and a day longer if they lie over here two days. So we will rest three days here.

I wrote you to direct me a letter to Greensboro. Direct in care of Lt. Smith instead of Capt. Tyler as I am detached with him. I want you to get this note Saturday.[184]

The cause of my writing, I want my wool hat and if you can get this

---

[184] Probably George H. Smith from Charleston, who served as a second lieutenant in Company D, 5th South Carolina Cavalry. Ibid., 51.

Sunday, you can send my hat to Ceder Grove Sunday to Mr. Elias Sease or Mr. Jefferson Drafts, son of Daniel Drafts, and ask them to bring it to me.[185] They belong to Capt. Caughman s Company and are at home on furlough. Send someone that can tell them. Bill will know them. If they are at Church, send to D. Drafts. I expect they will be at Church as it is a two day meeting.

1st Direct your letters to:

James M. Barr
Greensboro, N.C.
5th Regt. S.C.C.
Col. Donavant

Next letters to Richmond, Virginia
c/o Capt. Tyler
24344

My horse is looking better. Rest will help him. I hope he will stand me. The sun is about to come out. After you write to Greensboro, you must write to Richmond till I tell you otherwise.

I hope to hear from you and our little ones and Father and Mother soon. I hope we will not stay in Virginia long. Banks says we will come back next Spring if the War lasts that long. If I only can have my health and get back safe. May the Good One take care of us and permit us to meet again, that we may once more be happy.

Your Husband,
James

---

[185] Elias S. Sease from the Lexington District served in Company F, 5th South Carolina Cavalry; Jefferson L. Drafts from the Lexington District served in Company F as well. Drafts was wounded in action during the Battle of Trevilian Station, Virginia, on June 11, 1864. Ibid., 18, 49.

———⊰◦◦◦⊱———

Salisbury, N.C.
April 24th, 1864

My Dear Wife:

It is with pleasure that I am again permitted to write you a few lines to let you know where I am and how I am getting on.

Our Detachment got to Charlotte last Wednesday evening. I stayed Friday night with the Company. Saturday morning we left the regiment, stayed at Concord, N. C. last night, a nice little village. Tonight we are here at Salisbury, a nice little town.

We had a bad day to travel, rained the most of the day. We all got wet, but we are by a stove so we can dry ourselves. The distance from here to Charlotte is about forty miles. We travel about twenty miles per day.

I found Aaron, Charlie, Sam, Phillip in fine spirits. I would like to be with them, but prefer being as I am, one day in advance of the Regiment. I fare better and my horse is sheltered at night as we get stables for our horses. My fare is no better than if I was back with the Regiment. If I go to a Hotel, they charge five dollars for a meal and nothing but ham, biscuits, coffee and molasses.

When I wrote my last letter, I did not know Fink had gone back home, so I guess you will send my hat by him.

Our horses are not looking so well. Their backs have galded pretty baldy. My horse has reduced down considerable. If he breaks down, I will want the Hugh's horse, so they will have to keep him in as good order as you can.

I have seen a good deal of good land since I left Columbia. Some very broken at Concord. They have a large factory. I was not in it, only passed by it.

Tonight I would go to Church, but I cannot because I must write to you. Yes, to you the Dearest One on Earth to me, but My Dear One, when will we be permitted to see each other again? We may never, but let us pray if we are not permitted to see each other on this Earth to meet in Heaven. I trust that I will be allowed to live through this War and again be happy with you and our dear Children.

I cannot write you anything about the farm for I do not know what to write about. I told you to tell Walter he better give a note for the bacon. I don't want the note to draw interest. Say on the back. "This Note is not to draw any interest till called for. 200 lbs. bacon at $3 and 100 lbs. at $3.50." Bacon in Columbia sells from 4 to 5 dollars. Life is uncertain and if he gives a note, all is right.

I hope I get a couple letters from you on the 29th. We will get to Greensboro on that day. We will stay there till the Regiment comes up.

Sam got a letter from Sallie at Charlotte.

My love to all. Kiss the children for your dear Husband. Remaining as ever your true Husband.

Good Night my Dear Wife.
James M. Barr

Greensboro, N.C.
April 27th, 1864

My Dear Wife:

We arrived here today about 12:00 o'clock. We came from James Town today, ten or twelve miles. James Town is at deep river. It is a small place. Night before last we stayed at Lexington, a nice little town. Greensboro appears to be a pretty large place. We will stay here three nights as the Regiment is two days behind us. Thrown back a day in crossing the river.

The people in this State are quite tasty. They have find houses, or the most of them.

I am standing the trip finely, yet our fare is rough. Some days no meat. We draw for so many days, 3 days, but I could eat it all in one day. I could buy something but have not got the funds to buy with. I have three dollars left besides my stamps, so you see I am getting pretty low down in funds. I will pay $1.00 out for washing today as I have stripped and put on clean clothes after taking a good washing in a branch in a pine thicket.

I think the people here are mostly Unionist. They are very tired of the War, so much so that I believe they would have peace on any terms.

I hope that I will get a letter from you today.

Some of the men have gone down to the Office.

When we passed Glenn Anna Female College, the young Ladies made their handkerchiefs fly waving them at us. Gleen Anna is at Thomasville. One Lady waved a flag as we came in. It livened up our little detachment.

We are now about two hundred miles from Columbia and it will take us yet about three weeks to get to Richmond.

Our boys that ran the blockade were arrested the day before we left Columbia. I hear they were all put in jail till today. To-morrow they will be carried on to Richmond under guard. The boys did wrong going home without leave.

I received two letters today. I am glad you got my short note before Mr. Fink left for I am very anxious to get my hat.

I told Bill to plant Sugar Cane six feet apart, never told him how wide to plant the millet as I only planted it three feet. Thought he would know. If they have planted it too wide, you had better plant a row between every row. Make it three feet apart.

You had good luck in catching the hawk in the chicken coop.

I am glad to know that you are all well and getting on so well.

I will write to William in a few days. He will keep Lady Gray till she gets in foal if no longer. If he does not keep her, you will have to get along as well as you can without the mule. He says if he wants the mule, he will send after it. I would like for him to take the mare so I would not have to pay out any money. Yet, I would not pay any boot between her and the horse as she is a good farm nag. If he take the mule, I would rather pay him off in cotton. I believe I will write him and tell him so.

Tell Jimmie and Johnny to be good boys for Pa. Keep them from the well and millpond. Give my love to Pa & Ma, Spann and all kindred. My horse is doing tolerably well.

Your True Husband,
James M. Barr

Greensboro, N.C.
April 28th, 1864

My Dear Rebecca:

I forgot yesterday where to tell you to direct your next letters. Direct to Keysville, Richmond and Danville R. R. Virginia, Care of Capt. Tyler, in Care of him for fear I may not get them.

Tell Spann not to listen to Bill. I know he thought I had little judgement in planting millet. It is too much ground to tend for so few rows of millet. You will make none if you do not plant it closer. I would plant between the rows, making them three feet.

I think John C. is wrong as he would get more to get his property.

I hear Aiken would start about the first of May.

We will get to Keysville in eight or ten days.

Every ten days we will lie up three.

I write this so you may be able to write me. It will not cost much. I hope to hear from you soon.

I will close to send this off. I wrote William this morning. As ever

Your Affectionate Husband
James

Hillsboro, N.C.
May 2nd, 1864

My Dear Wife:

It is again with pleasure that I embrace this opportunity of writing you a few lines.

Yesterday we had a bad day to march as it was raining, but this morning the Sun is shining. I think we will have a fine day.

We left the Regiment at Greenville, N.C. They lay over there yesterday, will be here tonight. We will leave here at ten o'clock, will have about eighteen miles to Rocksboro. We will strike across for the Richmond and Danville R.R.

The boys were all well and appeared to be enjoying the trip finely. Philip seems to be fattening every day. I took supper with them on the last day of April. They had bacon, molasses and duck, flanked I guess.

I have no guard duty to do nor roll call to attend by being ahead.

My Dear, on the last day of April my thoughts all day were about home. One of the crowd said I was in such a deep study that he spoke to me and I did not notice him. It is true that I was in a deep study.

We will get to Keysville about the Sixth and to Amelia Court House on the 9th. Phil says to tell Jane he will be at Amelia Court House on the 9th of May and to direct after that time to Richmond.

I would like to see you and our dear children, but do not think I will have that pleasure till Winter.

You must try and make the corn hold out and if it will not, perhaps you can borrow some. I could have gotten some from Preston, but he did not send me word at what price.

I hope Henry can stay with Pa and Ma as I know they need him.

I am well, getting on very well.

Your Affectionate Husband,
James

Clarksville, Virginia
May 5th, 1864

My Dear Rebecca:

We arrived here yesterday about four o'clock and walked out on the street. The ladies passing us would throw flowers at us. A Miss Rosa Young threw one at me. We asked their names. Miss Young and Miss Wood. I told the boys, as there were three of us, we would go to Miss Youngs. We met a Negro and asked where Miss Young lived. He told us and said they were looking for some of the soldiers there for supper. Of course we made tracks for the Youngs' house. We were treated very kind, offered a bed and asked to come back to breakfast. We accepted all but the bed. Sorry to say I did not get to see Miss Rosa as she stayed out with a friend.

The ladies took me to be a single man, inquired of some of our boys who I was and said I had such a pretty beard. Mrs. Young asked me if I was a married gentleman. I told her I was. A lady asked me to Oak Hill, so you see I must take pretty well with the ladies. They are very kind, especially at this place. I wish we could lay over here a day.

Clarksville is here on the Roanoke River. We will cross it this morning and to Christianville and from there to Keysville where I expect a letter from my dear one.

I wrote Henry at Oak Hill but will enclose both together at Keysville when I get to the Railroad as it will go home as soon.

Your Devoted Husband
James

———◦◦◦———

Christianville, Va.
May 5th, 1864

My Dear Wife:

We arrived here from Clarksville about three o'clock this evening and find the place quite a sorry place. Only a few houses, bacon Seven Dollars per lb., butter Six Dollars per lb. Mr. Salmon and I have ordered three dozen biscuits and three slices of meat for Six Dollars, so we will have supper if the place is poor.[186]

The land we passed through today is very good. I would like to own some of it.

If Walter pays you any money and you need homespun, get Spann to get Love Gamillion or someone to get it for you in Graniteville. I do not know what you need. You must look out for yourself as I want you to have anything you need.

I am getting on finely, only my nose has fared rather badly for the want of shade. I am standing the trip much better than I expected I would. We will get to Keysville to-morrow, it is twenty two miles from here.

I have some money yet. Lt. Smith loaned me Twenty dollars, five dollar bills are now at a discount. Don't take any as you will have to lose so much. That is why I can't sell bacon at 3 & 31/2 and take five dollar bills, The Old Issue. (I borrowed ten dollars from Henry.)

Your Devoted Husband,
James

---

[186] In all probability Luder Sahlman, who served as a private in Company D, 5th South Carolina Cavalry. Ibid., 48.

Keysville, Va.
May 6th, 1864

My Dear Rebecca:

We arrived here about one o'clock today. It is an awful hot day.

I was sadly disappointed in not receiving a letter from you. Perhaps you did not get my letter written on the Twenty-eighth in time to answer it.

I hear we whipped the Yankees yesterday in Virginia.[187]

It will take us five days to get to Richmond.

I think that if we are successful this Summer, we will have peace. This is the opinion of most men that I have seen in Virginia. They say the battle will terminate the War, that is the pending battle before Richmond.

This leaves me well. My horse is standing it tolerably well.

Your Devoted Husband,
James

Wellsville, Va.
Near Petersburg
May 10, 1864

My Dear Wife:

We leave here on the cars for Petersburg, twenty miles from here.

Don't be alarmed for me. I came here to fight for our freedom.

Phil, Aaron and Charlie are on the cars. I am back here with the Advance Guard. We are five miles in advance. We were the Advance Guard for two days.

---

[187] Barr was referring to the Battle of the Wilderness, which initiated Grant's 1864 campaign against Lee's army. Eleven months later Lee surrendered the Army of Northern Virginia at Appomattox Court House.

I will write you the first opportunity, but it may be that I may not have an opportunity in several days.

Gen. Beauregard has gone on.[188]

Sam is behind with the horses.

We were ordered Sunday to Petersburg. We are now on our way.

If you write to Petersburg, I may get your letter and may not. Don't know.

Your Devoted Husband,
James

<hr />

Petersburg, Virginia
May the 10th, 1864

My Dear Rebecca:

I wrote you a few lines this morning, but as I wrote in a hurry I will write you a few more lines to let you know where we are and how we got here. We left Wellsville this morning for this place on board the cars. Our horses were put in the cars and we rode on top of the cars. We had quite a lively time as the ladies were cheering us onward from every house.

We expected to get into a fight as soon as we got here, but it seems that the Yankees had gotten wind of our reinforcements and took to their heels. On Sunday morning, at the Junction we heard the Yankees, three thousand strong, black and white were at some Eighteen miles from the Junction with

---

[188] In early 1864 General Beauregard was transferred from the Carolina coast to Virginia. He would be involved in bottling up Union Major General Benjamin F. Butler's force near Petersburg at Bermuda Hundred, in defending Drewry's Bluff south of Richmond, and in organizing the early defenses of Petersburg.

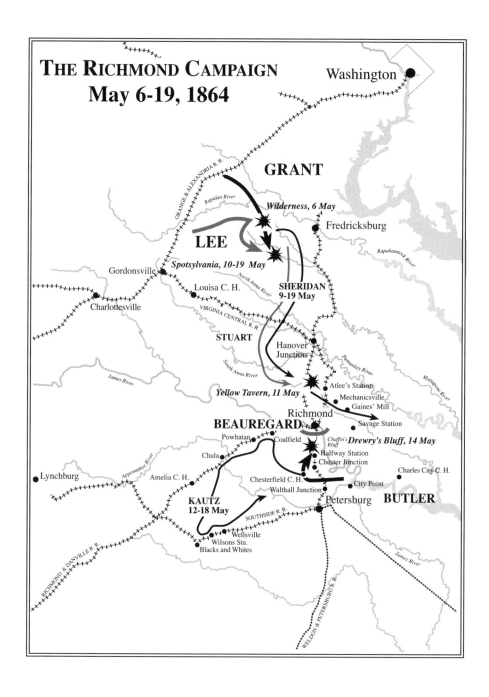

THE RICHMOND CAMPAIGN
May 6-19, 1864

Washington

GRANT

ORANGE & ALEXANDRIA R. R.

Rapidan River

Wilderness, 6 May

Fredricksburg

LEE

Spotsylvania, 10-19 May

Rapahannock River

Gordonsville

Louisa C. H.

North Anna River

SHERIDAN
9-19 May

Charlottesville

VIRGINIA CENTRAL R. R.

STUART

Hanover
Junction

Pamunkey River

Mattaponi River

James River

South Anna River

Yellow Tavern, 11 May

Atlee's Station

Mechanicsville

Gaines' Mill

Richmond

Savage Station

BEAUREGARD

Powhatan

Coalfield

Chaffin's
Bluff

Drewry's Bluff, 14 May

Appomattox River

Chula

Halfway Station

Chester Junction

Charles City C. H.

Lynchburg

Amelia C. H.

Chesterfield C. H.

City Point

Walthall Junction

KAUTZ
12-18 May

SOUTHSIDE R. R.

Petersburg

BUTLER

RICHMOND & DANVILLE R. R.

Wellsville

Wilsons Sta.

Blacks and Whites

James River

WELDON & PETERSBURG R. R.

only our little Detachment there and the Regiment a day behind.[189]

We had to go on picket there. Frank Drafts and I were sent together.[190] We had a hot place under an old sycamore tree. If it would have had leaves on it we could have shaded ourselves. We had a splendid dinner. An old man sent us plenty of ice. We then went ahead as an advance guard this morning. We were five miles in advance of the Regiment when we were called back. We had a splendid supper, but just as breakfast was ready the Courier came, so we could not stop to eat it, but the Lady sent us two plates of biscuits, which was quite acceptable. When we got back to Wellsville, Capt. Green, our Quartermaster, told us to go to his tent and get breakfast. He had a ham boiled and flour bread, so we fared well.

Soon we took the cars for this place, which was thirty miles. We were on the second train. The third brought our Wagons and mules and some loose horses. Some of our horses are still behind. Sam and some few men and the Negroes are yet to come. We are looking for the train to-morrow. I hear we will go for Richmond as we will not all be needed here.

I think the Yankees had better quit. Grant has been whipped. I heard today that Lee was driving him back. I can't tell you of the Battles as I have heard, but you will see it in your paper. We know that Lee has whipped him (Grant) and that badly. I can't tell you the number we lost, but a good many.[191]

I wish our Regiment could get together. It is some twenty-five miles from here to Richmond, but our boys may not be there as I suppose they were in the fight. The loose horses would be in our way if we were to get into an engagement. I hope when we get to Richmond that we may find the boys

---

[189] On Monday, May 9, 1864 Union commander Benjamin F. Butler ordered his force to advance on the Richmond-Petersburg Rail Road and the Confederate lines of communication at Petersburg. After a series of miscues and false starts, Butler ordered his force back to its original lines on May 10. Barr was apparently referring to Walthall Junction, where 2,500 Confederates under Major General Bushrod Johnson had held off more than 8,000 men of Butler's army.

[190] Possibly Jacob Franklin Drafts, who enlisted at age 24 as a private in Company F, 5th South Carolina Cavalry. Drafts died of disease at his home on October 21, 1864. Ibid., 18.

[191] By May 10, 1864 Grant and Lee had been fighting continuously since the Union Army of the Potomac crossed the Rapidan River on May 4. By this time Grant had been stopped by Lee in the Wilderness and had attempted to place his army between Lee and Richmond by way of Spotsylvania Court House to the south. By the May 20, after two weeks of fighting, Grant will had lost about 36,000 men while the Confederates suffered less than half as many casualties.

there. I think there are troops enough here to meet the enemy. The Yankees were within two miles of here (so I hear).[192]

We have short rifles, twenty inches long, so they are not much in our way. They shoot 300 yards. They were sent from Richmond to us at the Junction of the Danville & R.R.R.[193]

Phil said you must tell Jane of what I write and that he will write to-morrow or when he gets to Richmond. He is now on guard and has no chance to write. Tell Jane to direct her letters to Richmond to be forwarded. You must do the same.

We are all well, but had a hot place in the sun on the cars.

Your ink is very bad. Can't you get better? I hope you can.

I must close. Hoping this will reach you all well.

Your Affectionate Husband

James

Direct to me instead of Colonel, will you.

Petersburg, Va.

May 11th, 1864

Dear Rebecca:

I am still here, but expect to leave to-morrow morning. Soldiers have been passing all day long. I suppose some 30 or 40 thousand are here or not more than six miles from here.

---

[192] Barr apparently was still in the advance as the men traveled by train to the front. Upon arriving, the regiment was stationed between Richmond and Petersburg, where it fought on foot at Chester Station on May 10, at Drewry's Bluff on May 12, at Atkinson's Farm on May 17, and at South Side on May 18. Brooks, *Butler*, 250; Knudsen, "5th SC," 4.

[193] Matthew C. Butler's Brigade was armed with two-band Enfield Rifles and would do most of its fighting in Virginia on foot as dismounted cavalry. But it would be a mistake to list them as mounted infantry as Colonel Zimmerman Davis of the Fifth recalled, "The chief fighting was done on foot with the rifle, but there was not wanting the brilliant dash and headlong charge with sabre and pistol." Brooks, *Butler*, 241 350-351.

All of our men that have come on, except some 1/2 dozen who will be left here, went on today about 12:00 o'clock. These 1/2 Dozen with the Negroes will care for the men's horses that were on furlough. Phil, Charlie and Aaron have gone. Sam is with the horses, the ones that were led from Columbia.

We are within 25 miles of Richmond, but then we will have to go 80 miles around to save our horses and wagons.

Send me twenty or thirty dollars if you can. I don't know whether Fletcher has sent you the Hundred Dollars or not. If not, Spann or Smith will let you have it or you can get it from Henry, but if you can get the new issue, I would like it better.

I hope you are well, you and children Pa and Ma and all relatives.

I am faring better by being ahead of the Regiment as I can stay in houses and shelter my horse. He is now in the Livery Stable at this place.

Sam, Aaron and Capt. Tyler received letters here or at least I have them for them.

I must close to get this off tonight.

Send my wool hat if you can.

Your Devoted Husband,
James

—————◦◦◦◦◦—————

Editor's note: On May 19, 1864 Barr wrote his wife to describe his first experience in a large scale engagement in Virginia.

Near Chafins Bluff, Va.[194]
May 19, 1864

My Dear Wife:

It is through the mercy of God that I am alive and permitted to write you. Unto him be all the praise.

On Sunday our Regiment was ordered to Drury's Bluff.[195] Monday morning we were in our saddles by day light and by day the ball opened. We went in on foot as skirmishers. Two men were killed in our Company, Robert Hays and Corporal Gleaton.[196]

I never want to be in a hotter place than I was. The balls were as thick as hail. We charged and ran the Yankees. They rallied and brought a Brigade against us. Of course, so few men as we had, had to fall back. We did in good order. They poured a perfect volley after us. They came close. We were in the woods, the balls pealing trees all around. Hays and Gleaton were killed on the retreat. As soon as we retreated back, our field pieces opened on them and our boys followed them on.

---

[194] Chaffin's Bluff is on the north side of the James River just east of Drewry's Bluff.

[195] The Battle of Drewry's Bluff took place on May 16, 1864 as General Beauregard took the offensive, attacking Ben Butler's forces that then threatened the Confederate fortifications on the bluff. Dunovant's 5th South Carolina Cavalry was thrown into a hastily organized infantry brigade under Major General Robert Ransom, Jr. Ransom placed the 5th on his left near the James River, where, he reported, they "did admirable service." Although the attack began well for the Confederates, thick fog and miscommunication prevented Beauregard from achieving a complete victory. After being driven back, the Federals reorganized and pushed Beauregard's men back. Both sides reported around 4,000 casualties, and as a result, Butler decided to return to his Bermuda Hundred lines, where he would be "bottled up" for the rest of the campaign. *OR*, vol. 36, p. 213.

[196] Robert H. Hays was a farmer in his thirties from the Barnwell District and had enlisted as a private in Company I, 5th South Carolina Cavalry. Although the battle occurred on May 16, 1864, he was listed as being killed in action on May 11, 1864 at Drewry's Bluff. Corporal W. W. Gleaton of Company I, 5th South Carolina Cavalry was killed in action during the Battle of Drewry's Bluff , May 16, 1864. *1860 Census*, Barnwell District, South Carolina; Knudsen, "5th SC," 24, 27.

They are near the James River, close to their gun boats. I think Butler will have to leave. I hear they had a fight yesterday or a skirmish fight.

We were on the extreme right of the enemy lines. I never was so near outdone. If the enemy had managed well, they could have blanked [flanked] us. We were under a cross fire nearly all the time. I shot many a ball, but do not know what damage they did. I felt very cool, took it much better than I feared I would. I would be willing to do it again under the same circumstances. We ought not to have made a charge as we were Cavalry and had no bayonets to our guns.

We were relieved from the South side of the James River this morning. We are on the North side and don't know where we will go from here. I suppose to watch the enemy.

In the fight Monday, I think our losses were as great as the Yankees. We took a good many prisoners, killed some two or three hundred. I mean the loss in killed was as great as ours. Several men were wounded in our Regiment, and some six killed I heard yesterday. Some Eighty were killed and wounded, but I don't think they know.

Our horses and men had a narrow escape coming from Petersburg. They passed Chesterfield Court House and in one and 1/2 hours the Yankee Cavalry, 2000 strong, were there. Our Squad under Lt. Smith were to go there for the night. We were sent in a different direction. A Courier was sent after us saying they intended to go by Chesterfield Court House and we must go there that night, so we were going in when a little boy came running, saying, "If you go in you all will be captured." We took reconnaissance and got with the Regiment the following evening. All thought we were captured. [197]

Phil and Charlie are complaining, have been for several days. Aaron and Sam are well. I was the only one or rather Shealy and I were the only ones in the fight when we had the heavy skirmish Monday evening, I mean in our

---

[197] On May 12, 1864 Union Brigadier General August V. Kautz with his 2,800-man cavalry division launched a raid on the Danville Railroad from Butler's lines at Bermuda Hundred. During his advance, Kautz had little trouble driving pickets of the 5th South Carolina Cavalry from their front at Chester Station and capturing Chesterfield Court House and other posts. After destroying a great deal of Confederate supplies and railroad tracks and pushing as far west as Blacks and Whites (present day Blackstone, Virginia), Kautz and his men returned to Union lines at City Point on May 17, 1864. August V. Kautz, "Operations South of the James River," Robert U. Johnson and Clarence C. Buel, eds., *Battles and Leaders of the Civil War*, 4 vols. (New York: Thomas Yoseloff, 1956), 4: 533-534.

mess, though they, Sam and Aaron, were skirmishing all day.

I have not received but two letters from you since I left home. I got those at Greensboro. My horse is looking very bad. I have had very little corn to feed him for three or four days.

I am well and hope this will find you all well. I wrote this in a hurry.

Your Devoted Husband,
James

Ten Miles N. E. of Richmond, Va.
May 23rd, 1864

My Dear Wife:

I have been on the go ever since I left home. I told you about being so near captured at Chesterfield Court House, only eight of us. All the Regiment thought we were captured. They were proud to see us come up.

The fight on the South side of the James was a hot one. I told you we lost two men, Rob Hays and Gleaton. The enemy charged our company with 2 columns. They poured a perfect Volley at us with Grape and Canister besides their mine balls. We were in a hot place. The balls passed us like hail or as thick as hail falls. It was only through the goodness of God that I was saved. They came within 20 yards of us. Capt. Tyler shot with his pistol. Our men were killed on the retreat.

We were in the woods, charged the enemy and ran them. They were reinforced and we had to fall back. Capt. Tyler was with us. We were under a cross fire. It is a wonder that we escaped.

Wednesday we were ordered on the North side of the James and Thursday night we passed through Richmond to Hanover Junction to reinforce two Brigades. The enemy, after burning two culprits [culverts] on the Railroad, left so we did not get into a fight with them. They say they numbered some ten or fifteen thousand. They are the same raiders that Stuart fought when he was killed. I saw a good many dead horses on the battle ground. It was very unpleasant and the stink was awful. When the Yankees left Saturday morning they killed several horses that had given out. They would either shoot them or cut their throats to keep us from getting them.[198]

We rode all night Thursday night and part of Friday night. A part of every night we are riding. When we hear of the enemy, we cut across to meet them. Their object is not to fight, but to destroy all they can and cut off all communication from Lee's Army.

I am sitting here in the hot sun grazing my horse. We are all grazing, some three thousand. Our horses get no corn.

I wrote Wesley to bring me one of my horses. I want Jim or Pa's old Pete. I know the Hughs horse can't stand me here. If my Gray won't do, I will swap Pa my Hughs horse for old Pete. I can't care for a fancy horse here and an old horse stands it best. I told Wesley I, would give him $200. and pay his expenses here and back. I want to send Jeff Davis back home. I want him to come as soon as he can before she gets too poor to go back. I want to send Ance back as he is never with me. He does not do me any good here and if Wesley will come soon, Ance can ride Hays' horse home.

We are now within six miles of Richmond and think we will go back there in a day or two to organize in one Brigade. It will depend on where the enemy is.

I have not received a letter yet, but hope to get one soon as the Post Office is now distributing letters.

Give my love to Pa and Ma. My love to you, My Dear Wife, and our dear Children. I am more anxious to see you all than ever. When you write, tell me all the news. I have to write by chance.

Your Devoted Husband,

J. M.B.

Our Service here is awful hard. Phil is better.

---

[198] On May 11, 1864 the numerically superior Union cavalry under Major General Philip Sheridan met and defeated the Confederates north of Richmond at Yellow Tavern. In the fight , flamboyant Rebel cavalry commander J. E. B. Stuart was mortally wounded. In the days following the battle, Sheridan found his cavalry corps almost entirely surrounded between the defenses of Richmond and Lee's army. After resupplying his men with provisions from Butler's Army of the James, Sheridan marched north to rejoin Grant's army on May 24, 1864. As they retreated, the Federals killed any horses that gave out in order to prevent them from falling into Southern hands. Stephen Z. Starr, *The Union Cavalry in the Civil War*, vol. 2, *The War in the East From Gettysburg to Appomattox, 1863-1865* (Baton Rouge: Louisiana State University Press, 1981), 97-115.

Camp Lee, Va.
May 27th, 1864

My Dear Wife:

We are within two miles of Richmond, came out here to camp. We will leave in a few minutes for Richmond to have our horses shod. Then we will go back towards Hanover Junction to meet the Regiment as they made their way up that way yesterday evening.

I cannot tell you of any news as I have not the opportunity of getting the news. I will send you a paper showing you where we have been since we have been in Virginia on our march to Charles City.[199]

John C. Hanbey shot himself accidentally through his left hand. His hand, I hear, was cut off yesterday. I am very sorry for him as he was a good Soldier.[200]

We lost no men in the engagement at Charles City, had two or three wounded in the Regiment, but not in our Company. We lost two horses, killed in Capt. Whilden's Company by a shell.[201] It is a wonder that more were not killed.

I did not get to Charles City. My horse became very lame and I was left behind with a good many others that were lame, so I was not nearer than five

---

[199] On the night of May 23, 1864 Major General Fitzhugh Lee assembled a force that he intended to use to drive off two regiments of black troops that had been landed on the north side of the James River at Wilson's Wharf near Charles City Court House. Elements of the 5th South Carolina Cavalry participated in the all night march and skirmish the next day. Upon surrounding the black troops, Lee issued an ultimatum, demanding the surrender of the garrison and promising the black soldiers fair treatment as prisoners of war. If they refused, Lee insisted, he could not be responsible for the conduct of his troops. Upon reading the ultimatum, Union Brigadier General Edward Augustus Wild stated, "We'll try that," preferring to take his chances on the battlefield before surrendering. After several dismounted assaults on the Union position, Lee backed off and by the next morning had left the field in Union hands after suffering the loss of some twenty men. OR, vol. 36, part 2, p. 270-271.

[200] Most likely John C. Hanberry who had enlisted at age 20 as a private in Company I, 5th South Carolina Cavalry. Knudsen, "5th SC," 26.

[201] Captain Louis Augustus Whilden from Charleston commanded Company E, 5th South Carolina Cavalry. Whilden had been wounded during the fight at Drewry's Bluff and died of wounds on August 4, 1864. Ibid., 58.

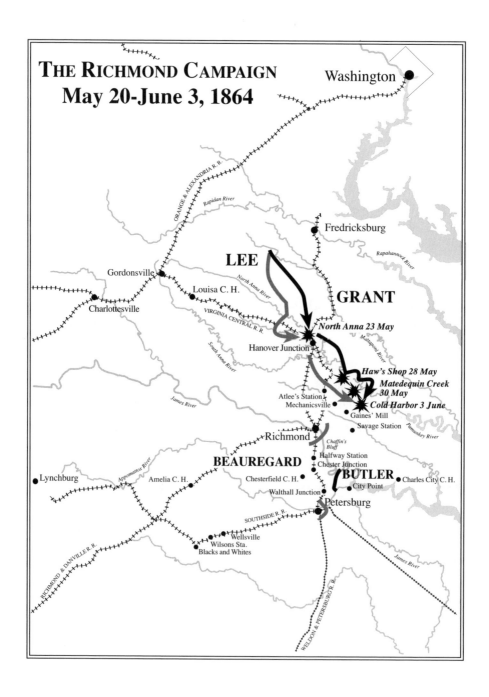

THE RICHMOND CAMPAIGN
May 20-June 3, 1864

or six miles, but was in the enemy's lines for two days. We rode very hard. We get very little corn for our horses and slim rations for ourselves.

We got some fifty horses and mules from the enemy and a few beef cattle. We killed some, but had no salt on anything to cook it in, so we had to broil on the coals. I cooked my first bread in the ashes yesterday. It looked nice. Don't you wish you could have seen it? We wrap the dough up in leaves then bake it. We were a jolly crowd cooking our days rations.

Our horses are looking badly, riding them hard and feeding them so little. I hope Wesley will come out here and bring me a horse and carry Ance back as he is very little use to me. I have not put on a clean shirt since I have been here, not having the chance to do so as my saddlebags were not here. Ance has them now and I hope to shift soon, but we are all in the same fix nearly.

Charlie is here, has been sick, but will leave here today for Atlas Station.[202] Lt.Rice is here in the Hospital with some three others from our Company. I think we will establish a Camp at Atlas Station temporarily for the sick men and sore back horses.

I am well pleased with the land out here. It is splendid land and I have seen a good many acres since I have been here on our ride to Charles City. I thought the land rather good, but considering how good the land is don't keep me from wanting to get back to South Carolina.

I am satisfied to never get in another fight. Hope I may not, but if duty calls me I shall be in our Service. It is hard and will be so all the summer following up the raiders.

I would like to know the result of Lee's fight, but it is thought he has gained a decisive victory over Grant. Grant's Army is not satisfied, suppose he will be superseded. I trust and pray that we may soon have peace.[203]

I have not received a letter from you since I have been in Virginia, but hope I will get one soon. Give my love to Pa and Ma and Kindred and to you

---

[202] Atlee's Station.

[203] By May 27, 1864 Grant had battered away at Lee's army in the Wilderness, at Spotsylvania, and along the North Anna River. But unlike previous Union commanders, Grant did not return to the defenses of Washington after each setback; instead, he relentlessly continued southward after Lee's army.

all the love of a devoted husband. I wish to see you and our dear children. How I would like to see the little fellows. Tell the Negroes "Howdy" for me and tell them to do their duty.

Your Husband,
James M. Barr

———∋⚬◉⚬∈———

Editor's note: Barr included the following in his letter of May 27, 1864.
May 1864

3rd.	Regiment camped in Richmond except horses.
10th.	Part Regt. engaged Enemy at Chester.
12th.	Part Regt. engaged Enemy at Halfway Station.
12th.	Narrow escape from Raiders. Horses arrived at Richmond in part.
13th.	Started to Coal pits to meet Spires Raiders.[204]
15th.	Night marched to Drury's Bluff - Met the boys.
16th.	General engagement., drove the Enemy back and lay on the battle field.
17th	Drove the Enemy back to Gun Boats.
18th.	Crossed the Pontoon on the James River below Richmond.
19th.	Night, started to Hanover Junction - fell in with Lomax & Wickhams Brigades - marched all night.[205]
20th.	Night - Started to Hanover Court House to meet Raiders.
21st.	Pursued them-bivouaced at Dr. Prices.

---

[204] On May 12, 1864 Colonel Samuel P. Spear of Kautz' Cavalry Division from the Army of the James led his 2nd Brigade, consisting of the 5th and 11th Pennsylvania Cavalry, on a raid of the South Side coal pits, where it destroyed part of the Danville Railroad. *OR*, vol. 36, part 2, p.1006.

[205] The cavalry brigades of Brigadier General Lunsford Lomax and Brigadier General Williams C. Wickham of Fitzhugh Lee's Division.

22nd.   Marched toward Richmond.

23rd.   Started to Charles City Court House to meet Enemy -Marched all night.

24th.   Continued the march and met and engaged the Enemy at Wharf 38 miles below Richmond.

25th.   Returned toward Richmond - bivouaced in old field nine miles from Richmond.

26th.   The Regiment went toward Hanover Junction. Some Seventy-Five came to Richmond to have horses shod. I am among the crowd. Was in Richmond about three hours. Will have our horses shod tomor row - then we will go back to Regiment. There is no rest here in Virginia. Always going.

I send you this so you can see how we have marched since we have been here.

J.M. Barr

Near Atlas Station, Va.
May 29th, 1864

My Dear Rebecca:

I wrote you a letter a day or two ago, but to let you know how I am and where I am I will write you again. I always have to write in a hurry as I never know how soon we will leave and never can write you a good letter in haste, but you can hear from me and know how I am getting on.

I got back to the Regiment yesterday evening from Richmond. The boys had just come out of a fight. They had a hot time. They say they were driven back by the enemy. We had to fight Cavalry and Infantry. [206]

Poor Nick Hartzog was mortally wounded and died about Nine o'clock last night. He said before he died that he knew he would die and said he knew it would nearly kill his mother. He told Frank Rice and Crum to tell his brothers that he was not a member of any Church, but he had a hope of heaven, that he had been praying and to tell them to meet him in Heaven.

Irbe Segris, neighbor of Capt. Tylers, was wounded and fell in the Yankee's hands.[207] Sgt. Hair was shot in the leg, they think he will lose it.[208] Lt. Whetstone was shot through the ankle, so we had one killed and three wounded.[209]

---

[206] The Battle of Haw's Shop on May 28, 1864 was the first major cavalry engagement for General Matthew C. Butler's Brigade and the 5th South Carolina in Virginia. The battle began as Sheridan, commander of Grant's Cavalry Corps, sent Brigadier General John Irvin Gregg's brigade southeast of Grant's army in order to ascertain the whereabouts of Lee's Confederates. Near Topopotomy Creek in Hanover County and almost a mile from Haw's Shop, the Federals met the Confederate cavalry divisions of Wade Hampton and Fitzhugh Lee. Butler's newly unified brigade, including the 4th, 5th and 6th South Carolina, made up part of the line. As the battle progressed, the Southerners dismounted and went into a defensive position behind temporary field fortifications made of logs and rails and protected by swamps and artillery. Butler's men were more than a match for the dismounted Union troopers of Gregg's Brigade. Armed with their short Enfield rifles and protected by fortifications, they held off the Federals for five to seven hours. By the end of the day Sheridan ordered up the ostentatious Brigadier General George Armstrong Custer and his Michigan Brigade. Custer's men were forced to dismount as well, and with their band playing and their seven-shot Spencer carbines blazing, the Wolverines found themselves in their most desperate struggle of the war. One of Custer's veterans remembered, "The South Carolinians, the most stubborn foe Michigan had ever had met in battle, refused to yield and filled the air with lead from the muzzles of their long range guns as fast as they could load and fire." After a brief and bloody encounter, Custer's men began to drive Butler's Brigade, including the 5th South Carolina, from the field. Some of the Carolinians refused to surrender, and as one witness put it, they "exhibited a foolhardy courage never seen anywhere else so far as my knowledge extends." In his official report Custer stated, "Our loss in this battle was greater than in any other engagement of the campaign." This was a dramatic statement, coming as it did from the commander of a brigade that had the distinction of having the highest Federal casualty rate of the war. The Richmond papers reported that Colonel Dunovant of the 5th had been wounded by a pistol-shot in his left hand, and went on to add that "Most of our loss is attributed to the fact that nearly all the force engaged on our part were new men, whose only idea was to go in and fight, which they did most gallantly and creditably." Brooks, *Butler*, 209-213; Starr, *Union Cavalry*, 217-219; J. H. Kidd, *Personal Recollections of a Cavalrymen with Custer's Michigan Cavalry Brigade in the Civil War* (Ionia, MI: Sentinel Printing Company, 1908) 225-8; *OR*, vol. 36, part 1, p. 821-822; Ibid., part 3, p. 362.

[207] There is no record of Irby Sergis in the 5th South Carolina Cavalry, however W. D. or U. D. Sergrist of Company I, 5th South Carolina was captured and died in Federal captivity at Washington, D.C. on June 17, 1864. Knudsen, "5th SC," 49.

[208] E. R. Hair is listed in the rolls as a corporal from the Barnwell District in Company I, 5th South Carolina Cavalry. Hair was wounded in action during the Battle of Haw's Shop, and on July 4, 1864 he died at Richmond's Chimborazo Hospital. Ibid., 26.

[209] John C. Whetstone from the Barnwell District served as a second lieutenant in Company I, 5th South Carolina Cavalry. He was listed as wounded in action during the Battle of Haw's Shop. Ibid., 58.

I received a letter from you this morning dated the 1st and 4th of May and received one yesterday dated the 15th and one from William dated the 10th.

I regret not being with the Regiment yesterday morning. Tom and John C. came to see us. Phil and Aron saw them. They were both well and looking well. I regret very much in not seeing them. Aron says John C. looks rather thin. They have gone down the Tappahannock.

I think Cavalry service is the hardest service out here as we fight any way and always on the go.

We will soon be without horses if we continue as we have begun with very little to feed our horses. A feed of corn perhaps in three days, graze them on clover when we can, and ride a whole day without watering. Horses and Riders suffering for what? For Our Independence. Oh, how we aught to fight! Up about Charles City they have ravished the Ladies, I was told by reliable men.

My horse will soon be done. He will soon go up the spout as the boys say, but many others are the same way.

I want Wesley to come after Ance. I cannot draw anything for him to eat and draw very little myself, so you see I cannot keep him here. I divide with him when I can.

The mail is going.

I am well and hope this will find you all well.

Your True Husband,
James

—❖—

Near Atlas Station, Va.
May 29th, 1864

Dear Rebecca:

This morning I had to write in a hurry so the letter could get off. I write you now on account of the money Preston wants to pay you. First, I would like to know how much it is. Second, I would much rather for it to be paid on the note that the Estate holds against me. Why? Because it is drawing interest against me. Thirdly, if we receive the money to any amount, your share may be paid off in Confederate money and your Brothers may not all receive it, so I think it best not to receive any unless you hear from me. I will receive a couple hundred dollars if all the rest do the same, but want what they intend for me to be paid on the note I gave Elijah. Be careful how you receive money for you may want something else at a division, Preston ought to tell you how much money he wanted you to take. I don't know what use you will do with the money. I am willing to do what is fair if all will do fair. I won't receive old fives for they are worth no more than $3.33. I have to pass them here for Three Dollars, so you see I lose two dollars out of every five. It is considerable in a larger amount. Ask Preston if all are receiving the money and how much he wants you to take and tell him you will not receive it unless all do the same. I think you should be very careful how you receive money unless you can put it to a good use.

If Wesley comes out here, he will need two hundred dollars. I do not know what in the world to do with Ance if Wesley don't come. I do hope he will come. My horse cannot last me. He is too young for service-an old horse, if he is clear footed, is the best. It does not make any difference out here how a horse looks. I don't care anything for looks.

The Hughs horse only kicks when a Crupper is on him.[210] Hill Winn don't know more than that about him and I knew that much before I traded for him and never thought enough about it to even tell you about it.

---

[210] A crupper is a seed filled molded tail dock that stabilizes the saddle by running from directly under the tail to the hilt of the saddle.

Phil and Aaron are both about sick, but keep with the Regiment, in the rear with the wagons.

Your True Husband,

J.M. Barr

———○○○○———

Near Gains Mills, Va.[211]

May 31st, 1864

My Dear Wife:

Yesterday our Brigade had a sharp fight.[212]

Col. Donavant was wounded in the arm the day Nick Hartzog was killed.

Yesterday we had none killed or wounded in our Compnay. Lt. Col. Jeffords was wounded in the thigh.[213] Several killed and wounded in our Regiment. Hendrix was killed.[214] We have been in some seven or eight engagements since we have been out here. They fought us against too greater odds yesterday. They were supposed to have had twenty to our one. They

---

[211] Gaines's Mill.

[212] The Union Cavalry continued forward after the fight at Haw's Shop, and on May 30, 1864 again faced the Confederates and Butler's Cavalry along Matadequin Creek, some four miles north of Cold Harbor. Being in advance of the infantry, both sides recognized the importance of holding the crossroads and Cold Harbor, and Sheridan threw his forces forward. Once again both sides engaged in a dismounted fight, with Butler's Confederates posted behind breastworks along Matadequin Creek. According to one Union account, Butler's men "held their ground with the same obstinacy they had previously shown" until once again the bold troopers of Custer's Michigan Brigade were ordered forward to drive them out. And again Union troops complemented Butler's Cavalry. One noted, "Butler's men behaved with great gallantry." But evidently they had learned their lesson at Haw's Shop for they "were ready to surrender when the logic of the situation demanded it. They made no such resistance as in the former action." Starr, *Union Cavalry*, 120; Kidd, *Recollections*, 330.

[213] Lieutenant Colonel Robert Josiah Jeffords had joined the army in Charleston at age 28. After serving as captain of Company A, 5th South Carolina Cavalry, he had been promoted to lieutenant colonel. Jeffords was later killed in action on Oct., 27, 1864 at Burgess' Mill, Virginia. Knudsen, "5th SC," 32.

[214] Franklin M. Hendrix enlisted as a private in Company F, 5th South Carolina Cavalry, from the Lexington District. The muster roll states that he was wounded on May 30, 1864 at Cold Harbor, Virginia, and died of his wounds on June 25, 1864. Ibid., 28.

came very near cutting us all off.

We have fought the Infantry in every fight. We have won a name as fighting stock. Gen. Butler said yesterday that it was mortifying to him to call on the 5th Regiment so much, but it was the only Regiment that he could rely on. His horse was shot in his hip but not killed.

Some of our Brigade behaved very badly on the battle field. The 20th Georgia behaved very badly. They ran, thought the enemy was after them and their horses ran away with them, killing three or four by throwing them off. This morning they were hunting up their horses, lost hats and everything. They had a regular stampede.[215]

My horse got a bait of corn for the first time in two days. You would not know him if you could see him.

I have not seen Ance in seven or eight days. He has gone back to Camp Lee and hired himself out at two dollars a day and his rations. If I only could get him home.

We were relieved about eleven o'clock and are now in the woods resting. Heavy firing this morning towards Hanover.[216]

I saw John C. last Sunday. He came to see us. He said he had not received a letter from you in some time. Said you were very prompt to answer his letters for a long time.

I am nearly worn out for the want of rest.

---

[215] On the evening of May 30, 1864, as Butler's Brigade went into bivouac at the Old Cold Harbor crossroads, a Georgia cavalry captain reported to Butler. The captain and part of his battalion of inexperienced troops had just arrived from Georgia and were on the way to join Brigadier General Pierce M. B. Young's Brigade. Since it was late and the Georgians had missed the fighting that day, Butler decided to place the captain and his men to the front as pickets for the night. The general sent along a veteran officer as a guide and gave the Georgians instructions to proceed down the road until they could see the enemy or were fired upon by the Federal videttes. Upon making contact with the enemy they were to drop back and establish their picket line in safety.
One of Butler's men remembered, "We were spreading our blankets . . . when, without a word of warning or report of trouble, we heard the rush of horsemen coming on us like a cyclone from a clear sky." It was the 20th Georgia Battalion, who fled after being fired upon by a solitary Union sentry. "Imagine our surprise and astonishment," one Carolinian recalled, "when the troops sent on picket came rushing down upon us, in a wild stampede, though tree laps, over fences, ditches and every thing in their path." Assuming that they were about to be overrun by a large enemy force, many members of Butler's Brigade "took to the bushes" as well. Butler finally regained control of his men by calling upon the 5th South Carolina Cavalry, who "came up with out a 'bauble' and restored order." Some of the Georgians, however, continued in their flight six or seven miles back to Mechanicsville. Although hardly at fault, Butler's veterans would hear many friendly jibes over their "stampede" at Cold Harbor. Brooks, *Butler*, 227-229.

[216] No doubt the preliminary skirmishing leading to the Battle of Cold Harbor, June 1-3, 1864.

Tell Walter that you cannot take money for more than you can pass it for.

Kiss the little fellows for me and I trust this will find you all well. My love to Pa and Ma. I remain as ever

Your True Husband,
J.M. Barr

———⊰∘∘∘⊱———

Near Gains Mills, Va.
June 3rd, 1864

Dear Rebecca:

I have received several letters from you. The last one was written on the 22nd I think of May. You said you received four letters from me at once. I received the letter you wrote to Keysville. Yesterday I received my hat and Thirty dollars you sent by Mr. Fink.

Get Fulmer to tan the hides if he is still home and send them to him at once.

Tell the Negroes that if you have to write to me again about their stealing your chickens that I will write to Mr. Spann to make them make away with all of theirs. If those that have them don't steal them, they ought to know which ones do it.

I have been having fever for the last four days, but feel better today. I am back with the Wagon Train. All the sick are with the Wagon Train. We have lost one hundred men, killed, wounded and missing out of our Regiment since we have been out here.

Heavy fighting about Gains Mill today.[217] I hear we captured five hundred wagons and three Regiment of Yankees this morning. It may not be so,

---

[217] June 3 marked the culminating attack by Grant's army on the Confederate defenses at Cold Harbor. With Richmond only eight miles away, Grant believed a break in the Confederate line at Cold Harbor might end the war. His headlong attack upon the Confederate trenches, however, cost the Union some 7,000 men in less than an hour, and in the end the Southern lines held.

but suppose we did capture a good many. You will see it in the paper before I get the news.

We will have hard fighting here for the next ten or twenty days. John C. says all the prisoners they captured were drunk, so Grant has to make them drunk to fight. Yet, I know some fight well without being drunk. Last Monday they fought well, yet we were (Our Brigade) were contending against too great odds. Some say they had twenty to our one. We lost none in our Company. We have been in some six or seven engagements since we have been out here.

We are faring very well, get plenty of bacon and corn bread. Now the soldiers are very well fed. Out here a tenth of every man's farm goes toward feeding our Armies. The people ought not to grumble about the law for it is a good one. Yet, I did not know it until I came out here.

I have not been paid off yet and have no money and won't be paid till the fighting is over. I have a two dollar bill in State money. I will send it home the first chance I have.

My horse is looking very bad. Several have gone up the spout. The saddle is hardly ever off of him.

You need not be uneasy about me. If I get sick so I can't write, I will get someone else to write you. I will tell you just how I am so you need not be uneasy.

Trees are full of fruit here. Peaches, apples and cherries are the best I ever ate.

Your Affectionate Husband,
James M. Barr

Savage Station on the York River
Some ten Miles from Richmond, Va.
June 5th, 1864

My Dear Rebecca:

Yesterday we were ordered here. We found the Regiment bivouaced near the above station in the woods. We were not here long before the horn sounded for saddle up and mount. The Regiment is now some five miles off watching the movements of the enemy and will fight if opportunity offers.

Our Cavalry force is now strong, supposed to be some fifteen thousand, would make a right nasty fight.

Thursday and Friday the enemy was repulsed at every point with heavy losses. Our loss was comparatively light, given at about five hundred killed and wounded. The enemy's loss some six or eight thousand. Our men fought behind breastworks, so that accounts for our not losing more men. We lost in prisoners some two hundred out of Beckinridge's Command. We captured some six hundred prisoners, eight hundred wounded.[218]

Longstreet's Corps were engaged so Tom and John C. were in it, Fletcher too. I have not heard from them, but hope they are not hurt. I would like to hear from them.

Phil and I are still back with the Wagon Trains. I am better, have a little fever, but my bowels are the worst. I think if I keep mending that I will be able to go with the Regiment in a day or two. Phil is complaining with his old disease.

Have you gotten my Army saddle home that Smith's negro got for Mr. Fink to ride to Columbia? If not, send after it and put it in the Store House.

Ance came back to us last night. He made ten dollars while he was away.

I received your letter dated the 24th of May and was so glad to get it. How anxious a Soldier is for a letter here. I am so glad to hear that you are all

---

[218] Former vice president of the United States and major general in the Confederate Army, John C. Breckinridge had part of his command overwhelmed during the Battle of Cold Harbor and lost some two hundred men.

well and getting on so well with the farm. Some of the Sugar Cane rotted so that is the cause of it not coming up better. I told Bill when it got <u>up knee</u> high to run a furrow with a <u>half plough close up</u> to it, <u>throwing</u> the <u>dirt from it</u>, then <u>fill</u> that <u>furrow full</u> of <u>manure</u> and put the dirt <u>back to it</u>.

My horse is poor and does not look like himself. He would make a pretty good match for the Hughs horse. I hope Wesley will come and bring me Jim or Pa's Old Pete. You may not think they will do, but we don't want fine horses here. All we want is a horse that will not fall down. It don't make any difference how ugly he is. If Wesley will come, and surely he will, I don't think it will cost him much if he does not stop in the towns. He can graze on clover and grass and stop with some citizens at night.

You will have all of the news before you get this letter.

Col. Kitt was killed Thursday and his body was sent home.[219]

I will finish this at some other time.

(June 5th, later)

The battle field was from MacCormicksville to McClellan's Bridge, a line of Seven Miles. The heaviest cannonading I ever heard and the small arms were one continuous roar. On Friday night they tried to charge our works, desperate firing. I know many a brave fellow was killed.

As for Grant, I do not know where he intends to fight again. He is back I think some distance. I think he had better quit. I don't think he will ever gain anything by his "on to Richmond." I don't think he will ever get there. It does not seem that he can get as far as McClellan got. I have passed over the ground where he fought (McClellan) and camped. Plenty of old clothing and everything thrown away. I hope this War will soon end.[220]

We get plenty to eat, but we see a hard time here. We are now in the War sure enough. We have seen service since we have been in Virginia. The

---

[219] There is no record of Colonel Kitt in Butler's Cavalry Brigade.

[220] On June 5, 1864 Grant's army was licking its wounds from the disaster at Cold Harbor. In the last month his army had been in continuous combat, suffering more than 50,000 casualties or 41% of its original number, while Lee's army had lost 32,000 men—men that could not be replaced.

Cavalry says the service is much harder here this Spring than it has ever been.

Remember me to all.
Your Affectionate
James

———◦◦◦———

Virginia
June 6th, 1864

Dear Rebecca:

I have just received your letter dated the 29th.

I wrote to Wesley to come out here after my horse and Ance. I told him if my Jim horse would not do to try and get Pa's old Pete, but I want him to come. I am afraid to send Ance through the country by himself. I offered Wesley two hundred dollars to come. If he sends me a horse, I may not get him or his back may be ruined before he gets here.

If a man gets sick, they give his horse to another man to ride — someone in the Regiment and no care is taken of him or his back. I have seen horses that were given to other men to ride in a horrible fix. I never saw horses with such backs in my life. I would hate awfully to give up my horse to any man. Yet, they were about to take him from me. I told them that I would go on my horse sick before I would give him up. If a man loses his horse, he is put in the Infantry service, so it stands a man in hand to watch his horse and take the best care of him.[221]

I imagine my horse would stand me awhile longer if I can get corn plenty or grazing. He has distemper badly. If Wesley does not come out here, I don't know what to do unless I send Ance alone home with my horse, but

---

[221] The Confederate government continued to follow the disastrous policy of requiring cavalrymen to furnish their own horses. While this policy gave Southern horsemen an advantage over their Northern counterparts during the first months of the war, in time, the attrition of field service destroyed the Confederate cavalry.

will wait until I get money enough to send him home — that is if Wesley should send me a horse instead of coming out here himself.

I am now in the front with the Brigade. Phillip has been sent back to a Hospital in Richmond. I have heard since I came to the Regiment that Phil would be assigned to some light duty. Perhaps in a Hospital. I heard that the Dr. recommended him for light duty. He will either be sent to a Hospital or a Government Stable, but to a Hospital I would guess.

I am well.

Glad to hear that our little boys remember their Pa. I would like to see you and them.

You must feed the horses on oats and wheat and keep them up the best you can.

Give the flour to the Negroes as you think best.

You must manage the best you can with the advice of Mr. Spann.

You must not be troubled about me. Only pray that the Good One may shield me from harm.

We are all lying in an old field resting, expect to stay here till tomorrow morning unless some fighting takes place.

You said something about our being settled. I don't think we will be settled this Summer and think it better for our health not to have a regular camp.

If we had a Regimental Hospital to send the sick it would be better. On rainy nights if we stop to stretch and rest, I use my oil cloth to shelter me.

I write this on account of receiving your letter after writing yesterday. This will not afford you much pleasure to read as it is so bungled. Yet you must put up with such as I cannot do better writing the way I have to do it.

Your Husband,
James

CHAPTER SIX
IT WAS A TREMENDOUS LICK

On June 11 and 12, 1864 Barr's regiment participated in one of the most hotly contested cavalry fights of the war; the Battle of Trevilian Station. As General Ulysses S. Grant continued to hammer away at Lee's army around Richmond, he sent Major General David Hunter with a small army though the Valley of Virginia and on to the west of Richmond in an attack on the Confederate supply center at Lynchburg. On June 5 Grant sent two divisions of his cavalry, some 8,000 men under Philip Sheridan, northwest in order to support Hunter's drive. Sheridan planned to link up with Hunter at Charlottsville and then destroy the Virginia Central Railroad to Hanover Junction. Upon learning of Sheridan's movement, Confederate General Robert E. Lee sent two cavalry divisions under Wade Hampton — perhaps 4,700 men — north to intercept the raiders. Hampton led his own division that included Butler's Brigade and the 5th South Carolina Cavalry and Major General Fitzhugh Lee's Division.

On the morning of June 11 Hampton moved to block Sheridan's cavalry along the Virginia Central Railroad about twenty-five miles from Charlottesville near Trevilian Station. Fitz Lee's Division and Hampton's men were still separated by several miles when the fighting began. As Butler's men made contact with Union General A.T.A. Torbert's First Division in their front, they believed that Lee's Division would move quickly up from Louisa Court House and support them on their right. However, Brigadier General George

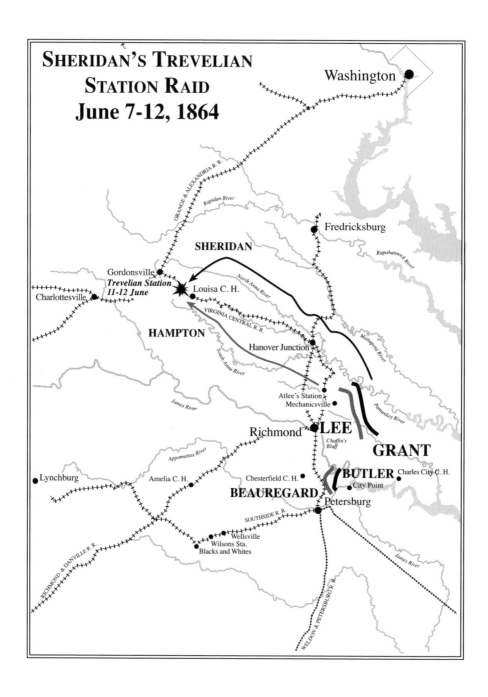

SHERIDAN'S TREVELIAN
STATION RAID
June 7-12, 1864

Washington

ORANGE & ALEXANDRIA R. R.

Rapidan River

Fredricksburg

Rapahannock River

SHERIDAN

Gordonsville
Trevelian Station
11-12 June
Louisa C. H.

North Anna River

Charlottesville

VIRGINIA CENTRAL R. R.

HAMPTON

Mattaponi River

South Anna River

Hanover Junction

James River

Atlee's Station
Mechanicsville

Pamunkey River

Richmond   LEE

Chaffin's
Bluff

GRANT

Lynchburg

Appomattox River

Amelia C. H.

Chesterfield C. H.

BEAUREGARD

BUTLER   Charles City C. H.
City Point

Petersburg

SOUTHSIDE R. R.

Wellsville
Wilsons Sta.
Blacks and Whites

James River

RICHMOND & DANVILLE R. R.

WELDON & PETERSBURG R. R.

Custer and his First Brigade of Torbert's Division had other plans. Finding their way between the two Confederate divisions, Custer's men first stopped Lee's advance from Louisa then attacked the rear of Hampton's dismounted division. Custer's horsemen were soon among Butler and Hampton's led horses, supply wagons, and ambulances and threatened to encircle Butler's South Carolinians. Upon discovering the calamity in his rear, Hampton reversed his division to avoid complete destruction. When Hampton ordered Butler to retire, Butler found himself in a dangerous situation. He told the courier to "Say to General Hampton it is hell to hold on and hell to let go. If I withdraw my entire line at once the blue coats will run over us." Showing considerable discipline, Butler withdrew each regiment individually to retrieve what horses they could find and successfully extracted the brigade. After a confusing mêlée that included mounted saber charges and dismounted assaults, the Southerners were fortunate to drive off the Wolverines and recapture their 800 animals and wagons, while also capturing many of Custer's men and supplies, including his personal headquarters wagon.

Although the fighting around Trevilian Station on the 11th had been a near total disaster for Hampton, he retreated only a short distance and had his men dismount and fortify a position behind part of the Virginia Central Railroad bed. The fighting on June 12 went differently for the Southerners. Sheridan concentrated his dismounted attack upon a bulge in Butler's line. Each time Sheridan's cavalry formed to charge the men of Butler's Brigade would open fire with their long-range Enfield Rifles and drive the Federal troopers to cover. After seven separate charges, the South Carolinians refused to budge, and Sheridan broke off the engagement after suffering heavy casualties. Sheridan, unable to support Hunter's raid, returned south to rejoin Grant's army. Both sides lost around 1,000 men during the Trevilian Raid, and the 5th South Carolina Cavalry reported that six men were killed, 41 were wounded and eight were missing.[222]

Barr was one of the wounded. After being hit, he came close to becoming a prisoner of Custer's Brigade before being rescued and brought to the relative safety of a barn that was being used as a field hospital. Later he was transferred to a Confederate general hospital in Charlottesville, Virginia. [223]

---

[222] Starr, Union Cavalry, 136-150; Brooks, Butler, 236-258; Battles and Leaders, vol. 4, 233-239.

[223] McDaniel, Correspondence, 252.

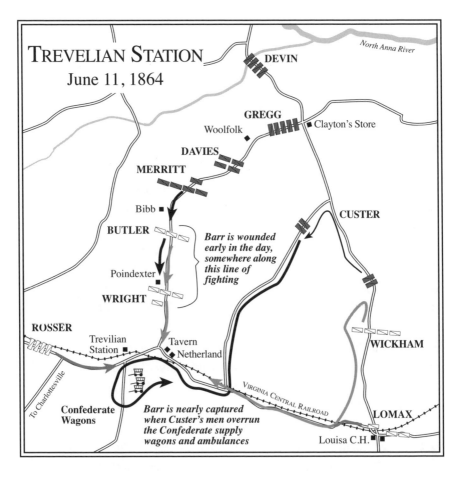

Charlottesville Hospital
Tuesday, June 14th, 1864

My Dear Rebecca:

I am now in the above named Hospital, was wounded in the leg last Saturday, the 11th. I was shot about one inch below the cap of my right knee on the inside. The ball I think went down the bone and around, coming out some four inches below where it went in, coming out on the other side of the leg.

I was on my knees when the ball hit me. I could not walk off of the battle field. In about one hour, I was carried to the rear, was put in an ambulance. There I fared bad as the Yankees were trying to flank us and did succeed in getting some 3 ambulances and some of our wounded for a short while when they were recaptured. Sgt. Boylston they had, but he is now here with me. He is shot in the hand.[224]

I have no use of my leg. If I want to move it, I have to call for help, but I have gotten good attention so far.

I hope to be able to go home soon, yet the Dr. said I could not go in three or four weeks unless someone came for me. I don't know how long I will stay at this Hospital. I would like to go to Richmond. I have no clothing here, all back near Richmond.

Capt. Tyler, I heard was wounded in the foot on Sunday, the 12th. I am expecting him here today.[225]

We have the best of the fight. The fight was not far from Louisa Court House, some 90 miles from Richmond.

I will write again soon. I am doing tolerably well.

Your Dear Husband,
James M. Barr

Charlottesville, Va. Hospital
June 14th, 1864

My Dear Wife:

Sgt. Boylston I expect will leave here this evening or to-morrow morning. All will leave that can walk. They will have to walk some 20 or 25 miles.

I get plenty to eat here. Tell Johnny that Pa had strawberries for dinner.

---

[224] Samuel Reed Boylston served as the first sergeant of Company I, 5th South Carolina Cavalry. He was wounded during the battle of Trevilian Station, VA, June 11, 1864 and died in Richmond on June 20, 1864. Knudsen, "5th SC," 9.

[225] On June 12, 1864 Captain Thomas W. Tyler, commander of Company I, 5th South Carolina Cavalry, was wounded in action at Trevilian Station, Virginia. Tyler later returned to duty. Ibid., 56.

I would much rather be in Richmond. I am afraid the Yankees will capture us here. I hope they may not.

The Doctor says my wound is eight (8) inches long. It is pretty sore and will be for some four or six weeks.

No one could well come for me as I am too far from Richmond.

Our forces are about Louisa Court House.

I am writing lying on my back.

I know you will be uneasy for me, but try and not be. I am waited on well, but would rather be at home.

I don't know how our Company suffered on Sunday. Only heard Capt. Tyler was wounded in the foot. I saw a good many from other Companies that were wounded on that day on Saturday, the day I was wounded. I cannot give the number, but it was large. Only 3 from our Company, Col. Aiken, Capt. Humphry and his first Lt. . in the 6th Regt. are a number of wounded men.[226]

I will not write any more now, but if I have a chance I will write more later.

Your Husband,
James M. Barr

Morning of the 15th of June, 1864

Dear Rebecca:

I feel quite pert this morning. I have just washed and combed and had my wound dressed, but yet my leg is still in my way. I hope I may be soon able

---

[226] Colonel Hugh K. Aiken, commander of the 6th South Carolina Cavalry, had been shot through the right lung. Most observers believed that the wound would be mortal, but Aiken made a full recovery only to be killed in action in February 1865 in South Carolina. Captain Moses B. Humphery commanded Company F, 6th South Carolina Cavalry. Brooks, *Butler* 244-245, 544.

to move it about. I have only been wounded five days, but feel nearly worn out lying on my back. Yet, if I have to stay here for four or six weeks longer I may complain.

I heard yesterday that Henry and Jim Quattlebaum were wounded. Jim very slightly.[227]

EVENING:

I feel much as I did this morning.

Capt. Tyler was sent here last night so I have heard. I have not seen him. We may stay close together for some time and not see each other.

As soon as I get able, I will ask for a transfer to Richmond. If the cars are running, then I will try and get home. I expect they will keep me six weeks before they give me a furlough. I think if I mend fast and someone would come for me, that I could get off, but I will write whenever I think I am able to go home.

You can't come here and I can't go away on account of the Rail Road. The Yankees have burned and torn up the tracks.

MORNING: JUNE 16th, 1864

Sgt. Boylston will leave this morning and mail this letter in Richmond. I wrote a few days ago to you, but now the letter is here in the office as no mail leaves here.

My Dear, I suffered severe pain all night, but feel easier this morning. I am sitting up. There are some men here who were wounded five weeks ago. They could go home if the cars were running.

I was hit on the right leg 1 inch below the knee cap, ball hit the bone and passed down and around, coming out on the opposite side of my leg making a wound 8 inches long.

Your True Husband,
James M. Barr

---

[227] Henry R. Quattlebaum and James Quattlebaum served in Company B, 6th South Carolina Cavalry. They were both wounded on June 12, 1864 during the Battle of Trevilian Station. Brooks, *Butler*, 249.

———⟨◦⟩———

Charlottesville, Va. Hospital
June 16th, 1864
AFTERNOON

My Dear Rebecca:

I do not know whether my letters will get off today or not. I am doing as well as a wounded man can do for a Wound sometimes requires weeks, yes, months to get well. I think in three or four weeks I can go anywhere on crutches and perhaps in less time.

There are sixteen wounded soldiers in the room that I am in. We are in a very large and airy room. This house before the War was a Hotel. The wounded, or the most of them, are quite lively. We have one man that was shot in the hand that I think will die. Part of his hand was cut off on Sunday. He now lies senseless, poor fellow. His comrads hardly know where he is. He is from Georgia. After a wound commences running, they say it is not near so painful.

I am afraid you will see in the papers that I am wounded before you get this, but I want you to hear it from me. If I cannot send these letters off today, I will write again tomorrow.

I was hit on the right leg on the inside, one inch & 1/2 below the knee cap, ball hit the bone, passing down and around through the Calf of leg, coming out on the other side of leg, making a wound eight inches long. I don't see what prevented the ball from smashing the bone to pieces for it was a tremendous lick.[228]

I had to lie on the battle field about one hour. Then two men toted me off to a hollow, then got a litter, put me on it and carried me to an Ambulance and I assure you I had a rough time in it running from the Yankees. They did not get me, but my leg was awfully bruised as the roads were so rough.

The Yankees got Sgt. Boylston, Col. Aiken and Gregg and several others,

---

[228] Had the ball shattered the bone, in all probability Barr's leg would have been amputated immediately

but we recaptured them all. I expect Col. Aiken is dead by now.[229] We got a good many prisoners.

I am now feeling no pain.

I have written you as near as I could what happened.

Your
James

<hr/>

MORNING
Delavan Hospital
Charlottesville, Va.
June 22, 1864

My Beloved Wife:

This morning I will try and write you a few lines to let you know how I am. I cannot get in any position that I can write. I am now writing with my elbow resting on the bed. Very tiresome and I cannot half write.

My leg is swagged down a good deal. They poultice it twice a day. It has run considerably. I still have no use of my leg, but the Doctor says the ball passed through the bone. You don't wonder then that I have no use of it. I thought it quite strange for the bone not to be broken and I could not move my leg. I think my leg is safe now. I think it will get well. It pained me so for two or three nights after I wrote you that I thought it would have to come off, but I think now that I am doing as well as I possibly can. The wound looks healthy and my leg is nearly down to its usual size. My foot and ankle are swelled a good deal.

All the wounded are doing tolerably well. In this room the man that I thought would die is now pert and can walk about.

I have no idea when I will be able to leave here and I am out of money,

<hr/>

[229] Captain James J. Gregg of Company B, 6th South Carolina Cavalry had been wounded in the arm, captured by Custer's men, and later liberated by the Confederates. Brooks, *Butler*, 244.

but that is the general cry among all soldiers.

Captain Meetze from Lexington Court House is here on duty.[230] He told me anything I wanted that he could do that he would do it with pleasure. Said he would come to see me every day.

Capt. Tyler is in about 300 yds. of me. I wrote him yesterday to come and see me as soon as he could. He sent me word he would come to see me as soon as he gets able. I think I will get to see him soon. Perhaps he may see me as far as Columbia.

I need not talk about going home yet for a few weeks.

I have plenty of everything to eat, yet I think they cook bad. The ladies are very kind.

Hope this will find you all well.
Your Devoted
James

<u>EVENING</u>
June 22nd, 1864

There are a great many wounded and sick soldiers here. I cannot describe the place that I am in, but think this house was built for a Hotel.

I would write to Charlie to send Ance home with my horse if I had money or if he had as much as One Hundred and fifty dollars. I don't see how he is to get home unless someone comes out for me and if I could go, <u>who</u> would come here is a puzzle.

Sure there are some that could come if they would. If William can't come, I don't think anyone else will. I feel like I will be able to go home by the 15th of July or perhaps I could go sooner.

Your
James

---

[230] Captain George W. Meetze served in the 13th South Carolina Infantry. *OR*, vol. 16, p. 682.

—————⊲◦⊳—————

Editor's note: On June 22, 1864 Barr's brother-in-law and messmate Sam Guess wrote the following to Rebecca Barr.

June 22nd, 1864

Dear Beck:

You no doubt will be surprised to receive a letter from me. I suppose you have heard long before this that the Major was wounded. I have not been able to see him since nor hear from him. I did not know where he was until yesterday. He is at Charlottesville, Virginia Hospital, which is 100 miles above Richmond.

I was in the fight with him when he was hit, but did not see him as I was on the extreme left and he on the extreme right of the Company.

I hope the Major will be able to come home soon. I know he would like to be there now.

Charlie and Aaron are both well. Aaron was in a fight yesterday. I have not heard from him since as the Company has not returned yet.

I have Anderson and the Major's horse in charge. The horse is doing badly. I wish I could send him and Anderson home. I would have sent them several days ago, but I have no money to pay his expenses home and don't know when I will be able to get it. The Major has not told me or any of us what to do with his horse and boy, but I know he wants them sent home as soon as possible and I am going to send them just as soon as I can get the money to do it. We have not been paid off since we have been in Virginia and I can't tell when we will get any pay. It will take at least $40 dollars to pay Andersons and the horses expenses home. I have tried to borrow the money here, but can't find anyone who has it.

If you want me to send Anderson and Jeff home soon, you had better send me about $40 dollars to pay his expenses or if you think best, I will keep him here until we draw money from the Government and then I will send him, but we have no use for him here at all and the Major was wanting to send him home before he was wounded and I think myself it would be best to get them home. They should be sent as soon as possible for neither the horse nor boy are doing well here. If you send me the money, I will start them home as soon as I get it. I intend to start them any how as soon as I get the money, but it may be some time before I get it unless it is sent to me.

I am quite well, hope you all are.

Give my love to Mr. and Mrs. Barr and family. My love to you and family.

I would like to hear from you soon. Let me know what to do.

Yours Respectfully,
Sam Guess

Direct your letter:
S.D. M. Guess
Richmond, Virginia
Co. I, 5 Regiment, S. C. Cavalry
Butler's Brigade
Hampton Division
Care of Capt. Tyler

P. S. You must excuse this badly written letter or note. Sallie and Jimie were well when I last heard from them.

Sam

———◦◦◦◦———

Charlottesville Hospital, Va.
July 1st, 1864

My Dear Wife:

I am trying this morning to write to you. I have a board set on my bed and I am lying on my back trying to write.

Tomorrow will be three weeks since I have been wounded and I am not much if any better off. The swelling has gone out of my leg and it has run a great deal, but on the calf of my leg where the ball came out is a bad place. Pains me a great deal, a continual burning pain for the last three or four days. The Doctor put something on it this morning that has eased the pain some.

I know that you would like to be with me, but it can't be. If I had some one to stay and look after me, I would do better. A good many little attentions I miss.

My appetite is not very good. They have plenty here, but it is not half cooked, no salt in anything.

I am still quite weak, can't sit up yet. I can move my leg now myself. The wound at the knee and thigh is doing very well. I think it is healing.

The flies bother me a great deal, also the green ones. They want to blow my leg. I am afraid they will, but I am conscious to keep the spread well tucked down.[231]

I received your letter written on the 12th of June.

Now I have no idea when I could or will be able to go home. I do not think that I could go under three or four weeks and I will have to mend fast in that time. I have fallen off a great deal and it will take time to strengthen up. The Doctor would not give me a furlough unless the wound is near about healed up unless someone would come after me. I will be too weak to think about a furlough to try and go home alone. I cannot go now as my wound is too bad. It is sluffing off instead of healing. I hope it will turn for the better in a short time.

I feel as if I would like to get up and walk about. If I had the strength and it would not hurt my leg I would try. It would do me good, but I could not manage crutches.

I do not know how Capt. Tyler is. I have not seen him. He is not yet able to get out of his room. I heard he got live things in his foot.

I heard yesterday that old Mr. Fort was dead and old John Hendrix married.

I have been looking for a letter as the cars are now running every day.

It seems that the raiders have been pretty well thrashed. Hampton reports in todays paper, or rather Lee's, shows what a drubbing they got.

---

[231] Blowflies and other insects deposit eggs in rotting meat in a process known as "blowing."

My Dear, I must close. I wish you could be with me. I cannot write for anyone to come for I don't know who would come.

Your Husband,
J.M. Barr

———⟨⟩———

Editor's note: On July 5, 1864 Rebecca Barr's mother sent her the following letter.

Home,
July 5th, 1864
My Dear Daughter:

I am truly sorry to hear of the Major's misfortune, but while my sympathies are aroused in his behalf, I am glad it is no worse. I hope he will soon be able to come home and perhaps his would [wound] will prove for his and your good. For if he had not been wounded, he might have been killed before this awful War is ended and as he is wounded, he may not be able to take up arms again, but be allowed to remain quietly at home with you.

I was in hopes that all my children would escape being hurt, but I know he is wounded and I fear the other boys are. We have not heard from them in two weeks. John C. wrote regular twice a week until now. Oh, that we could again be blest with Peace.

You must muster up all the fortitude you can and bear your affliction the best you can. Be assured, my Dear Child, that you have my sympathy.

I am sorry to say that little George Emma is still in very bad health.[232] If she is improving any, it is very slowly, had high fever all last week. Her fever has been lighter for two last days. She can't stand alone nor sit up, but a short time (alone). Poor little creature has a hard time breathing.

I hope your little Johnnie has missed the fever before this. It appears there is a great deal of sickness among the children.

---

[232] George Emma Dowling may have been the daughter of William Preston Dowling. McDaniel, *Correspondence*, 274.

Generally we have had very dry, warm weather down here until yesterday. Had a good rain, which rendered the weather more pleasant. This morning Preston is nearly done ploughing corn. He says we have a good crop if the
Season holds out. It looks well at present. My garden was suffering for rain.
I had a fine garden until it turned off too dry for it, but the worst luck with
Poultry in the world. I have ten young turkeys, three goslings and a few
chickens, too few to count.

Dear Daughter, we have a Union Prayer Meeting going on in this neighborhood. One Wednesday at Spring Town, the next at Orange Grove (The
Methodist Church), preaching every Sabbath. I pray often twice a day. Sarah
(your sister) and her Babe were complaining when I heard from them last.
Mary Cox has been quite sick, but is better. The rest of the family is quite
well. Write soon and let me know when you hear from the Major and how he
was getting on. Preston's wife & Johnson join me in love to you. Kiss the children for me.

Your Loving Mother,
E. S. Dowling

*Editors note: On July 8, 1864 Captain George W. Meetze of 13th South
Carolina Infantry wrote Rebecca Barr the following.*

Charlottesville, Va.
July 8, 1864

Mrs. James M. Barr:

By request of my friend, Major Barr, I write a few lines to inform you of
his condition.

His wound has not done well since here and day before yesterday it took
a change for the worse, so much so that his leg had to be amputated. His leg
was taken off above the knee. The operation was performed yesterday about

ten o'clock. I spent the night with him. This morning he is doing very well.

He desires that you come on at once. Said you must get your Brother, the Doctor, to come with you.

I can assure you that he has the best of attention and seems to be in good spirits. He is a warm friend

of mine and anything I can do will be done.

Hoping that you may soon be with him and that he will soon be well enough to return Home with you, I remain yours with

Great respect,
Geo. W. Meetze

Editor's note: On July 14, 1864 Barr's sister Sue Guess wrote him the follow-ing letter.

Lexington Dist., S.C.
Thursday P.M.,
 July 14th, 1864

My Dear Brother:

Your letter of the 1st inst. came to hand Tuesday & as Rebecca had left to go to you, I took the responsibility upon myself to open it as we were all so anxious to hear from you, hoping it might be written after the dispatch you sent Rebecca, but to our disappointment, it was written before. We are all still very anxious to hear from you and hope you are better.

Rebecca left home Sunday morning to go to you, but we are afraid she will not succeed in getting there. She left Bamberg Tuesday morning. George, who carried her down, returned home today.

The children are all here. They are doing remarkably well. Jimmie and Johny are scarcely any trouble at all. Charlie is doing much better than I was afraid, he would, as he had been quite sick before his Ma left. I know she is uneasy about him. I expect she will be with you before this reaches you, if she can get to you at all, if she is, this will tell her about the children. I think I may say Charlie is well though Dennis nurses him all the time. He will not let any of us take him. He appears quite bashful, is a little cross sometimes.

Anderson came home Tuesday morning. He left Camp on the fifth inst. He started by private conveyance to bring your horse and clothes home. The horse gave out, so he had to leave him and come by the cars. I will give you a copy of what the gentleman, with whom the horse was left, wrote on the back of Anderson's pass:

"July 8th, 1864. Green Bay, Prince Edwards Co. Va.

Mr. Barr, your boy Anderson got to my house yesterday with his horse which gave out and is not able to travel any further and had to leave him, and hope the people will aid him in his route home. I will do all I can for the horse which is subject to your order.

William J. McGehee"

His address is Green Bay, Po. Off. Richmond & Danville, R.R. Prince Edwards County, Va. Mr. McGehee told Anderson to give the paper to Pa and tell him to write to him. Pa will mail a letter to him tomorrow telling him to take good care of your horse and he shall be paid for it. If you wish, Pa says you can write to him also. He had me to write you a copy of what he wrote.

Anderson said Sam was sick when he left and was going to the Jackson Hospital in Richmond, said Sam said he had Typhoid fever. We have not heard from Thomas in some time.

Eliotte Steadman and Henry Quattlebaum are at home.[233] Jim Quattlebaum could come no farther than Richmond as a section of the Rail Road was torn up and he could not walk. Cary Mitchell's second son (Ridgell) is dead. Tom Bates' son (Andrew) was killed last week on James Island and buried today. Bud was home on a furlough last week, left for Camp Tuesday.

Mr. Guess came to see me last week only staid four days. He has been ordered back to his company. I feel anxious to hear from him as there has been a good deal of fighting about Charleston recently though the Company was at Green Pond Station when I last heard from it.

Tell Rebecca (if she is with you) that I will comply with her request and

---

[233] Eliotte Steadman served in Company B, 6th South Carolina Cavalry. Chapman, *History*, 463.

write to you or herself often if it is only a few lines to let her know how the children are. I have made Johny a bonnet which he wears finely.

All the children sleep in Pa's room. Mother doesn't appear willing for either Anna or myself to take them. Charlie sleeps in his cradle. The others on a pallet.

As I have no news to write, I will close. Hoping you will soon be able to come home. Mother & Pa join me in love to you and Rebecca. The children send a kiss to you both. Ma and Pa are not very well.

With much love I am as ever your
Affectionate Sister
Sue Guess

P.S. Excuse this writing. My pen is very bad.

Editor's note: On July 22, 1864 Rebecca Barr's brother John C. Dowling wrote his sister the following.

Petersburg, Va.
July 22nd, 1864

My Dear Sister:

I take my pen in hand this day to give you some notice of my where abouts and my luck in the present campaign.

I am quite well at the same glorious little Petersburg. The place I enjoyed myself so well last Summer, but Mr. Grant gives it a different appearance to what it did then, but still there is some likeness, but the Yankees shell it so much till there is but little pleasure in being on the street. There are several business houses open yet, but they are not as full as they were before Grant got so near, but he can't get the little place I am confident.

Dear Sister, I have just received the sad news of the misfortune of Major

Barr. Oh, how awful War is. Just to think that a couple of months ago he was safe and sound and in the enjoyment of good health and now he is probably suffering in some hospital for the want of proper attention. It may be that he is mortally wounded, and if so, you may never behold his gentle features again, but as in everything else I hope for the best and hope he is now with you on a long furlough and doing well.

There would be some consolation in getting a wound if they could all be very slight and be the cause of getting to go home. I don't know that I would not take a slight one myself, but when a soldier expects to get a slight one, he very often makes a mistake and finds a messinger to warn him to his long eternal home. That is very often the case.

I am very anxious to hear from the Major. I had the pleasure of seeing him twice since he has been out here, but it has been some time since I have heard from him.

I must close. Give my regards to Sue and Mr. & Mrs. Barr. Write soon and tell me all the news.

I remain your
Affectionate Brother,
J. C. Dowling

AFTERWORD

Upon learning of her husband's condition, Rebecca Barr made the decision to travel to Charlottesville, Virginia. According to family tradition, it was not an easy choice for her to make. She was about five months pregnant and in addition, her infant son Charlie was so ill she feared the child would not survive until she returned. Preparing for the worst, as she left her children with her sister's family, she carefully laid out the cloths she wished the child to be buried in.

Rebecca's brother, Elijah Henry Dowling, escorted her to Virginia. It was a difficult trip made even more so by the disrupted rail system in the South. For much of the trip Rebecca and her brother traveled on open flat cars with Rebecca sitting on a chair. Further on they found sections of the line blocked and they traveled on by renting or borrowing horses. Upon finding a rail link to Virginia, they were again thwarted by a train master who informed them that they were too close to the front lines to be permitted to continue on the train. Dowling recognizing a fellow Mason, countered with a Masonic sign of distress. To Masons the signal represents a life or death situation for a fraternity brother. They were permitted to remain on board and were successful in reaching Virginia and eventually Charlottesville.

At the Charlottesville Hospital they found that James Barr's condition had continued to deteriorate. Evidentially infection had spread up the stump of his leg and it forced the surgeon to amputate a second time. Although

Rebecca was able to spend several days nursing her husband, it was too late; Barr died August 29, 1864.

The prudent thing for Rebecca Barr to do at that time would have been to make arrangements in Charlottesville for the internment of her husband. Near all of the Confederate General Hospitals in Virginia are the graves of thousands of Southern soldiers who died far from their homes, and Rebecca could not have been questioned for taking care of her husband in the same manner. On top of the fact that she was pregnant, her brother Elijah had already left for home and she would have enough difficulty skirting the front and Union raiders in her own journey home. But, rather than leaving her husband's body in Virginia, she boarded a flat car with his remains and began the trip back to South Carolina under the hot August sun. Along the route she sent word ahead to Leesville to have Anderson and one of the other slaves meet her at the train station in Columbia, South Carolina, with a wagon and a buggy. The night she arrived she wasted no time, had the wagon loaded and headed home. The last leg of the journey would prove to be memorable for her as she struggled to keep her servants awake through the middle of the night during the final thirty miles to Leesville. As soon as it was practical, Rebecca Barr held a service for her husband and had him laid to rest in the Barr Family Cemetery near his home.

After her husband's death Rebecca left her farm and moved with her three sons to her brother Elijah Dowling's home in the Barnwell District. On December 6, 1864 she gave birth to a daughter who died the following day and was buried near her father in the Barr Cemetery. Later Rebecca would return with her bother and sons to reclaim the overgrown fields of her farm and establish a grain and saw mill. On November 18, 1883 Rebecca married Franklin Asbury (Tom) Warren. Warren had served during the war in Company A, 1st South Carolina Infantry. Rebecca and Tom are buried together in the Leesville Cemetery.[234]

---

[234] McDaniel, *Correspondence,* 7-13.

BIBLIOGRAPHICAL ESSAY

This is not a listing of all sources consulted in the editing of this work, but rather it is intended to help interested readers find more information on the 5th South Carolina Cavalry. For Barr, his family, and his associates, the *Eighth Census of theUnited States: 1860* (population and slave schedules from Lexington and other districts in South Carolina) is an important starting point, as is John A. Chapman's recently reprinted *History of Edgefield County* (Clearwater, S.C.: Eastern Digital Resources, 1998). For a general history of southern agriculture at this time, there exists few better places to start than the venerable *History of Agriculture in the Southern United States to 1860* (2 volumes, Gloucester, Mass: Peter Smith, 1958; originally published 1933) by Lewis C. Gray.

The volume at hand, of course, is based upon the work of Ruth Barr McDaniel, who compiled the Barr letters for her *Confederate War Correspondence of James Michael Barr and Rebecca Ann Dowling Barr* (Taylors, SC: Ruth Barr McDaniel, 1963). The original letters remain in the possession of the McDaniel family. Other letters from the 5th South Carolina Cavalry can be found in Olin Fulmer Hutchinson, Jr., *"My Dear Mother & Sisters": Civil War Letters of Capt. A. B. Mulligan, Co. B, 5th South Carolina Cavalry—Butler's Division—Hampton's Corps, 1861–1865* (repr. Spartanburg, SC: The Reprint Company, 1992). The most complete and detailed study of the 5th South Carolina Cavalry is in an unpublished manuscript by Lewis F. Knudsen, Jr., titled "5th South Carolina Cavalry Regiment (Provisional Army of the Confederate States), 1861–1865:

Muster Roll, Officer Registers, and Muster Roll Records and Events"
(Columbia, SC: Lewis F. Knudsen, Jr.,1999). The best primary source on
General Matthew C. Butler's Brigade is U. R. Brooks, *Butler and His Cavalry
in the War of Secession, 1861–1865* (repr. Camden, SC: J. J. Fox, 1989).

Other sources of information on the unit and other South Carolina
troops can be found in Janet B. Hewitt, ed., *South Carolina Confederate
Soldiers, 1861–1865*, 2 vols., (Wilmington, NC: 1998) and Randolph W.
Kirkland, *Broken Fortunes: South Carolina Soldiers, Sailors and Citizens Who
Died in the Service of Their Country and State in the War for Southern
Independence, 1861–1865* (Spartanburg, SC: 1995). And of course no
detailed study of Civil War soldiers would be complete without consulting
the National Archives and Records Administration's, *Compiled Service
Records of Confederate Soldiers Who Served in Organizations for the State of
South Carolina, 1861–1865*, (Microfilm No., 267) and the South Carolina
Department of Archives and History, *Confederate Historian: Rolls of South
Carolina Volunteers in the Confederate States Provisional Army*, Vol., 4—
Cavalry and Artillery (microcopy No., 16). Other sources include A.S.
Salley, *South Carolina Troops in Confederate Service*, vol.1(Columbia, SC: The
State Co., 1913) and R.A. Brock, *The Appomattox Roster* (The Southern
Historical Society: 1887) and S.E. Mays, Jr., compiler, *Genealogical notes on
the Family of Mays and Reminiscences of the War Between the States* (Plant
City, FL: Plant City Enterprise, 1927).

General works that describe the movements of the 5th South Carolina
Cavalry include General August V. Kautz's "Operations South of the James
River" in the fourth volume of Robert U. Johnson and Clarence C. Buel,
eds., *Battles and Leaders of the Civil War*, vol. 4 (New York: Thomas Yoseloff,
1956) and Stephen Z. Starr, *The Union Cavalry in the Civil War*, vol 2, *The
War in the East From Gettysburg to Appomattox, 1863–1865* (Baton Rouge:
Louisiana State University Press, 1981) as well as J. H. Kidd, *Personal
Recollections of a Cavalrymen with Custer's Michigan Cavalry Brigade in the
Civil* War (Ionia, MI: Sentinel Printing Company, 1908). Finally, no editing
of Civil War-era documents should be undertaken without consulting the
United States War Department's *The War of the Rebellion: A Compilation of
the Official Records of the Union and Confederate Armies*, 128 Vols.
(Washington, D.C: Government Printing Office, 1880–1901).

INDEX